WHAT SMART STUDENTS KNOW

WHAT SMART STUDENTS KNOW

MAXIMUM GRADES.
OPTIMUM LEARNING.
MINIMUM TIME.

adam robinson

 THREE RIVERS PRESS
NEW YORK

Published by Three Rivers Press, New York, New York.
Member of the Crown Publishing Group.

Random House, Inc. New York, Toronto, London, Sydney, Auckland
www.randomhouse.com

THREE RIVERS PRESS is a registered trademark and the Three Rivers Press colophon is a trademark of Random House, Inc.

Printed in the United States of America

Design by Parham-Santana Design and Philip Yee

Electronic Pre-Press Production by Philip Yee

Library of Congress Cataloging-in-Publication Data
Robinson, Adam.
   What smart students know : maximum grades, optimum learning,
minimum time / by Adam Robinson.
      Includes index.
   1. Study, method of.   2. Students—Time management.   3. Test-taking
skills.   I. Title.
LB1049.R57   1993   93-20437

ISBN 0-517-88085-7

20 19 18 17

About the Author

For more than a decade, Adam Robinson has helped thousands of students discover their academic potential. In 1980, Robinson devised and perfected the now-famous "Joe Bloggs" approach to taking standardized tests. This revolutionary method formed the foundation of The Princeton Review's early success, a nationwide company he helped create in the early 1980's.

His innovative work in education has been hailed by the *Wall Street Journal*, *The New York Times, The Christian Science Monitor, Forbes,* and *Rolling Stone.* The country's leading educational pioneer, Robinson has sold over 2 million books, including a *New York Times* best-seller. For this book, his seventh, he has drawn on his years of working with the students to uncover the common denominators among the successful students.

Robinson was born in 1955. After attending Evanston Township High School in Illinois, he graduated from the Wharton School before earning a law degree at Oxford University in England. Robinson is a rated chess master and includes boxing among his hobbies.

I'd Like to Hear from You

As an authority in the field of education, everything I've learned has come from students like you. In this book I've shared the experience of hundreds of smart students. After reading this book, you might have some interesting anecdotes, tips, or comments you'd like to share with me. I appreciate all your feedback, both positive and negative. I promise I'll do my best to respond as promptly as I can.

You can reach me at the following address:

Adam Robinson
284 Fifth Avenue
New York, NY 10001

Acknowledgments

Some twenty-five years ago, my mother handed me a new book she thought I might like to read. *How Children Fail,* written by a teacher named John Holt, was one of those rare books that becomes an instant classic. My parents were always giving me books they thought I would appreciate. Still, I have no idea why my mother thought this particular book would interest her ten-year-old son. Certainly she knew I had absolutely no interest in school. Indeed, perhaps that explains why she thought Holt's book would appeal to me.

In any event, I read it and quickly moved on to other things. I don't recall the book having made any major impact at the time. But today, as I try to trace the genesis of my ideas, it is impossible to overestimate Holt's influence. I freely and fully acknowledge my profound intellectual debt to the late, great John Holt. No one has ever had a clearer understanding of how children learn, nor more clearly expressed those insights. We are all fortunate that his torch of education reform has been ably taken up by John Taylor Gatto, three-time New York City Teacher of the Year, New York State Teacher of the Year, and author of *Dumbing Us Down* and *The Exhausted School.*

Later, my ideas on education were shaped by my own experience working with hundreds of students individually, and thousands more in groups. My observations were influenced by recent work in motivation theory as well as cognitive science and cognitive psychology. I would like to single out the work of three professors whose work has had a major influence on my thinking: Mihaly Csikszentimihalyi, former chairman of the Department of Psychology at the University of Chicago and the author of *Flow: The Psychology of Optimal Experience;* David C. McClelland, former professor of psychology at Harvard University; and W. Edwards Deming, visiting Professor at Columbia University and the world's leading expert on quality management.

A big collective thanks to Eve Levy, John Kremer, Joan Margolis of the Brooklyn Learning Center, Carrie Seares, Jessica Dorf, Sarah Leberstein, Jill Rothstein, John Kremer, Eve Levy, Laurie Laba, Neale Eckstein, Benjamin Eckstein, Lisa Eckstein, Sabrina Padwa, Kara Stern, Brandon Michael Smith, and Lori Etringer for all your help and suggestions in shaping the final manuscript.

Thanks to my editor, Dick Marek, for believing in the project. Thanks also to his able assistant Jason Graham, and to all the other folks at Crown who helped make it happen: Andrew Martin, Steve Magnuson, Jim Davis, Ken Sansone, Kay Schuckhart, John Sharp, Andrea Connolly, Debra Kampel, Hilary Bass, Helen Zimmermann, Arlene Dion-Borg, Phyllis Fleiss, Michelle Sidrane, and the dynamite sales force. I realize I'm not the easiest author to deal with.

The following individuals deserve special mention: Jerry Speyer, for encouraging me to make a difference; George and Nancy O'Sullivan, and Brad, Ryan, and Christina, for their friendship and support; Kerry Conrad and the guys at O'Sullivan Graev & Karabell for their help over the years; Claire Wyckoff for helping out with the marketing effort; Joe Spencer, for refining the Smart Student logo; Genevieve "Alfalfa" Williams, for her impeccable aesthetic sense; and Ellen Lewis, for all her help and sense of humor in the eleventh hour.

I am especially indebted to the following individuals:

- Bethany Chamberlain, Diana Amsterdam, Durrae Johanek, and Estelle Kleinman, for their invaluable editorial suggestions;

- Julie Coopersmith, for representing me over the years and being a friend (again, I realize I'm not the easiest author to represent);

- Alex Knowlton, Richard Tesoro, and John T. Parham of Parham-Santana Design for designing the book and giving visual shape to the concepts;

- Paige Williams and Gail "Legs" Eisenberg, for their wit, enthusiasm, and outstanding editorial input (Paige is also responsible for the student notes throughout this book);

- Sam Nisson, Shane Nisson, and Bessie Wohl, three frighteningly smart students at Brown, Columbia, and Harvard respectively, for their brilliant feedback.

- Matthew Robinson, for going above and beyond the call of duty as a brother, pitching in to help out every aspect of the project;

- McDonald Comrie, for his strategic planning;

- Jeff Smith, for his legal and business acumen;

- Noah King, for his insights into students and his outstanding help on the manuscript;

- Julie Parham, for her support and all her help in selling the dream;

- Charles Nunn, for his profound wisdom; and

- Philip Yee, all-round Macintosh computer god and the closest thing to Star Trek's Scotty that I'll ever find. James Brown may be the hardest working man in show business, but Phil is the hardest working man in the Mac world.

Finally, a very special thanks to Amy Margolis for helping me articulate my ideas. Amy is an outstanding tutor in her own right and without her suggestions this book would not be what it is today. She deserves much credit for the final format of the methodology.

I dedicate this book to my mother, Joan Robinson, for giving me the courage to pursue my ideas; to my late grandmother, Claire Robinson, the goodliest, saintliest woman I have ever known; and above all to my late father, Walter Wendell Robinson, the person who taught me how to think.

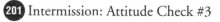

# of Contents

WHAT SMART STUDENTS KNOW

What This Book Will Do for You

IMAGINE...

You are in a room with thirty other people. You are all about to begin playing a long and complicated game, so a referee is on hand to enforce the rules and keep score.

You look around to size up the competition. Here's what you observe. A few players seem very talented or skillful. Some are highly motivated and have put in extra hours of hard preparation. And a few seem unprepared or indifferent. But most players, like you, have average talent and experience. They have prepared for the game with a fair amount of practice.

The referee blows a whistle and everyone begins playing hard. As the days pass, the game progresses. All the players are earning at least a few points, but you notice increasingly more of them becoming discouraged, falling behind, and not trying as hard.

You notice something else. Certain players consistently rack up most of the points. There's something odd here, because these are neither the most talented nor the hardest working players. You can't figure out why they are succeeding while others struggle and fail.

There's another odd thing about this game: you all play, even though the referee didn't explain the rules. In fact, if you were to ask the referee something as basic as how points are scored, he wouldn't be so sure himself!

Who can compete in a game with no established rules, and what kind of game is this, anyway?

THIS ISN'T JUST A GAME

This is school.

The referees are your teachers, the players are you and your classmates, and the point totals are your grades. The unspoken rules are the arbitrary criteria teachers use to determine grades. And remember: not even the referees—your teachers—are exactly sure how they do this!

Now, if neither the most talented nor the hardest working students earn the highest grades, who does?

The ones who know the rules, the ones who know how teachers actually determine grades. The smart students.

Smart students not only get higher grades than their classmates, they also learn more, in less time, and get more satisfaction out of the entire process. This book shows you how they do it.

The founding fathers in their wisdom decided that children were an unnatural strain on their parents. So they provided jails called school, equipped with tortures called education.

JOHN UPDIKE

1

Of course, there's more to school than grades. School is also a place for you to make friends, join clubs, compete in sports, and discover what you're all about. But the primary reason you're in school is to get an education.

WHO SHOULD READ THIS BOOK

If you're in high school or college, this is a practical guide for improving your academic performance. If you are younger, the material may be a little sophisticated to handle on your own, so you may want to ask someone older (a friend, a parent, a teacher) for some guidance.

But even if you're not in high school or college, this book has much to offer. It's for parents who want to know what they can do to improve their children's learning skills. It's for teachers who want to see school through the eyes of their students so they can teach better. It's for adults who want to take up a new subject and teach themselves. And it's for voters, educators, politicians, business leaders, and policymakers who are concerned about the real crisis in our nation's classrooms.

WHY YOU NEED THIS BOOK

*Education may be
defined as that period
during which you are
taught facts you do
not want to know, by
people you do not
know.*

GILBERT KEITH
CHESTERTON

Until now, your learning methods have probably been hit-or-miss—frustrating, inconsistent, and inefficient. **No one bothered to teach you the most important academic skill: <u>how to learn</u>.** Your teachers (and perhaps you) assumed that the ability to learn in a school setting was a natural gift—either you were born with the knack or you weren't.

This belief is entirely wrong.

Learning is a natural ability, but learning in school is another matter. If school were structured in a way that better conformed to how you learn naturally, you wouldn't need me or anyone else telling you how to learn. After all, you don't need anyone telling you how to learn a subject you're passionate about. If school didn't distort the natural learning process and make learning itself an alien experience, this book wouldn't be necessary.

Most students exhaust themselves with inefficient, laborious, and sometimes completely counterproductive study methods because they have misconceptions about what actually goes on in school. They don't know how grades are determined, why textbooks are so hard to read, or what it means to understand something. Their mistaken ideas about school and learning lead them to adopt the wrong goals and strategies. They've been conditioned to accept school as it is instead of molding school to their needs. What's more, they've come to believe (wrongly!) that any difficulty they have is their fault, rather than school's.

It doesn't matter whether you're getting straight A's or struggling to get C's; your misconceptions about school and the learning process are probably making school a lot tougher than it has to be. Whatever grade you are in, whatever subjects you are studying, whatever marks you are getting, you could be learning more in less time, earning higher grades, and having more fun in the process. In this book I'll show you how.

I wish I had known back in high school the skills and techniques you are about to learn. Like you, my perceptions and attitude got in my way. It wasn't until college that I realized how painless—even fun—excelling at school could be.

This book debunks the myths that stand between you and academic success. It's going to be a long time before school systems change, but you can change your experience today. You could learn how to become a smart student on your own through years of trial and error, but why bother? This book shows you how to do it by sharing the experience of hundreds of smart students.

TWENTY QUICK AND EASY TIPS TO STRAIGHT A'S!
TRIPLE YOUR READING SPEED IN THIRTY MINUTES!
SPEED LEARN ANY SUBJECT IN A WEEK!

If you believe claims like that—and I hope you don't—you've got the wrong book. But if you want to excel—and who doesn't?—if you're frustrated by how little you learn, or want to spend less time learning more, this book is for you.

For every person wishing to teach, there are thirty not wanting to be taught.
W. C. SELLAR

If you're in college, you probably picked up this book for yourself. If you're in high school, I'll bet a parent bought it for you. "Gee thanks, Dad! What a terrific present. I think I'll skip the movies Saturday night and read this book!" You were probably so overcome with enthusiasm that you immediately flung it on your bookshelf.

I don't blame you. When I was in school I never read books on how to study either. Sure, I picked up a few study guides over the years. I even started to read one or two, but I rarely got beyond the first chapter.

These guides were as boring as the textbooks they were supposed to help me understand. Their advice was either obvious, trite, or impractical. I tried to follow some of their recommendations, I really did, but I lacked the super-discipline their suggestions apparently required. I figured that any student who could do half the things these books advised wouldn't need help in the first place.

A few pseudo-hip guides claimed to teach students how to earn high grades without learning much, but these guides missed the point. I wanted to learn as much as I could and earn high grades; I just didn't want to sacrifice my waking hours in the process.

THIS BOOK IS DIFFERENT

Other books assume that if you're not doing as well in school as you'd like, something is wrong with you. **I start from the premise that something is wrong with school.**

I'll show you how <u>your perceptions of school affect</u> not only <u>how well you</u> do and how much you learn but also <u>how you feel about yourself</u>. Then I'll show you how to alter your perceptions and get your subconscious attitude working for you instead of against you.

This book lets you in on the secrets of smart students. It provides you with proven skills culled from observations of and interviews with hundreds of successful students. Smart students do not all learn in precisely the same way, but surprisingly there are many common denominators. I've taken what smart students do instinctively, or have learned through trial and error, and created a system out of it: the CyberLearning method.

CyberLearning turns you into a <u>self-propelled learning machine</u>. It allows you to rework and personalize any subject so it becomes an extension of you. Using CyberLearning, you can take any subject, no matter how alien, and master it so well you'll own it!

Even if you're already a smart student, you'll pick up pointers. You'll discover dozens of tips and techniques on how to maximize your grades while increasing how much you learn, including the following:

- how to read in a way that keeps you concentrated, involved, and interested
- what to do when you can't understand your textbook
- how to personalize any subject and make it your own
- how to take notes that improve your understanding
- how to decide what information is important to know, and what can be safely ignored
- how to remember what you need to know
- how to anticipate what kinds of questions will be on tests
- how to take different types of tests
- what to do when you're stuck on a test question
- how to express your ideas most effectively in papers
- what your teachers look for when determining your grades

In short, I'll teach you how to play and win the game of school. **I'll show you not just what to do and why, but also what *not* to do.** I'll step you through the entire process, from first assignment to final exam, so that you can see how the various learning skills work together.

If you hate studying—even if you love studying—I'll show you how to get more done in less time. With the time you'll save you can pursue things you'd like to do, rather than things you were assigned to do: take up a new sport, run for student council, write for the school newspaper, get a part-time job.

HOW TO READ THIS BOOK

This book will introduce you to an entirely new way of looking at school. A few ideas and techniques will take some getting used to. Whenever the text bogs you down, take a break. Don't try to read this book straight through in one sitting. I strongly suggest you skim through the entire book leisurely to get acquainted before settling down to business. **Start by skimming the headings and bold text. You'll also find practical tips and summaries highlighted in gray boxes.**

I recommend that you read the chapters in the order presented, as each chapter builds on the previous one. Each part, however, is a complete unit, so if you have an exam coming up or you're under a deadline to write a paper, you might want to turn immediately to the relevant sections. If you feel like skipping around, you should at least begin with *Part I: How Smart Students Think About School*. Whatever you do, be sure you take the quiz beginning on page 15 before doing anything else.

To change your perceptions about school, I'll be using terms you will not be familiar with. For example, instead of "preparing" for an exam, smart students use the term "rehearsing" for one. If you're looking for a specific topic that you don't find in the *Table of Contents*, check out the *Index* on page 273.

ANYONE CAN BECOME A SMART STUDENT

Smart students learn more, in less time, earn higher grades, and have more fun in the process. This book shows you how to become one. And if you're already a smart student, I'll show you how to become even smarter.

Sound good? Here's the catch.

I'll provide the basic blueprint for academic success—CyberLearning—but you'll have to tailor specific methods to your unique needs and learning style. And simply reading about it is not enough; you'll have to work through some exercises to get the full benefit of CyberLearning.

I wish I could say that getting straight A's is a snap once you know a few simple techniques, but it isn't that easy. CyberLearning enables you to learn more efficiently than other students, but you must still make an effort.

That is, you'll still have to think. Unlike passive listening or reading, thinking requires active effort. Smart student techniques are demanding. They require you to work with greater concentration. But they do work!

It will take some time to give up your old habits and get used to the new techniques you will be mastering. This change won't happen overnight; after all, your learning habits have formed over years. These smart student techniques will save you an amazing amount of time, but initially you'll have to spend some time mastering them; figure a few hours a week for the next couple of months. If you practice these methods a little each day, they'll soon become automatic habits.

School days, I believe, are the unhappiest in the whole span of human existence. They are full of dull, unintelligible tasks, new and unpleasant ordinances, and brutal violations of common sense and common decency.

H. L. MENCKEN

MY PROMISE TO YOU

My method requires small changes in your learning habits and a big change in the way you see school. These changes will require some effort on your part—at times a prodigious effort—but they will lead to startling improvements in how much you learn and the grades you receive. What you are about to learn will benefit you for the remainder of your academic career—indeed, for the rest of your life.

WHY I WROTE THIS BOOK

Education is the state-controlled manufactory of echoes.
NORMAN DOUGLAS

I'm not an educator, a teacher, a scholar, or a psychologist. If you've read any of my other books, you know that I developed a system that cracked wide open standardized tests like the SAT, GRE, GMAT, and LSAT. The few simple techniques of my system enable tens of thousands of students each year to improve their scores dramatically. But becoming a smart student involves more than learning test-taking strategies. My goals in this book are much more ambitious. I wrote it to show you how to improve your grades by mastering an entirely new way to learn.

I confess to having mixed feelings about this. Most students are far too concerned with grades and not concerned enough with genuine learning. Sadly, this distorted priority is reinforced in all too many classrooms.

Earning high grades and learning as much as you can are not the same thing, nor do grades measure how much or how little you learn. Grades reflect everything from penmanship to popularity, and are frequently used to reward "good" behavior or punish "bad" behavior.

If you don't know the rules of the game, it is possible to learn a lot and still receive mediocre marks. It is also possible to learn very little and receive high marks. There's really no big secret to how you do this. All it takes is figuring out what's on tests and what kind of answers your teachers expect.

Granted, high grades do make your life easier, but don't just settle for getting by. **You invest a significant chunk of your life in school; you have a responsibility to demand more of yourself than just achieving a high GPA.**

I wrote this book to improve your academic performance by returning *you* to the center of the learning process. Your school experience has probably been less than ideal. I am convinced that little substantive learning takes place in our schools as they are now organized. This book demystifies the learning process and shows you how to teach yourself.

I am not against schools, and I am not against teachers. I am for you—the student. I am adamantly against anything that interferes with your developing genuine understanding and an independent, questioning, self-confident state of mind.

Although school might be the problem, you are the solution. **I wrote this book to change the way you see school, to change the way you see the world, and to change the way you see yourself.**

THIS IS YOUR WAKE-UP CALL!

What Smart Students Know is a manifesto. It urges you to rebel against those who attempt to spoon-feed you an education and force you to learn their way. It's time to achieve intellectual and academic success on your terms as well as theirs. And once enough students do this, they'll set off an earthquake under the educational establishment. Then maybe we'll see some real changes in the school system.

You are playing for enormous stakes—the education you get today will be with you for the rest of your life. Starting today you are going to take charge of your education. After you finish the next chapter *(The Real Secret),* you will never again see school—or yourself—in the same way.

Are you ready? Because once you begin to take control of your educational destiny, there is no turning back. Once you decide to become the driver rather than a mere passenger, you won't ever again be content taking the back seat. From now on, how much you learn and how well you do will be entirely up to you.

Go for it!

BY THE WAY

This chapter is really the introduction. I didn't call it one, however, because it contains important information and I know you don't always read introductions or pages numbered with Roman numerals. Sorry about the minor deception.

P.S.
Any student trying to memorize anything in this book is *completely* missing the point.

How Smart Students Think About School

PART I

The Real
Secret

SMART STUDENTS AREN'T ANY "SMARTER" THAN OTHER STUDENTS

We all know, or have known, students who don't seem to be that much smarter than anyone else, or to work that much harder, and yet they consistently excel. I'm not talking about brainiacs or kids who live at the library. Yet compared with their classmates, smart students learn more in less time, receive higher grades, and have more fun in the process.

How do they do it?

Motivation is one factor, but smart students are not motivated to work hard for its own sake, or to learn because it's expected of them, or to please anyone else. Smart students mainly try to please themselves.

As for working hard, smart students are always looking for better, more efficient ways of doing their work. In many respects, smart students are much lazier than their classmates!

Intelligence is another factor. Now, when I say "intelligence," I don't mean high IQ. The kind of intelligence necessary in school, as well as in many aspects of life outside school, is not some kind of mysterious, inborn ability. Instead, it's a habit. Smart students are in the habit of asking certain sorts of questions. We'll get to these questions later. In the meantime, rest assured that if you can read this book, you have sufficient intellectual capacity to handle your studies.

Academic skills certainly play a part in their success: smart students know how to read efficiently, get the most out of their classes and lectures, understand and memorize material, prepare for and take tests, and write well. But these are not natural abilities. They, too, are skills that can be mastered.

WHERE DO SMART STUDENTS LEARN THESE THINGS?

Sometimes it's a matter of luck. A student will stumble onto the secrets of doing well. A few resourceful students discover these secrets for themselves, learning the hard way through patient observation and persistent trial and error. Sometimes a parent or an older brother or sister who learned the hidden rules of the game will pass them on. **And many smart students were originally inspired somewhere along the line by a great teacher.**

Yet most smart students assume (wrongly) that everyone approaches school in the same way they do. To them there is nothing special about how they study and learn: it seems to come naturally. But it doesn't. Whether they were conscious of it or not, at some point smart students learned how to learn. Fortunately, you can, too.

You cannot teach a person anything; you can only help him find it within himself.
GALILEO

Yet these techniques are not the real explanation for the success of smart students.

SO WHAT'S THEIR REAL SECRET?

Smart students do not simply study more efficiently than their classmates in the way, say, that an Olympic track star runs more efficiently than a weekend jogger—smart students do completely different things. **Smart students have different skills, goals, habits, priorities, and strategies because they see school, the learning process, and even themselves differently.** In a very real sense, smart students and their classmates attend different schools.

ATTITUDE—THE CRITICAL DIFFERENCE

It's all attitude. Attitude is the way you define and interpret your experiences. Your attitude is the sum total of your beliefs, assumptions, expectations, and values. It determines the meaning or significance you attach to events, and your response to them. In short, your attitude is how you look at the world.

Your attitude about learning and your self-image profoundly affect one another. After all, when you're a student, school is the basis of your life. Your attitude determines how you experience school, what goals you set, and the techniques and strategies you choose to reach them. As a result, your attitude determines how much you learn and how well you do.

When I first started writing this book, I thought my job was a simple matter of describing how smart students study and learn. But the more I talked with students, the more one thing became clear: smart students use completely different study and learning methods because they see things in a completely different way. They have a completely different attitude. This is why they use completely different study and learning methods.

I can show you the techniques and strategies smart students use, but until you see things differently, these methods will affect your performance very little.

WHAT SMART STUDENTS' ATTITUDE IS NOT

Let's get something straight here. When I refer to the attitude of smart students, I'm not talking about the importance of having a "positive mental attitude." And I'm certainly not referring to the attitude you hear teachers talk about when they say things like "Sally has a good attitude, it's a shame her brother Billy has such a bad attitude." A good attitude in that sense usually means making a show of cheerfully doing whatever your teachers want.

WHAT SMART STUDENTS' ATTITUDE IS

Smart students know that you can teach yourself far better than any school possibly can. Because smart students have this extraordinary attitude, they approach every aspect of their schoolwork differently.

Think of it this way: Michael Jordan doesn't just play basketball differently from other players—he sees the game differently. He also sees himself differently. If you want to rack up those baskets in the game of school, you must change the way you see it. <u>You must also change the way you see yourself.</u>

THAT'S THE HARD PART

Changing your learning habits and techniques isn't that easy, but it's a piece of cake compared with changing your attitude. Your attitude is deep-rooted, even subconscious. And you'll have to work doubly hard at changing it. As you will see, the school system reinforces damaging attitudes every day in many subtle (and not so subtle) ways. Changing your attitude is so critical to becoming a smart student that throughout this book we will be working through exercises designed to do just that.

Forget passively accepting what the education system has to offer: <u>being a smart student means taking charge and teaching yourself.</u> Becoming a smart student means taking responsibility for your education. The central message of this entire book can be summed up in a sentence: **<u>No school can teach you the way you learn best, so how much you learn and how well you do is up to you.</u>**

ACCEPTING RESPONSIBILITY

<u>Becoming a smart student means that you'll have to demand more of yourself.</u> It means you'll have to get over the fears that go with being independent. It means you'll have to <u>do more than your teacher asks you to do</u>. And it means <u>no more excuses.</u>

Sometimes you'll <u>be stuck with</u> a <u>boring teacher</u>, a <u>stupid assignment</u>, or a <u>lousy textbook</u>. It's <u>still your job to find ways to master the material so you can ace your papers and your exams.</u> You may feel uncomfortable with this notion. <u>You may believe that simply listening to your teachers and completing your assignments means that you'll learn your subjects and that you're entitled to good grades.</u> You better get over that feeling soon because I'm telling you right now: there is <u>no such guarantee</u>.

You may have to get over feelings of guilt. You may actually discover a moral conflict about doing better in school with less work. "No pain, no gain" sound familiar? Smart students work hard when they must, but they don't want to work any harder or longer than absolutely necessary. <u>Smart students hate wasting time or energy.</u> They would <u>rather spend half an hour in intense, concentrated study than spread that effort out over several hours of aimless and superficial review.</u>

<u>Remember their motto: "Maximum grades, optimum learning, minimum time."</u> When smart students work hard—and there's no getting around it when you teach yourself—it's because the hard work is immensely satisfying.

The notion that hard work can be satisfying may sound weird at first, but if you look at the activities you most enjoy, you'll see that these are the activities you work hardest at. Few things are as satisfying as hard work that gets results, or as frustrating and demoralizing as hard work that doesn't. Smart students don't mind working hard—when they have to—because their hard work pays off.

Of course, if you enjoy studying all night without learning much, and want only the grades you "deserve," you may not like this book. But if you want to learn more in less time and earn higher grades, you'll *love* this book.

Take This Quiz!

(Twenty Reasons You Could Be Working Harder and Longer Than You Have to, Yet Learning Less and Receiving Lower Grades)

IF YOU WANT TO BECOME A SMART STUDENT

You have to see things the way smart students do. As I mentioned in the previous chapter, attitude is the critical difference between smart students and their classmates, and changing your attitude is no easy task.

You may already have the right attitude without realizing it. Or you may feel guilty about that attitude, as if something's wrong with you for having it. We will keep returning to your attitude throughout the book (in periodic *Attitude Checks*), but first let's take a basic inventory.

There is too much education altogether, especially in American schools.

ALBERT EINSTEIN

YOUR INITIAL ATTITUDE INVENTORY

This is just a questionnaire, not a test you're being graded on. It is designed to give you insights into your attitude, so it is crucial that you put down the response that best reflects what you truly think and feel, not what you think is the "right answer." If your opinions have already been influenced by what you've read so far, select the option that best indicates how you felt before you picked up the book.

ATTITUDE CHECK

Instructions: Next to each statement below, put a 1 if you agree with it and a 0 if you disagree. Read each one carefully. These are not trick questions, so take them at face value. This is an important exercise. Don't agonize over your selections, but do give each statement some thought before responding. Take a stand and answer every question.

---

[0] 1. You are not naturally good at or even interested in learning, so you need to be told by a teacher what to learn and how to learn it.

[0] 2. You cannot be expected to learn on your own or from other students.

[0] 3. You learn in essentially the same way and at the same rate as every other student in your class.

[1] 4. Textbooks are the best resource from which to learn a subject.

[0] 5. Since you are not good at learning, subjects need to be simplified and broken down into a series of skills (tasks, units, objectives) that are presented as drills or workbook exercises. You find such exercises especially rewarding.

[1] 6. Your teacher telling you something is the same thing as teaching it, and you understand that material when you can repeat what the teacher has told you.

[1] 7. The more facts you can repeat, the more you understand.

[0] 8. You would not be interested in learning if you were not "motivated" with rewards like good grades and public praise, or with punishments like bad grades and public criticism.

[0] 9. You would not be interested in learning if you were not tested frequently.

[0] 10. Calling on you randomly in class and expecting an immediate response is a particularly effective teaching method.

[1] 11. Grade competition increases how much you learn and brings out the best in you and your classmates.

[0] 12. If you find, say, history boring, this is because the subject is dull rather than because of the way you are forced to learn it.

[0] 13. There is a certain body of key cultural information that you and everyone else should know; if you do not learn this information by the time you graduate, you never will.

[0] 14. The important information that you need to know is on tests; if something is not on a test, it's not important.

[0] 15. Teachers determine your grades on a consistent, objective basis.

[0] 16. Your marks on tests accurately reflect how well you understand the course subject matter; your grade point average is a good indicator of how much you have learned in the past and how smart you are.

[1] 17. If you listen to what your teachers say and do what your teachers tell you to do, you will learn as much as you are capable of learning.

[0] 18. The faster you learn, the more intelligent you are.

[0] 19. Any learning that takes place in school is a result of your teacher's teaching you; not learning is your fault.

[0] 20. If the way school is run causes you to become confused, discouraged, or rebellious in any way, something is wrong with you.

Add the individual responses to compute your total score. Total Score: ___5___
The maximum possible score is 20, the minimum is 0. We will discuss this quiz and what your score means in the next chapter.

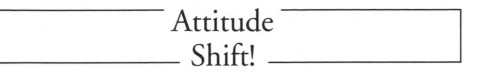

Attitude Shift!

OKAY, LET'S TAKE A LOOK AT THE QUIZ YOU TOOK

1. You are not naturally good at or even interested in learning, so you need to be told by a teacher what to learn and how to learn it.

   Jeepers, I hope you disagreed with this one. You learn best from a trained teacher, who should be in total control of the learning process. Sorry, but no teacher knows how you learn best. And you'd better find out quickly if you don't already know!

2. You cannot be expected to learn on your own or from other students.

   Smart students strongly disagree with this statement. Before entering school we manage to teach ourselves the fundamentals (with a little coaching from parents). And there's no reason you can't learn as much from your classmates as from your teachers.

3. You learn in essentially the same way and at the same rate as every other student in your class.

   Nonsense! Every student learns differently, which is another reason why you and only you know how best to teach yourself.

4. Textbooks are the best resource from which to learn a subject.

   Textbooks separate subjects from real life and spoon-feed you isolated and disconnected facts. How many adults do you know who learn their jobs from textbooks?

5. Since you are not good at learning, subjects need to be simplified and broken down into a series of skills (tasks, units, objectives) that are presented as drills or workbook exercises. You find such exercises especially rewarding.

   I don't think so. Next.

6. Your teacher telling you something is the same thing as teaching it, and you understand that material when you can repeat what the teacher has told you.

   Sorry, but telling you something and having you repeat it does not mean that you understand that material. Don't confuse memorizing with understanding.

7. The more facts you can repeat, the more you understand.

   Gong! When was the last time a trivia expert won a Nobel Prize?

I am always ready to learn, but I do not always like being taught.

WINSTON CHURCHILL

8. You would not be interested in learning if you were not "motivated" with rewards like good grades and public praise, or with punishments like bad grades and public criticism.

 Take my word for it—you *are* interested in learning. The ever-present threat of bad grades encourages anxiety, not true learning.

9. You would not be interested in learning if you were not tested frequently.

 See my previous comment. Of course you're interested in learning. What you're not interested in is *not* learning, wasting your time, or feeling stupid.

10. Calling on you randomly in class and expecting an immediate response is a particularly effective teaching method.

 Give me a break! This "teaching" method achieves little more than a classroom atmosphere of general panic and possible humiliation. Learning through intimidation? Not interested.

11. Grade competition increases how much you learn and brings out the best in you and your classmates.

 Competition in school is corrosive. It most certainly does not bring out the best in anyone trying to learn. Instead, it creates the impression that learning is worth doing only if you're being graded on it. And since everyone learns at different rates and in different ways, what could grade competition possibly be about? Smart students don't need the spur of grades to make them learn. And ironically, anyone more interested in grades than in learning is going to be beaten in the grade game by someone who's more interested in learning. I can't stress this concept enough.

12. If you find, say, history boring, this is because the subject is dull rather than because of the way you are forced to learn it.

 More likely it's the other way around.

13. There is a certain body of key cultural information that you and everyone else should know; if you do not learn this information by the time you graduate, you never will.

 Who says learning takes place only in school?

14. The important information that you need to know is on tests; if something is not on a test, it's not important.

 Obviously the information you're tested on is important, but tests don't cover everything important in a subject. And they certainly don't cover all the information you need in your life.

Desire for approval and recognition is a healthy motive; but the desire to be acknowledged as better, stronger, or more intelligent than a fellow being or fellow scholar easily leads to an excessively egoistic psychological development.... Therefore the school and the teacher must guard against employing the easy method of creating individual ambition, in order to induce the pupils to diligent work.

ALBERT EINSTEIN

15. Teachers determine your grades on a consistent, objective basis.

    No way! Grading couldn't be more inconsistent, subjective, or arbitrary.

16. Your marks on tests accurately reflect how well you understand the course subject matter; your grade point average is a good indicator of how much you have learned in the past and how smart you are.

    Schools seem to think so, but I hope you don't. Grading is far from being an exact science. Your marks on tests reflect a number of things, of which your understanding is only one factor; your awareness of what your teacher thinks is important also plays an important role.

17. If you listen to what your teachers say and do what your teachers tell you to do, you will learn as much as you are capable of learning.

    That's a comforting thought, but completely wrong. Following orders doesn't guarantee learning.

18. The faster you learn, the more intelligent you are.

    Where was this ever proven? There are sprinters and there are marathoners; everyone learns at a different pace.

19. Any learning that takes place in school is a result of your teacher's teaching you; not learning is your fault.

    Please tell me you disagreed with this one. Students who have difficulty learning as school insists everyone learn are unfairly labeled lazy, stupid, misbehaved, unmotivated, or "learning disabled."

20. If the way school is run causes you to become confused, discouraged, or rebellious in any way, something is wrong with you.

    More likely something is wrong with school.

INTERPRETING YOUR "SCORE"

By now you probably realize that the lower your score, the better. The higher your score, the more you've been brainwashed by the school system. Not to worry. Together we're going to change that. I'll be working on your attitude for the rest of the book, and you'll see how you're progressing with periodic *Attitude Checks.*

If your grand total was a zero, congratulations—yours is the attitude of a smart student. Welcome to the club. But perhaps you haven't thought of yourself as a smart student. Many potential smart students have the right attitude about school and the learning process, but they've been made to feel guilty about their beliefs. Like their classmates, they've been brainwashed by school to think something is wrong with them, when in fact there's something wrong with school.

WHAT YOU'RE UP AGAINST: HERE'S WHAT SCHOOLS THINK ABOUT *YOU*

You don't acquire your attitude in a vacuum—it's shaped to a large extent by the viewpoint of the school system. This viewpoint is not publicized, but it's not hard to see what it is. To discover how the school system sees *you*—its subject—we should not listen to what it says, but observe what it does. If we take an unflinching look at the typical school experience, if we examine how school is structured, how classes are run and what class time is devoted to, how subjects are taught, what books are used and how they are written, what assignments are given, and what kinds of tests are administered, it becomes very clear how schools view you and your ability to learn.

To find out, simply turn back to the attitude quiz you just took. The purpose of it was to give you a chance to see how much your attitude has been indoctrinated by the school system. **You see, our school system strongly agrees with every one of those statements!**

DOES THAT SURPRISE YOU?

To me the worst thing seems to be for a school principally to work with methods of fear, force, and artificial authority. Such treatment destroys the sound sentiments, the sincerity, and the self-confidence of the pupil. It produces the submissive subject.

ALBERT EINSTEIN

It should. Of course, not all schools or teachers believe all those things about you. If you asked, most teachers would probably deny many of them; some might even be insulted. But while you may not be aware of these institutional attitudes, be assured that they are embodied in our education system.

Unfortunately, you, too, have been conditioned by school and probably share at least some of these beliefs. As a result, you spend more time and energy than you have to, while learning less and receiving lower grades. It is hard to escape their influence because these attitudes are reflected and reinforced in every aspect of school life. Indeed, these notions are so ingrained in the American consciousness that most people have difficulty accepting that they are in fact myths.

THE SMART STUDENT'S CREDO

All smart students, consciously or unconsciously, share twelve beliefs or principles about school and the learning process. Study this list:

Principle #1:	Nobody can teach you as well as you can teach yourself.
Principle #2:	Merely listening to your teachers and completing their assignments is *never* enough.
Principle #3:	Not everything you are assigned to read or asked to do is equally important.
Principle #4:	Grades are just subjective opinions.
Principle #5:	Making mistakes (and occasionally appearing foolish) is the price you pay for learning and improving.

Principle #6:	The point of a question is to get you to think—*not* simply to answer it.
Principle #7:	You're in school to learn to think for yourself, not to repeat what your textbooks and teachers tell you.
Principle #8:	Subjects do not always seem interesting and relevant, but being actively engaged in learning them is better than being passively bored and not learning them.
Principle #9:	Few things are as potentially difficult, frustrating, or frightening as genuine learning, yet *nothing* is so rewarding and empowering.
Principle #10:	How well you do in school reflects your attitude and your method, not your ability.
Principle #11:	If you're doing it for the grades or for the approval of others, you're missing the satisfactions of the process and putting your self-esteem at the mercy of things outside your control.
Principle #12:	School is a game, but it's a very important game.

You don't have to memorize these principles; we'll be discussing and reinforcing them throughout the book. (**By the way, there's nothing magical about the number twelve. I just wanted to keep the number of principles manageable.**)

SEEING YOURSELF AS A SMART STUDENT

Taking a look at what amounts to the foundation for a new attitude, you probably notice that these principles reflect not just how you see school and learning, but how you see yourself.

I never let schooling interfere with my education.
MARK TWAIN

Your self-image has a powerful influence on your academic performance. Aren't all our efforts directed at proving our self-conception? If you see yourself as someone who can't learn, you won't, regardless of the techniques I'm about to show you. Your self-image is crucial to your becoming a smart student, and this is something you have to work out for yourself. If you see yourself as someone who can learn, you will, despite the difficulties you encounter.

The self-image of most students is greatly affected by how well they do at school, which is one of the reasons they find school so difficult. **Paradoxically, the self-image of smart students is not influenced by their performance in school, even though they excel.** Smart students are motivated to learn in spite of—not because of—school.

If you want to stop sabotaging yourself and your performance in school, you must first get some idea of what truly makes you tick. I can't change the way you see yourself—you have to do that—but I can change the way you see school.

What I've tried to do in this chapter is to begin to get you to see school and the learning process through the eyes of smart students. Once you see school in a new light, you'll begin to feel differently about yourself.

ONWARD AND UPWARD!

It's not enough for me to tell you what smart students believe. You must accept these things in your heart.

Your attitude has developed over your academic lifetime. It will not change overnight, but the process will pick up momentum the minute you begin. As your attitude begins to change, so will your success in school, which will lead to further changes in your attitude, and still greater achievements.

WHAT'S COMING UP

Changing your attitude is half the battle, the harder half, but still only half. We're now going to explore the techniques smart students use to teach themselves: CyberLearning.

How Smart Students Learn

PART II

Learning the Old Way

THROWING YOU IN THE DEEP END

Okay, let's get started. For some idea of the problems involved with reading and understanding a textbook—as if you haven't experienced this before—we're going to work through a sample textbook passage together. You'll learn how *not* to approach a textbook, and you'll see how a smart student would tackle it.

Sorry, but like most textbooks, the passage I've selected is overdense with information, dry, and—let's be frank—dull. I've chosen this particular geology passage for several reasons. First, its level of difficulty approximates that of most textbooks at the high school and introductory-college level. It allows me to demonstrate all the techniques smart students use to strip down and analyze complex and confusing text.

But I also selected the following passage because I think you'll have absolutely no interest in the subject matter. In fact, I'm fairly sure you will find nothing in the passage that seems even remotely relevant to anything in your life. I'm not trying to punish you. It's important for you to see that by using CyberLearning, you can take an interest in anything you read.

To get the full benefit of this book, you'll have to work through various exercises along the way. You don't have to agonize over them—we both know you're not being graded here—but try to give them a decent shot. More than just reinforcing my points, these exercises will get you into the habit of looking at information differently, actively. It's fun! It's empowering! It's the way smart students sail through their courses. Welcome aboard!

Two exercises follow. We'll be discussing them in the coming chapters. **Please do them in the order presented. By the way, since later exercises will refer to your work in earlier ones, do all your exercises on loose sheets of paper (not in a spiral notebook).** This way you'll be able to move pages and compare your work as it progresses. Write on one side of each sheet only, number the exercises, and keep them together.

┌─────────── EXERCISE #1 ───────────┐

Instructions: A little free-association. Before you read the following textbook excerpt, take a few minutes to jot down on a sheet of paper everything you know about rocks, or what they remind you of. If you think of any questions, jot down those, too. You don't have to write complete sentences; phrases or abbreviations are fine. Don't be afraid of being too obvious, simplistic, or farfetched. To get you in the spirit of things, I'll start you off with the first few thoughts and questions that popped into my head: *hard; old (How old? How do we measure?); boulders.*

└────────────────────────────────────┘

┌─────────── EXERCISE #2 ───────────┐

Instructions: Read the following passage as if you were in a course in geology or earth science, and your entire grade depended on a test you were going to have on this passage next week. Take notes and mark up the passage the way you normally would when studying for an important exam. (Of course, we both know you aren't going to take a test on it next week, but try to get into this exercise anyway.)

└────────────────────────────────────┘

The purpose of this exercise is to see how you read this passage and take notes on it, so you don't have to study it at length (though you'd get more out of the exercise if you did). As you read and take notes, try to be aware of your thoughts and feelings.

You're going to have to wrestle with this passage a bit; it's only 520 words, but it's fairly dense. To see how you handle plain text, I have removed the helpful headings, diagrams, italics, and other graphic and visual aids you might find in a textbook. Since this is a learning exercise, you'll have to make do without such clues and signposts.

ROCKS

Rocks are hard, natural masses of solid matter that make up the earth's crust. With a few exceptions (such as coal), rocks are composed of one or more minerals. Geologists classify rocks as either igneous, sedimentary, or metamorphic, depending on how they were formed.

Igneous rocks are formed from magma, the molten matter deep within the earth. There are two types of igneous rock. If magma rises toward the surface, it slowly cools and sometimes solidifies underground. The result is intrusive igneous rock. If magma reaches the earth's surface, it emerges from volcanoes or fissures (cracks) as lava. Lava cools rapidly aboveground, solidifying into extrusive igneous rock. Intrusive igneous rock, such as granite, can be identified by its large, clearly visible mineral grains (crystals). Because extrusive rock solidifies more quickly than intrusive igneous rock, it is characterized by tiny crystals. Basalt, with its fine texture, high density, and dark color, is the most common extrusive igneous rock, lying beneath the vast ocean floor. Pumice, another common extrusive igneous rock used in some abrasives, acquires its rough porous texture from the explosive release of gas that often accompanies volcanic eruptions.

Virtually all sedimentary rocks are formed when particles, known as sediments, accumulate in strata (layers). Most sediments are created when rocks of any kind are broken down by erosion or weathering. When these particles cement or compact together and harden, they form sedimentary rock. Shale, the most common sedimentary rock, is formed from mud and clay; sandstone, as its name suggests, is formed from sand. Some sediments, however, are created from animal or plant remains that have decayed or decomposed in water. Most limestone, for example, is formed from the minerals of decomposed shells or skeletons of marine organisms, while coal is formed from plants that have decayed in swamps. Sedimentary rock usually forms under water. It can frequently be identified by characteristic layers or by particles of different sizes, and often contains fossils.

Metamorphic rocks are formed when rocks of any type are changed by long periods of intense heat or pressure within the earth. This process, known as metamorphism, alters the texture, structure, and mineral composition of the existing rock, usually making it rougher and more dense. Metamorphic rock can sometimes be identified by its distorted structure, or by wavy bands. When the sedimentary rock limestone undergoes metamorphism, it becomes marble. Shale, another sedimentary rock, becomes slate under metamorphism, while the igneous rock granite becomes gneiss.

As hard as they are, rocks do not last forever. Rocks above ground are continuously exposed to weathering and erosion. Over thousands or even millions of years, they are broken down and worn away to sediments, which can later form new sedimentary rocks. Rocks below ground can also change. Any rock subjected to sufficient heat and pressure undergoes metamorphism and forms new metamorphic rock. And if the heat is great enough, any rock can be melted back into magma and later form new igneous rock. Thus, any type of rock can be transformed into one of the others. This dynamic, never-ending process of rock formation is known as the rock cycle.

HOW DID YOU FEEL?

We'll return to the passage and the exercises shortly. Before we do, though, let's talk about how you felt as you read it. Were you bored? Distracted? Confused? Did you resent being asked to do something? Were you overwhelmed by the facts? Did you feel pressured to remember everything as you were reading? How much do you remember? Did you understand the passage as a whole? Are you sure?

MEET JOHNNY, A TYPICAL STUDENT

Here's what Johnny was thinking about and feeling as he read the passage and took notes on it.

Johnny glances at the title and immediately begins reading the first sentence.

> *Let's see, how many pages is this stupid assignment? I hope it doesn't take all night. Great! A short passage on rocks. How hard can this be? Let's see here. Rocks are hard, solid matter—so tell me something I don't know. Minerals, yeah, I kinda knew that. Uh-oh, scientific words. Igneous, sedimentary, and metamorphic? I've never seen those before; better copy them down—they'll be on the test for sure.*

After reading each sentence, he takes notes on whatever seems important, trying to use as many of the author's words as possible. Since he owns this "textbook," he also highlights—a lot. He isn't following anything that he's reading, but somehow highlighting nearly everything reassures him that "he's not missing anything."

> *Intrusive igneous rock? What does that mean? Basalt has a fine texture, high density, a dark color, and lies beneath the ocean floor. I wonder if that's gonna be on the test. Strata? What's that? Who knows. Who cares. This stuff is incredibly boring; when am I ever going to need it in real life? Hey! What time is it? I wonder if I should call Diane.*

Johnny is trying hard. He really wants to finish this assignment, but he's having a hard time concentrating or even following what's going on. He's bored, confused, and overwhelmed; and, as the passage goes on, he's feeling pretty stupid.

> *Let's see here. Huh? Some sedimentary rock is made from animal remains. That's weird. I wonder how that happens. Oh well, I suppose I better copy that down, too; it might be important.*

Despite his struggles, Johnny is conscientious; he's determined to complete the assignment even if it takes all night. So he plods through the text, word after dull word, detail after dull detail, hour after dull hour.

> *Distorted structure, wavy bands. I'm not following any of this stuff; no way I'm gonna remember it all for the test! Wait a second—now they tell me any type of rock can become any other type of rock. What the heck! First they tell me there are different kinds of rocks and now they tell me any kind of rock can become one of the others. This is getting complicated. Maybe I should take a break. I'm getting hungry. I wonder if there are any munchies in the fridge. Hey! I forget. What's a rock?*

And so on.

Some time later, Johnny completes his assignment. Despite having taken detailed notes and reread them several times, he realizes that he doesn't understand or even remember more than a few words of what he read! Still, Johnny feels satisfied because he has done precisely what the teacher assigned. (Johnny is evidently unaware of Smart Student Principle #2: Merely listening to your teachers and completing their assignments is *never* enough.)

HOW *NOT* TO TAKE NOTES

Here are Johnny's notes on our sample passage (they had to be reduced a bit; don't worry if you can't read every word).

Rocks
 - hard, natural masses of solid matter that make up the earth's crust
 - composed of one or more minerals (except for coal)
 - 3 types: igneous, sedimentary, metamorphic, depending on how formed
 - Igneous: - formed from magma (molten matter within earth)
   - two types of igneous: if magma rises and cools underground: intrusive igneous r. if magma reaches surface, it emerges from volcanoes or fissures (cracks) as lava, cooling quickly: extrusive igneous r.
   - granite, intrusive; large visible mineral grains
   - extrusive, characterized by tiny crystals
   - basalt, under ocean floors, fine texture, dark color, high density
   - pumice (used in abrasives), porous, from volcanoes; gases
 - Sedimentary: - formed from particles (sediments), accumulate in layers (strata)
   - sediments created when rocks broken down by erosion or weathering
   - when particles cement/compact together, harder, they form sed. rock
   - shale (most common) formed from mud + clay
   - sandstone from sand
   - some sediments created from animal/plant remains in water
   - limestone formed from the minerals of decomposed shells/skeletons of marine organisms
   - coal is formed from decomposed plants in swamps
   - sed. r. frequently identified by layers, particles of different sizes; fossils

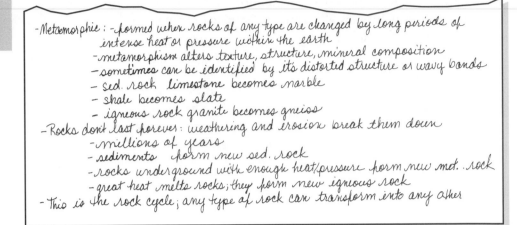

- Metamorphic : - formed when rocks of any type are changed by long periods of
                intense heat or pressure within the earth
        - metamorphism alters texture, structure, mineral composition
        - sometimes can be identified by it's distorted structure or wavy bands
        - sed. rock limestone becomes marble
        - shale becomes slate
        - igneous rock granite becomes gneiss
- Rocks don't last forever : weathering and erosion break them down
        - millions of years
        - sediments   form new sed. rock
        - rocks underground with enough heat/pressure form new met. rock
        - great heat melts rocks; they form new igneous rock
- This is the rock cycle; any type of rock can transform into any other

WHAT'S WRONG WITH THESE NOTES?

Plenty. Johnny took notes on each sentence as he read it, without waiting to see
whether the information was important or not. As a result, he took far too many
notes. He rarely used abbreviations or his own words. Notice that his notes give
everything equal emphasis; nothing stands out as especially important. Johnny's
notes follow the same linear format as the passage; it's impossible to see the
connections between the various facts and ideas.

These are the sort of notes you might take during a lecture, when you're
rushed and trying to keep up with your teacher. But as textbook notes they are
practically useless since all they do is repeat what the author says.

In the coming chapters I'll show you how a smart student would take notes.
Now let's take a look at Johnny's notations on the actual passage text.

HOW *NOT* TO MARK UP YOUR TEXTBOOK

Here's how Johnny marked up the sample passage.

ROCKS

Rocks are hard, natural masses of solid matter that make up the earth's crust. With a few exceptions (such as coal), rocks are composed of one or more minerals. Geologists classify rocks as either igneous, sedimentary, or metamorphic, depending on how they were formed.

Igneous rocks are formed from magma, the molten matter deep within the earth. There are two types of igneous rock. If magma rises toward the surface, it slowly cools and sometimes solidifies underground. The result is intrusive igneous rock. If magma reaches the earth's surface, it emerges from volcanoes or fissures (cracks) as lava. Lava cools rapidly aboveground, solidifying into extrusive igneous rock. Intrusive igneous rock, such as granite, can be identified by its large, clearly visible mineral grains (crystals). Because extrusive rock solidifies more quickly than intrusive igneous rock, it is characterized by tiny crystals. Basalt, with its fine texture, high density, and dark color, is the most common extrusive igneous rock, lying beneath the vast ocean floor. Pumice, another common extrusive igneous rock used in some abrasives, acquires its rough porous texture from the explosive release of gas that often accompanies volcanic eruptions.

Virtually all sedimentary rocks are formed when particles, known as sediments, accumulate in strata (layers). Most sediments are created when rocks of any kind are broken down by erosion or weathering. When these particles cement or compact together and harden, they form sedimentary rock. Shale, the most common sedimentary rock, is formed from mud and clay; sandstone, as its name suggests, is formed from sand. Some sediments, however, are created from animal or plant remains that have decayed or decomposed in water. Most limestone, for example, is formed from the minerals of decomposed shells or skeletons of marine organisms, while coal is formed from plants that have decayed in swamps. Sedimentary rock usually forms under water. It can frequently be identified by characteristic layers or by particles of different sizes, and often contains fossils.

Metamorphic rocks are formed when rocks of any type are changed by long periods of intense heat or pressure within the earth. This process, known as metamorphism, alters the texture, structure, and mineral composition of the existing rock, usually making it rougher and more dense. Metamorphic rock can sometimes be identified by its distorted structure, or by wavy bands. When the sedimentary rock limestone undergoes metamorphism, it becomes marble. Shale, another sedimentary rock, becomes slate under metamorphism, while the igneous rock granite becomes gneiss.

As hard as they are, rocks do not last forever. Rocks above ground are continuously exposed to weathering and erosion. Over thousands or even millions of years, they are broken down and worn away to sediments, which can later form new sedimentary rocks. Rocks below ground can also change. Any rock subjected to sufficient heat and pressure undergoes metamorphism and forms new metamorphic rock. And if the heat is great enough, any rock can be melted back into magma and later form new igneous rock. Thus, any type of rock can be transformed into one of the others. This dynamic, never-ending process of rock formation is known as the rock cycle.

WHAT'S WRONG WITH JOHNNY'S TEXTBOOK NOTATIONS?

Johnny gave as little thought to marking his textbook as he did to taking notes. Instead of deciding what was important and then underlining that, he underlined and highlighted everything that *might* be important. In other words, Johnny marks up his textbooks to avoid thinking while reading. Moreover, Johnny rarely if ever takes notes on *his* thoughts and questions.

I'll also show you how smart students mark up their textbooks later (page 99 if you want to peek ahead).

LEARNING THE OLD WAY: DOES THIS SOUND FAMILIAR?

I'll bet that your current approach to studying a textbook probably goes something like this.

1. You read the text, taking notes as you go along. If you own the book, you highlight anything that seems important, and underline anything that seems especially important.

2. You reread your textbook, perhaps more than once, to see if there's anything you missed.

3. If you're fussy, you might recopy your notes more neatly.

4. In the following weeks, you reread your notes as many times as possible. As exam time approaches, you'll do this more often, repeating the material and quizzing yourself to be sure you've memorized as much as you can.

You're not alone—this is how most students study. And like most students, you're probably often surprised by the difficulty you encounter on tests. You don't understand this because the material doesn't seem so difficult when you are "studying," or when you quiz yourself the night before.

So why do tests seem so much harder than you expected, and why don't you score better?

SUMMARY

I know that doing something again and again the same way is comforting. But the standard reading-highlighting-rereading approach to studying and learning is almost a complete waste of time. To list just some of its problems:

- **It's passive.** Although you feel as if you're busy "studying," passing your eyes over the text repeatedly, you're not really doing anything; that is, you're not doing any thinking. Trying to learn this way is about as active as watching television. If you ever have trouble concentrating while studying, it's because you're not doing any active thinking that engages your mind with the material.

- **It's boring.** Reading and rereading is by definition monotonous. And if you repeat information often enough, chances are that not only will you fail to understand it but it will become meaningless.

- **It's ineffective.** The standard approach to learning—reading and rereading—isn't an efficient way to memorize facts, much less to understand them. Studying this way ignores the way your mind works. For instance, try saying a word over and over—eventually it becomes meaningless!

- **It's not practicing anything important.** If you want to improve at football, practice football. If you want to improve your piano playing, practice playing the piano. You aren't practicing understanding when you highlight your textbook mechanically and reread your notes endlessly. What you *are* practicing is highlighting and reading; unfortunately, you will not be tested on how well you do these things.

The problem isn't you, it's your approach. The challenge is finding a learning method that puts you in control of the process, keeps you interested and engaged in the material you're studying, and produces genuine understanding!

Learning the New Way:
— Introducing CyberLearning —

UNLEARNING SOME BAD HABITS AND ACQUIRING GOOD ONES

CyberLearning may require some immediate changes in your study habits. Instead of reading a textbook over and over, you'll be reading it once thoroughly. Instead of highlighting every third sentence, you'll be taking notes. If you do mark up your textbook, you'll do so sparingly. Instead of taking notes on everything, you'll be selecting only the most important information. And instead of rereading your notes all term long, you'll be constantly changing and revising them, trying to reduce them eventually to a single sheet.

The one real object of education is to leave a person in the condition of continually asking questions.

BISHOP MANDELL CREIGHTON

WHAT IS CYBERLEARNING?

"Cyber" comes from an ancient Greek word meaning to pilot, or to be in control. CyberLearning is the dynamic process by which you (not your teacher, not some textbook author) take control and become the pilot in your own education.

CyberLearning begins with *dialoguing:* the process of asking a specific cycle of questions of the material you're studying. Gradually, by organizing and reorganizing the information, and by making connections between the new material and what you already know, you build genuine understanding.

DIALOGUING: A MODERN VERSION OF AN ANCIENT TRADITION

The process of using questions as a means of discovering knowledge and building understanding has been around for several thousand years. It is known as the Socratic method after the famous Greek philosopher. Socrates was immortalized in a number of *Dialogues* written by his equally famous student, Plato. (If you haven't read any of Plato's *Dialogues*, I highly recommend them. You'll find them highly entertaining, and you'll learn a lot about how to reason.)

The Socratic Manner is not a game at which two can play.

MAX BEERBOHM

The Socratic method has been used as a teaching tool for centuries in traditional European universities such as Oxford and Cambridge. The trouble with the Socratic method as typically used is that the teacher does most of the asking and the student does most of the answering. As you'll see, the teacher is then doing the hard work (asking the questions), not the student.

You should be asking the questions, not your teacher. **Knowing what questions to ask is much more important than merely knowing "the answers."** Once you know what questions to ask the answers will rarely be difficult to find.

I refer to this questioning process as "dialoguing" because you are setting up an internal dialogue between yourself and the material you're studying. By asking and answering your own questions instead of relying on someone else's, you become your own teacher. Once dialoguing becomes a *habit,* you'll be able to teach yourself any subject. The key is knowing what questions to ask and when to ask them.

CYBERLEARNING: THE TWELVE QUESTIONS

Consciously or unconsciously, all smart students ask the same twelve basic questions when they are learning a subject. These questions form the basis of CyberLearning. We'll be spending an entire chapter on each question, so for now I'll just outline them for you. Don't worry if they don't make much sense; once we get to the individual questions you'll see how a smart student would apply them to the geology passage and it will all become clear.

Here's a brief outline:

Question 1: What's my purpose for reading this?

Before you begin reading, you need to know precisely why you're reading so you'll know what you should be looking for. You'll find an in-depth discussion of this question in the chapter beginning on page 45.

Question 2: What do I already know about this topic?

After glancing at the title but still before you start reading, you should warm up by taking a couple of minutes to jot down quickly everything you know about the topic. Turn to the chapter beginning on page 49 if you'd like to see an examination of this question. Now it's time to make the first pass over the material.

Question 3: What's the big picture here?

Before you start reading the material closely, you skim through it to get an outline of the main points. We'll look at this question more thoroughly in the chapter beginning on page 53. Now that you've warmed up with the first three questions, you start reading the text closely.

Question 4: What's the author going to say next?

As you begin to read the material closely, you try to stay one step ahead of the author by anticipating what he or she will say next. We'll look at this question in greater detail in the chapter beginning on page 63.

Question 5: What are the "expert questions"?

Each subject asks a unique set of questions that you need to keep in mind as you read. The chapter beginning on page 67 explores this question at length.

Question 6: What questions does this information raise for me?

As you read, you need to be aware of the other questions the material should be raising in your mind. You'll find an in-depth discussion of this question in the chapter beginning on page 71.

Question 7: What information is important here?

As you're reading, you need to decide what information is important enough to include in your notes. What's important will depend on your purpose (Question 1). The chapter beginning on page 81 provides a closer look at this question.

Question 8: How can I paraphrase and summarize this information?

As you take notes on the important information you are selecting, you should translate the author's words into your own, using as few as you can. You'll find more on this question in the chapter beginning on page 89. After you've finished taking notes on the passage, you should not need to refer to the passage further.

Question 9: How can I organize this information?

Once you've finished taking notes, explore them to see how the information is organized and whether you can create any new groupings or links that make sense. You'll find a thorough discussion of this question in the chapter beginning on page 101.

Question 10: How can I picture this information?

Again looking over your notes, your goal now is to translate as much of the information into symbols and pictures as possible. I'll demonstrate how to answer this question in the chapter beginning on page 107.

Question 11: What's my hook for remembering this information?

Now that you've worked with the information and begun to understand it, you need a hook or gimmick to ensure that you'll be able to remember what you need to know for tests. You'll find a detailed discussion of this question in the chapter beginning on page 111.

Question 12: How does this information fit in with what I already know?

As you look over your notes, you should be trying to see how the new information fits in with what you already know—not just about that topic but about others as well. This question is examined in the chapter beginning on page 121.

Again, don't try to memorize these questions—you'll soon be asking them automatically! (By the way, it's just a coincidence that there are twelve questions as well as twelve principles.)

SOME GENERAL OBSERVATIONS

We will be working through the Twelve Questions in great detail in the coming chapters, but for now I'd like to make a few preliminary observations about the overall process:

Question 11:
What's my hook for
remembering this
information?

- **Depending on your purpose, some questions are more important than others.** If you're in a class where you are graded by papers instead of tests, for example, Question 11 (memorizing) is less important. So that you can see all the questions in action, however, I'm going to work through each one exhaustively as if you had to prepare for a final exam.

- **The same questions apply whether you are learning from your textbook and other readings or from your teacher in class.** There are of course differences between the two situations, which I will point out as we explore the individual questions. (The next chapter will be an intermission discussing classes and lectures.)

- **The order of the questions is approximate only.** Some questions overlap and you can combine them, some you ask simultaneously, and some you ask over and over.

- **Have some scratch paper ready.** Your brain has a limited processing capacity, so you'll need to jot down your thoughts. Since your brain handles visual images more easily than it handles words or abstract concepts, paper allows you to give concrete shape to your ideas.

BEFORE WE BEGIN: A FEW WORDS ABOUT YOUR SUPERSONIC BRAIN

In this and the coming chapters, you and I are going to be listening in on the thoughts of a smart student as he or she analyzes the geology passage. Don't be intimidated—this process is going to take us much longer to follow along than the actual thinking-involved took.

Let's take a simple example so you can see what I'm talking about. Imagine that you've just finished dinner. A friend calls you up and asks if you'd like to see a movie. Here are the thoughts (questions) that flash through your head:

- *Have I seen the movie?*
- *If so, do I want to see it again?*
- *If not, what have I heard about it?*
- *Do I want to see it?*
- *How will I get there?*

- *Even if I don't want to see this movie, would I still like to go with this person?*
- *Who else is going?*
- *How do I feel about that?*
- *Is there anyone I'm trying to avoid that I might run into at the theater?*
- *Is there anything else I should be doing?*
- *Can I afford the ticket?*
- *What's happening after the movie?*
- *How will I get back home?*
- *How late?*
- *What do I have to do tomorrow?*
- *Is there anyone who might object to my going?*
- *Do I have any other plans?*
- *If so, do I want to break them?*
- *How am I feeling now?*
- *How will I feel in a couple of hours?*
- *How would this person feel if I said yes?*
- *If I said no?*
- *Do I care?*
- *If I say no, do I want to offer an excuse or suggest an alternative?*
- *If I say yes, should I make any special requests?*

Phew! Twenty-five questions, and I probably missed some that occurred to you! Yet all these questions flash through your head, your amazing brain processes them faster than a mainframe supercomputer, and in a second or two you respond: "Sure! Sounds like fun! When can you pick me up?" Or you might say, "No, thanks, I'd like to but I've got exams coming up and I'm way behind in my reading." The point is that if we were to discuss each of these questions in detail, it might take us an hour or more to explore them adequately.

I mention this so you won't be intimidated by the length of the discussion that follows in the coming chapters. We may spend five pages discussing a question that you can answer in five seconds. I don't want you to lose your time perspective.

WHAT'S COMING UP

The next chapter is a brief but important intermission on classes and lectures. If you'd like to get right into the CyberLearning method, you can skip directly to the first of the Twelve Questions on page 45 and return to the intermission later.

SUMMARY

You may be feeling a little overwhelmed by the Twelve Questions. Perhaps all of it seems so new, so far from anything you've been taught, that you can't imagine becoming comfortable with any of it. Some elements of CyberLearning may already be part of your study habits, so don't panic.

In most classrooms, teachers ask questions and students look for answers. But asking the right questions is usually the hard part—the part that makes you think most about the material. Smart students' learning is self-guided. They ask their own questions. When smart students read about rocks (or about anything else), they maintain a dialogue between themselves and the text, constantly asking questions and searching for answers. So they aren't just reading the passage, they're engaging it.

The following chapters will explore the twelve fundamental questions that every smart student asks. These questions may seem like a lot the first time through, but with practice you'll be asking them automatically. Soon you'll be using these twelve questions to master any body of knowledge, adapting them to different types of classes, different subjects, and different situations. For now, though, grab some scrap paper, and get ready to take control of your education.

Intermission:

Applying the Method in
Classes and Lectures

GETTING INFORMATION FROM A TEACHER INSTEAD OF A BOOK

You listen in classes and lectures for the same reason you read your textbooks: to extract the important information you will need to process later for understanding. But listening to your teacher and reading your textbook are not the same, as you well know. When reading, you set the pace; when listening, your teacher does. And even more important, the person you listen to in class—unlike the person who wrote your textbook—is usually the one who determines your assignments, makes up your tests, and decides your grade.

In this chapter we'll examine the pluses and minuses of processing spoken (as opposed to written) information. Once you recognize these and understand how to use the Twelve Questions to unscramble the puzzle, you'll be well on your way to never being glazed, dazed, surprised, or mystified by a lecture again.

Let's consider the disadvantages first.

THE DISADVANTAGES

The major disadvantage of class lectures is that you are forced to keep up with your teacher. Also, even great lecturers are not always coherent, and jump from topic to topic. Your teacher not only sets the pace but also determines the general topic and does most of the talking. In other words you are thrust into a passive role. This is less true in a seminar or small class, or in classes where students are encouraged to ask questions and contribute to discussions. But in most classes you have little choice but to listen and take notes.

No matter how great the lecture, it's hard not to resent this role. Your passivity makes it difficult to concentrate and listen attentively. It also creates the illusion that you understand a topic simply because you can follow what your teacher is saying about it. Don't think that being able to follow a lecture means you'll be able to answer test questions on the material. After all, your teacher has done all the hard work—selecting and organizing information—for you. Listening to your teacher is like watching a gymnast perform a flip and saying, "I watched that carefully and it doesn't look so hard. I can do that."

While you are always limited by having to keep up with the teacher, there are ways for you to take a more active role during lectures. We'll cover these in the coming chapters. Now let's examine the advantages.

THE ADVANTAGES

While not the ideal way to learn, lectures are still the best way to discover what the teacher thinks is important. Teachers make it a point to cover everything they consider worthwhile. Given the way most students read and study, teachers can't be sure students are getting the information from their textbooks.

There also seems to be a universal unspoken agreement between teachers and students that anything not mentioned in class is off-limits as far as tests are concerned! In any event, most teachers feel guilty if they test you on something that was not at least mentioned in class.

Furthermore, your teachers, unlike the authors of your textbooks, know you and your classmates. They have a sense of what you do and don't understand, and can tailor their lecture to your needs and questions about their subjects.

The advantages of lectures far outweigh the disadvantages. Although attending lectures and keeping up with your reading are both essential, lectures are ultimately much more important to your grades.

CLASSES AND LECTURES: NUTS AND BOLTS

Here is some general advice about classes and lectures.

- **Complete any assignments from the previous class, especially assigned textbook reading.** Keep a step ahead. Don't wait to hear the lecture before you read the chapter on the topic. You may think this will save you time, since the teacher will stress the important material (instead of your having to figure out what's important by reading everything). But if you don't read the assigned chapter, you may have a very difficult time following the lecture at all. What's more, if you read the chapter beforehand, you will see where and how your teacher deviates from the textbook—a valuable clue for possible test questions. (**If you haven't done the reading—shame on you—try the following smart student tactic.** As soon as class begins, take the first opportunity to raise your hand and say something, no matter how straightforward. This way you'll lessen the chance your teacher will call on you later—when you may not know the answer!)

- **Review your notes from the previous lecture as well as the assigned reading.** Do this as close to the time of the lecture as you can. This allows you to add and connect what you learn in this lecture to what you already know.

- **Bring your textbook.** Your teacher may refer to it. An obvious point but worth noting.

- **Bring your notes from your textbook assignment.** You may find it faster to add the lecture notes directly to your textbook notes.

CLASSES AND LECTURES: NUTS AND BOLTS (CONTINUED)

- **Bring your notes from the last class only.** Leave your other notes at home. It's too easy to lose a semester's worth of notes as you run around. You can easily replace a lost textbook, but lost notes are a major headache.

- **Show up on time.** Lateness will be interpreted as disrespect or lack of interest or both, and you'll miss the important first few minutes of the lecture. Teachers often make announcements or summarize their main points during the first few minutes of class. If you know you have to leave early, let your teacher know before the lecture and sit near the door so you won't disrupt the class when you exit. If your presence won't be missed—like in one of those large college introductory courses that are held in rooms like coliseums—just slip out discreetly.

- **If you can choose your seat, pick one that encourages you to concentrate.** Some students prefer to sit near the front of the class because they get distracted looking at other students. Others find it more distracting to have students behind them, so they sit in the back. Others avoid window seats, and so on. Sit next to a friend (but not one who is talkative or makes you giggle!) so you can peek at his or her notes if you miss something the teacher says.

- **You don't have to suck up to your teacher, but don't go out of your way to create a bad impression either.** Don't slouch in your seat. Pay attention. Teachers like to see students who follow, or at least seem to follow, what they are saying. What they're looking for is a room full of heads nodding in agreement (*not* nodding out in sleepiness). Reading a book or talking with a friend is not going to win you any points with your teacher. You'd be surprised how far whispers can carry; if you've ever spoken in front of a group, you know how distracting even minor sounds can be.

- **Wait before asking a question.** If you have a question about something the teacher says, put a question mark in the margin of your notes and wait to see whether your teacher answers it. If not, raise your hand. If it is inappropriate for some reason to ask a question during class, ask your teacher afterward, or ask a classmate. (Be careful about asking questions if you haven't done the assigned reading, or you might be broadcasting that fact to your teacher.)

- **If you're confused about a specific point, ask your teacher for an example.** Examples are usually easier to understand than abstract explanations. If you don't understand the example the teacher provides, ask for another.

CLASSES AND LECTURES: NUTS AND BOLTS (CONTINUED)

- **When the teacher calls for a response from the class, think about the question before you raise your hand.** You shouldn't be the first person in the room to raise your hand. What's more, if you listen to the questions and insights of your classmates instead of volunteering your own thoughts, you'll be surprised at how much you can learn from them.

- **If you disagree with something the teacher says, voice your objections cautiously.** Don't come across as a know-it-all. Your teacher has an ego, just as you do. And don't think that ego isn't present at grading time.

- **Don't use a tape recorder unless you absolutely must.** Tape recorders simply double the amount of time you spend listening to your teacher. The sense of security they provide is false; as you will learn shortly, not every word your teacher utters is important.

- **Quiz yourself!** Right after the lecture—on your way to the next class, if necessary—take a minute or two to summarize to yourself what was just covered in class. You can jot this down on paper, or just do it in your head. Doing this helps "fix" the main points in your memory. You won't be able to remember every idea, but you should be able to sum up the main ones in a few sentences. Doing this is an excellent way to begin rehearsing for tests.

I'll have more to say about lectures in the coming chapters.

WHAT'S COMING UP

In the next chapter I'll begin demonstrating how smart students answer the twelve basic CyberLearning questions. I may use some terms you are unfamiliar with, and you may not understand everything I'm doing, but just pay attention and follow along. In a short time everything will become so clear and obvious you'll wonder why you weren't always approaching school this way.

Remember, you now know more about the ins and outs of lectures than you did a few pages ago. And it was relatively painless. Now it's time to move on to the core of an entirely new system of learning.

Okay, then. Ready? Let's begin with the first CyberLearning question.

Answering Question 1:
What's My Purpose for Reading This?

KNOW WHERE YOU'RE GOING AND WHAT YOU'RE LOOKING FOR

Do you ever go into a crowded grocery store with no real purpose, just to wander aimlessly among the canned goods and produce? Of course not. It would be a frustrating waste of time. Reading a textbook without a conscious goal is like aimlessly wandering the aisles of a store—only it has more disastrous consequences.

The way you shop in a store will vary depending on what your shopping goal is. Shopping for a pair of basketball sneakers is different from browsing for a birthday gift; doing your weekly grocery shopping is different from running to a corner store to cure a sudden case of the munchies.

The same flexibility of approach should be true of the way you read. There are many reasons you might be reading something in school:

- doing research for a paper
- studying for a final exam
- looking up important information
- scanning for general ideas
- preparing for a class discussion

Whatever your assignment, you probably begin by diving right into the material without considering why you're reading it. But you shouldn't do this, because the way you read and what information you get out of the material will depend on your purpose. If you don't define your purpose in reading, how will you know what information to look for? **Remember Smart Student Principle #3: Not everything you are assigned to read or asked to do is equally important.**

The way you study—that is, the way you ask and answer the Twelve Questions—depends greatly on what and why you are studying. The way you read your textbook should be different from the way you read a magazine article. Likewise, the way you study for a class in which your grade is determined by papers should be different from the way you study when it is determined by tests. For that matter, the way you study for a multiple-choice test will be different from the way you study for an essay test.

Question 1:
What's my purpose for reading this?

Question 2:
What do I already know about this topic?

Question 3:
What's the big picture here?

Question 4:
What's the author going to say next?

Question 5:
What are the "expert questions"?

Question 6:
What questions does this information raise for me?

Question 7:
What information is important here?

Question 8:
How can I paraphrase and summarize this information?

Question 9:
How can I organize this information?

Question 10:
How can I picture this information?

Question 11:
What's my hook for remembering this information?

Question 12:
How does this information fit in with what I already know?

Question 3:
  What's the big picture
  here?
Question 11:
  What's my hook for
  remembering this
  information?

QUESTION 1 SETS THE STAGE FOR ALL THE OTHERS

You don't need to write anything for this question, but it should always be in the back of your mind as you study. Although you can answer it in a few seconds, this question is crucial. because it forces you to assess how deeply you need to explore the other eleven questions.

For example, if your purpose is to scan for information for a research paper, Question 11 is less important than if you were preparing for a final exam. If you're skimming a magazine article for potential paper topics, then there's no reason to go much beyond Question 3. You'll learn more about how to answer this question in the coming chapters.

BE SPECIFIC

Keep in mind that you need to state your purpose precisely. It's not enough to say, for example, that your purpose is to study for a test—what type of test will it be? If it's an essay test you'll need to pay more attention to the general ideas, whereas if it's a short-answer test, the details will also be important.

I'm not saying that you should read and study *only* what will be on the exam, but that you should keep it in mind. Like it or not, the test is still the standard by which teachers judge your knowledge and ability.

ANSWERING QUESTION 1 ON THE ROCKS PASSAGE

In the instructions to Exercise #2 (page 26), we assumed that our grade in our hypothetical earth science course depended on a test we were going to take on the rocks passage. So that's your purpose: you're studying this passage so you can ace a major exam.

Now, let's say we figure that based on our teacher's previous tests, this one will include about two-thirds short-answer questions–multiple-choice and true-false questions–and about one-third essay questions. (In *Part IV: How Smart Students Get Their Grades*, I'll show you how to figure out what will be on your exams and how to prepare for them.)

Now you know what you're looking for as you study. Since it's a major test, you'll need to explore all the eleven other questions in detail.

ANSWERING QUESTION 1 IN CLASSES AND LECTURES

It is just as important to listen with a purpose as to read with a purpose. Question 1 now becomes *What's my purpose for listening to this?* Before class begins you should give some thought to the same considerations we have just discussed for textbooks. Will you be facing a paper or test? What kind? How deeply must we analyze the lecture material by exploring the remaining eleven questions?

Don't worry if this doesn't make complete sense at this point; you've just begun the process. It will all become clear shortly.

WHAT'S MY PURPOSE FOR READING THIS?

SUMMARY

It's easy to overlook this important question in your rush to complete assignments, but before you begin always take a minute or two to define your purpose. Your purpose is not simply to read the assigned pages. You need to be specific about why you are reading the material. Is it for a test (if so, what kind of test), is it for a discussion in class, or what?

As you know, reading academic material can often seem tedious and confusing. If so, you probably haven't fully defined your purpose. You must know what you want from the material if you expect to find it. Stating your purpose is the key that lets you unlock the material and make it work for you rather than confuse you. Once you begin to take control of your subject, you're ready to ask yourself the next CyberLearning question.

Answering Question 2:
What Do I Already Know About This Topic?

GETTING WARMED UP

You probably start most of your assignments without any preparation. If you're supposed to read a chapter in your history book, you sit down at your desk, open your book to the appropriate page, and immediately start reading. That's like going for a run without stretching your muscles first. Reading a complex text is a strenuous mental exercise. If you dive into difficult material without warming up, it won't go smoothly.

Of course, at the beginning of a term you may know very little about a topic. That's okay. You can warm up for your assignment by jotting down questions you have about the subject or a few notes about what you expect to learn in the reading. If your teacher has already covered the topic in a lecture, this step acts as a quick review.

HERE'S WHAT YOU DO

After you read the title but *before* you begin reading, *quickly* and *briefly* jot down the following facts and questions:

- what you know about the topic
- what the topic reminds you of
- what you'd like to know or expect to learn

You'll get more out of this step if you write things down rather than just "do it in your head." The physical act of writing actually activates more of your brain. You won't need to save your work, so you can just use your own shorthand on scratch paper. The point of answering this question is simply to prepare you brain to receive the new information, not to take notes you'll be studying from.

I realize that writing this information down takes a lot of self-control but Answering Question 2 should be easy and fun; treat it like a game and let your imagination go.

HERE'S WHY YOU DO IT

If you're used to rushing into an assignment, taking even a few minutes to warm up may seem silly. But hold on a second. Warming up is supposed to turn reading into a game by getting you curious: you'll be reading the material to see how closely you guessed what the author says.

Question 1:
What's my purpose for reading this?

Question 2:
What do I already know about this topic?

Question 3:
What's the big picture here?

Question 4:
What's the author going to say next?

Question 5:
What are the "expert questions"?

Question 6:
What questions does this information raise for me?

Question 7:
What information is important here?

Question 8:
How can I paraphrase and summarize this information?

Question 9:
How can I organize the information?

Question 10:
How can I picture this information?

Question 11:
What's my hook for remembering this information?

Question 12:
How does this information fit in with what I already know?

Warming up has other benefits, too:

- **It starts the process of generating questions.** As you become aware of what you know and don't know about something, you'll think of key questions that need answering.

- **It makes you aware of what you know and don't know about a topic.** You'll often be surprised that you know more (or less) than you thought.

- **It puts you on the lookout for new information.** It paves the way for the information you're about to absorb and helps you remember it by connecting new material with what you already know.

- **It's valuable practice in resourceful thinking.** Even if you know very little about a topic, being able to "make do" with what you already know will come in handy when you're faced with a test question you draw a blank on.

- **It acts as a review.** If you already know quite a bit about the topic, warming up gives you a chance to quiz yourself.

- **If makes you the authority.** Before you are influenced by the author's ideas and opinions, warming up gets you to express your own thoughts freely. Doing this lessens your dependence on the text and forces you to think for yourself.

Don't skip your warm-up! Again, I know this step seems like a lot of work but it should take five or ten minutes at most and can save you hours of wasted study later. I promise.

ANSWERING QUESTION 2 ON THE ROCKS PASSAGE

You answered this question when you completed Exercise #1 on page 26, and now I'll show you how I answered it. Take out your work and compare our responses to this question.

Again, there's no right or wrong way to answer this question as long as you put some genuine effort into it. Still, comparing is helpful—you may look at my sheet and say "I knew that; why didn't I jot it down on my sheet?" which will encourage you to push a little harder on the next exercise.

As I admitted, I know next to nothing about rocks. As I thought about what I knew about rocks (and what I didn't know—also very important), here's what I came up with in a few minutes:

- hard
- old (how old? how do we measure?)
- boulders
- what types of rocks are there?
- what are rocks made of? certain kinds of metals or minerals?
- soil
- sand
- what's the difference between soil, sand and tiny rocks?
- what's the difference between a stone and a rock?
- stone age
- mines
- quarries
- where are mines and quarries located?
- erosion
- pebbles
- gravel
- geology
- landslides
- concrete
- is concrete a sort of man-made rock?
- skipping stones
- fossils
- how do fossils get in rocks? where are they found?
- archaeology, paleontology
- coal
- diamonds
- is coal a rock? does it become one if it forms into a diamond?
- gems
- precious stones
- are gems or jewels special kinds of rocks?
- meteorites
- are meteorites rocks from outer space?

I told you I didn't know much about rocks other than general knowledge. That's okay. Now that I have some idea of the gaps in my knowledge I can begin filling them.

ANSWERING QUESTION 2 IN CLASSES AND LECTURES

Shortly before going to class or lecture, or while waiting for it to start, guess what topic the teacher will cover. As with reading, this step turns the lecture into a game and makes it more challenging and relevant. Since most teachers and lecturers discuss a topic after giving you an assignment to read, you should be able to write quite a bit in response. It forces you to recall what you read, and readies your mind for the new batch of information.

SUMMARY

Question 2 asks you to jot down briefly anything you know about a topic before you start reading. You may dismiss this step too quickly. Don't. It is imperative that you write something down—even if the ideas seem silly. Doing this will help you recognize what you know and don't know about a topic. It also forces you to stand on your two feet without relying on your textbook. In short, warming up forces you to think for yourself. Finally, Question 2 serves as a warm-up before you begin dialoguing with the text. Question 3 will continue the warm-up process.

Answering Question 3:
What's the
Big Picture Here?

YOU NEED A ROAD MAP

You've warmed up by answering the previous questions, but you're not quite ready to begin a close inspection of the text. First you should get an overview, the big picture.

It's difficult to understand text because information is presented linearly, one fact or idea after the next. Rarely do you get a chance to see how ideas connect or where the discussion is leading. To understand something you need to see the whole as well as the parts; you need to see the general structure.

Reading without an overview is like driving to an unknown destination, with someone next to you who waits until the last second to give directions: "Okay, turn right here, now turn left, now right." What you'd like is a general idea of the route and destination before you set out.

The big picture is your personal road map. This chapter shows you how to create one so you'll be in charge. You'll always know where you are and where you're going.

WHAT YOU'RE LOOKING FOR

When you concentrate on the big picture, you're not really trying to understand the material. Nor are you trying to memorize anything. Rather, you're just trying to get a general but solid sense of what you're reading. In short, you needn't spend a lot of time on this question.

Here's all you need to get the big picture:

- **Main Ideas and Themes**
  The typical chapter contains only a half dozen or so main ideas. Make sure you "get" these before you are swamped with confusing details.

- **Important Terms and Concepts**
  Don't try to learn them at this point; just familiarize yourself with them.

- **Overall Organization**
  While you read you'll need to keep in mind the order in which the main ideas and important concepts are presented.

For now you should skip most of the facts and minor details.

Question 1:
What's my purpose for reading this?

Question 2:
What do I already know about this topic?

**Question 3:
What's the big picture here?**

Question 4:
What's the author going to say next?

Question 5:
What are the "expert questions"?

Question 6:
What questions does this information raise for me?

Question 7:
What information is important here?

Question 8:
How can I paraphrase and summarize this information?

Question 9:
How can I organize this information?

Question 10:
How can I picture this information?

Question 11:
What's my hook for remembering this information?

Question 12:
How does this information fit in with what I already know?

Now that you know *what* you're looking for, I'll tell you *where* you'll find that information. Where you look to find the big picture will depend on whether you are reading a book or a chapter. We'll consider each separately.

GETTING THE BIG PICTURE OF A BOOK

To get the big picture of a book, read the following items in this general order:

- **Preface and Introduction**
  You may think these sections are a waste of time (since teachers rarely "assign" them) but they frequently summarize the entire book. No kidding! Read them carefully (yes, even if the pages are numbered with Roman numerals).

- **Author Biography**
  A brief biography is sometimes on the inside of the book cover, or in the back of the book. You can skim this quickly. Knowing something of the author's background helps you understand his or her point of view.

- **Table of Contents**
  Read each of the chapter titles, not just the chapter you are looking for.

- **Chapter Summaries**
  Of course, not all books include chapter summaries. If the summaries are long, read the first and last few paragraphs of each.

It's not a bad idea to get the big picture of an entire book even if you're going to read only part of it. This step doesn't take that much time, and an understanding of the whole will help you grasp the part you're reading.

GETTING THE BIG PICTURE OF A CHAPTER

To get the big picture of a chapter or a long article, read the following items in this general order:

- **Chapter Title**
  Spend a minute reflecting on the title. A well-worded title can summarize an entire chapter.

- **First and Last Paragraphs of the Chapter**
  Read the entire paragraphs, since they often sum up the few key ideas.

- **Section Headings**
  Glance at the subheadings, too.

- **Tables, Graphs, Charts, Pictures, and Diagrams**
  You might be tempted to skip over figures because there's that much less to read. Don't. Figures are often used to convey complicated ideas that are difficult to express in words. Spend a moment interpreting what information these graphic devices provide.

- **The First Sentence of Each Paragraph in the Chapter**
  The *last* sentence of each paragraph is also useful, but you can skip it on longer assignments. If it's a really long chapter, reading the first and last sentences of each subsection is sufficient.

The next two items are also very important for getting the big picture.

- **Chapter Summary**
  See if you can summarize the chapter based on your quick survey *before* you read the author's summary. It's an excellent way to build your understanding as well as to prepare for exams.

- **Questions at the End of the Chapter**
  Again, try to come up with questions on your own *before* reading the author's.

Getting the big picture of a short article is not much different. Read the first and last paragraphs carefully and skim the first sentences of all other paragraphs.

WRITE IT DOWN

It's a good idea to take rough notes on scratch paper when you're getting the big picture. Having a pencil in hand and jotting down your impressions forces you to think. It's also helpful to have a written road map that you can follow when you begin to read the material in depth as you answer the other CyberLearning questions. If you're going on a long and complex journey, referring to a tangible map is much easier than trying to remember a series of complicated directions in your head. (In a passage the size of the rocks passage, a written road map isn't really necessary; for a lengthy chapter it's extremely useful.) When you've finished the chapter or article, you can throw your big picture notes away.

For an individual, however, there can be no question that a few clear ideas are worth more than many confused ones.

CHARLES S. PIERCE

STEP BACK FOR SOME PERSPECTIVE

Imagine yourself in the following situations: painting someone's portrait, supervising the construction of a skyscraper, and driving a car. What do they have in common with learning? In each one you are constantly shifting your perspective back and forth between the details and the big picture.

As a painter you work on a particular feature, then you step back to see how the feature fits in with the rest of the portrait. As a construction supervisor, you need to inspect the work on each floor, but you also need to move away from the building to see how the overall construction is going. And as a driver you take in your immediate surroundings as well as what's happening down the road.

When you're learning something you must do the same. Step back periodically. Don't get so caught up in trying to memorize all the facts and details that you miss the few main ideas the course is trying to get across.

If you ever find yourself confused by something you're reading, you've probably just lost your bearings momentarily. A good way to reorient yourself is to go back to the big picture and get it firmly in mind before continuing.

QUIZ YOURSELF!

After you've gotten the big picture, you're ready to begin reading the material. But before you jump in, I recommend that you try the following two drills, which should take no longer than a few minutes.

Even though you have only a general idea of what the material is about (after all, you haven't even begun to read the material closely), give them your best shot. You can do them aloud or on paper, but have fun.

- First, try to summarize the entire chapter in a few sentences.
- Second, try to outline brief answers to the chapter questions at the end.

You'll probably miss a lot but that's okay. You'll be surprised at how much you can piece together from the few main ideas you've picked up already, and to think you've only just begun to attack the text. These drills will not only help you understand and remember the material—they're also great test-taking practice!

ANSWERING QUESTION 3 ON THE ROCKS PASSAGE

Well, let's see. What are the major ideas in our sample passage? Here's my road map:

> - rocks made of minerals
> - three types of rocks:
>   - igneous rocks formed from molten matter
>   - sedimentary rocks formed from particles in layers
>   - metamorphic rocks formed underground from other rocks under heat and pressure
> - any type of rock can change into any other

That's really all there is to this step for our passage. You don't have to write out complete or grammatically correct sentences; you're the only person who's going to use this road map.

ANSWERING QUESTION 3 IN CLASSES AND LECTURES

WHAT'S THE BIG PICTURE HERE?

As you know, one of the advantages of books over lectures is that you can skip around in a book. Still, you can usually get the big picture of what your teacher will say if you're alert.

First, most teachers assign something to read before covering it in class. Doing your assignment will give you a summary of the main points your teacher will cover in class and will make the lecture much easier to follow. This is one more good reason for completing assignments before class.

Second, if teachers cover new ground, they will often summarize their main point in the first few minutes of their lecture. So listen up.

SUMMARY

Getting the big picture is like becoming acquainted with someone you've just met. You don't begin by asking for intimate details of their lives; you get to know them first in a more general sense.

Reading is the same way. Getting the big picture for an article should take five, maybe ten minutes tops, while getting it for a complicated chapter might take up to half an hour. This is an excellent investment of your time and with practice it will become an efficient habit. Getting the big picture will focus your reading and give you a framework you'll need to make sense of new information. Without it, a reading assignment often seems like a long string of details. With it, you'll know the major points the author is trying to make, and you'll understand the relevance of the details.

This is a critical step and will save you a lot of time later, so don't skip it. In fact, for much of the reading you have to do in school, getting the big picture is *all* you have to do. If, for example, your teacher hands out a long list of "recommended" readings, it is usually enough to get the big picture of each by skimming the chapter summaries. (Of course, if you have the time and you'd like to study closely each recommended book, be my guest.) **Just remember Smart Student Principle #3: Not everything you are assigned to read or asked to do is equally important.**

You'll learn how to tell what's worth reading closely and what's not when we review Question 7 beginning on page 81. Before moving on to Question 4, let's take a break for a critical look at something near and dear to your heart—the textbook.

Question 4:
What's the author going to say next?

Question 7:
What information is important here?

Intermission:
The Trouble with Textbooks

GO FIGURE

Students are rarely encouraged or even allowed to learn from meaningful real-life activities, the way most adults outside school do. Rather, the primary educational tool in the classroom is the textbook. Why teachers rely so heavily on textbooks may puzzle you since you probably find reading one about as easy as wading waist-deep through quicksand.

It may come as no surprise to hear that as a vehicle for conveying information, textbooks leave an awful lot to be desired.

- **Textbooks present only one point of view.** This is true even though a great many textbooks are written not by experts with teaching experience but by teams of editors. The assembly-line fashion in which many textbooks are produced leaves them riddled with errors. I don't just mean typos or omissions or silly grammatical lapses; I'm talking blatant factual inaccuracies, including some real bloopers. A recent investigation of history textbooks, for example, came across one that told the famous story of how President Truman ended the Korean War by dropping a nuclear bomb (Eisenhower was president at the time, and the nuclear bombs they were thinking of were dropped on Japan in World War II.) So much for editorial review boards.

- **Textbooks are notoriously dull, poorly written, information–dense, and crammed with jargon.** No, it's probably *not* your fault if you find your textbook difficult to read.

- **Textbooks try to be everything to everybody.** Since publishing companies want their textbooks adopted by as many states and school districts as possible, they water down their subjects to the "lowest common denominator." There's no way any one textbook can conform to your particular needs and learning style.

- **Textbooks can't present the big picture.** Even if you had a textbook written just for you, it would still not be the ideal learning tool. As you know from the previous chapter, textbooks present subjects logically, which is not the way learning—a process of trial and error—takes place. Does this sound weird? It's not. Learning a subject is like putting together a puzzle when you have no idea what the final picture is supposed to look like. Textbooks help create the illusion that the only way to learn a subject is to break it down into topics and then present them in a specific order. Some teachers get around this by assigning chapters in a different order, but the essential problem remains: textbooks can only present information linearly, one piece at a time, while your mind needs to see how those pieces fit together.

I mention these things so you don't think it's your fault if you have difficulty reading your textbooks—everyone does, even smart students. As always, however, smart students do something about it. **Remember Smart Student Principle #2: Merely listening to your teachers and completing their assignments is *never* enough.**

DON'T BEAT YOUR HEAD AGAINST A WALL

Let's say you're having trouble with the rocks passage. What to do? You could struggle with it for hours, or you could seek out another source of information.

Another source of information? Your teachers and textbooks may be the only information sources you rely on now. These are the most obvious sources, of course, but why stop there? Libraries and bookstores contain others.

Don't limit your search to other textbooks. You can learn a lot from encyclopedia entries, magazine articles, and video documentaries. Anything that helps you understand a subject is great, so don't be proud—even a children's book on the subject can get your feet wet before tackling something challenging.

Even if you have no trouble understanding your primary textbook, consulting a supplementary resource on the subject provides benefits. Every author approaches a subject from a different point of view, explains it differently, emphasizes different aspects, and provides different examples. Exposing yourself to more than one point of view is an enormous advantage even in strictly factual subjects like geology, but it's especially advantageous in the humanities.

HOW TO CHOOSE A SUPPLEMENTARY INFORMATION SOURCE

Within the first few weeks of a new course, you should have found an outside textbook or other source of information that supplements your "official" textbook. Since academic materials cost almost as much as a small sports car, check out what your public library or school library has to offer before you purchase anything.

Here are some tips on choosing supplementary information sources:

- **Ask your teacher.** Most teachers will be impressed by your initiative and will be glad to suggest other books in the field. You might also ask someone who has already taken the class or someone majoring in the field.

- **Find a book that has lots of examples, detailed explanations, and questions (preferably with answers).**

- **Beware of popular outline or study guides.** Many of them are more difficult than the textbooks they pretend to replace! They also omit a lot of key information and are usually short on examples and explanations.

- **Find a different author and publisher.** Some publishers put out workbooks or outline guides to accompany their main textbook. If you're having trouble with the textbook, however, you probably won't be helped by anything else the author has written. In any event, you're trying to get a different perspective on the subject.

- **Choose an expert with real experience in the field, and preferably some of that experience in teaching.** Don't be impressed by a list of consultants or an editorial board of advisers; these books are compiled by committee. Look instead for a book that prominently announces the name of one or two authors.

- **Look for something that seems inviting to read.** On the other hand, don't be fooled by splashy graphics. Publishers will spend a ton of money trying to make a mediocre textbook look good, so be sure it reads as good as it looks. In short, don't judge a book by its cover.

- **The later the edition, the better.** Most new textbooks have kinks that take a few editions to weed out. A book that has survived over the years clearly has something going for it. You can find out the edition on the copyright page in the front of a book.

While we're at it, there's no reason you have to rely on just one outside source of information. One history textbook may have an excellent explanation of the Civil War whereas another textbook has a better explanation of Reconstruction—use them both.

HOW TO USE YOUR SUPPLEMENTARY INFORMATION SOURCE

Once you've chosen a supplementary source of information, look up your specific topic in the index or table of contents. For our passage, you would be looking up *rock*, *sedimentary rock*, *metamorphic rock*, and *rock cycle*, so you might have to skip around. After you have gotten a handle on the material, you'll have a much easier time when you return to the "official" passage.

I'm not saying you should rely exclusively on outside sources of information. You are still responsible for reading the material in your primary textbook since your class discussions and tests will be based on it, not on your outside source.

Be alert—there's also the possibility that your outside source will sometimes *contradict* the information presented in your primary textbook. If it does—great! Comparing the conflicting viewpoints will force you to think. (Of course, when it comes to actually answering a test question in such gray areas, the textbook your teacher uses is the safer choice to go with.)

WHAT'S COMING UP

Smart students are always on the lookout for anything that helps them learn. I realize that finding and using a supplementary information source for a course takes time, but it is time well spent. Having one handy will save you hours and hours when you hit those inevitable sections of your official textbook that just don't seem to make sense.

Let's move on to Question 4. The first three questions prepared you to read; the next question forces you to stay a step ahead of the author as you do.

Answering Question 4:
What's the Author
Going to Say Next?

NOW YOU'RE READY TO READ

Question 1 defined your purpose; Question 2 warmed you up by making you think about what you already know; and Question 3 gave you the big picture. Now that you've answered these questions, return to the beginning of the material. You'll be reading it closely to answer the next set of CyberLearning Questions, beginning with what the author is going to say next.

STAYING ON THE EDGE OF YOUR SEAT

Anticipating what someone is about to say is a natural and important part of communication. If I say "I like strawberry..." you're already thinking "ice cream" even though I might say "shortcake." For some reason, students stop thinking ahead when they read academic material.

But your brain never stops making connections. When you're reading your chemistry textbook about "strong acid reactions," what do you suppose the author will discuss next? Think about it. Even if you know nothing about chemistry you probably correctly anticipated "weak acid reactions."

You have a general idea what the subject is all about and you're ready to handle the specifics. It's time to dig out and extract the information you need by active reading. Anticipating what the author will say next while you read is a big part of the active approach; waiting is passive and boring. So don't wait to read what the author will say, *tell* the author what he or she is about to say.

Asking what the author will say next is not really a separate step, but something you do in the background as you read to answer the other CyberLearning questions. **In fact, as you read you should expect the author to answer your questions.**

Now you're beginning to see why I call this process "dialoguing." You've been creating a dialogue between you and the author, though obviously the other person is not present. When you carry on a dialogue with the author, you're forced to take an active role. You're not just passively listening to the author; you're talking with the author, too. Since the author does not "hear" your questions, you'll have to be patient; the author might not "respond" immediately. The answer may appear several pages later or may not appear at all.

That's fine, because the point of this question is simply to keep you actively involved in the material and give you feedback. It hooks you into what you're reading and turns what might be a dull task into a fun exercise—now you're

Question 1:
What's my purpose for reading this?

Question 2:
What do I already know about this topic?

Question 3:
What's the big picture here?

**Question 4:
What's the author going to say next?**

Question 5:
What are the "expert questions"?

Question 6:
What questions does this information raise for me?

Question 7:
What information is important here?

Question 8:
How can I paraphrase and summarize this information?

Question 9:
How can I organize this information?

Question 10:
How can I picture this information?

Question 11:
What's my hook for remembering this information?

Question 12:
How does this information fit in with what I already know?

reading to answer your questions and to see if your guesses were correct. If they weren't, it's a tip-off that you need to reevaluate your thinking—and better now than during an exam.

THE CLUES

The two main clues that help you anticipate what the author will say next are organizational and grammatical. Let's consider each.

Your ability to anticipate will depend on what you already know about the subject. If the subject is new to you, you may not be familiar with its common organizational patterns. In history, for example, conflicts lead to events. In physics, laws are followed by formulas and examples. In psychology, experiments are followed by conclusions. In mathematics, theorems are followed by proofs. In novels, goals are followed by obstacles, which are followed by resolutions.

Once you become familiar with the basic structure of a subject, it is easier to anticipate what the author will say next. Here are some more general organizational patterns:

- problem followed by solutions
- definition followed by examples
- general rule followed by exceptions
- claim followed by reasons
- whole followed by its parts
- question followed by answer
- cause followed by effects

If you're reading about a problem, you can expect that a discussion of possible solutions will follow; if the author is claiming something, you can expect the reasons to follow.

Grammatical clues include the words and phrases that tell you what the author is about to say next. Some signal words alert you that the author is about to

- introduce a new idea: *but, although, nevertheless, despite, however, except*
- elaborate on or emphasize the idea under discussion: *and, moreover, also, furthermore, in addition*
- offer a conclusion: *so, therefore, as a result, consequently, thus, hence*
- provide reasons for a conclusion: *because, since, owing to, as a result of*
- provide a list of items: *first, second, next, last*

You get the idea.

These lists are incomplete, so don't bother memorizing them. They are simply intended to give you a sense of what to look for as you try to stay one step ahead of the author.

ANSWERING QUESTION 4 ON THE ROCKS PASSAGE

Here are the thoughts (in italics) that went through my head as I answered this question on the first two paragraphs of the passage. Notice that I started with the title.

That's a pretty general title, I guess this is going to be a general review discussing the different types of rocks, what they're made of, and how they're formed.

ROCKS

Rocks are hard, natural masses of solid matter that make up the earth's crust. With a few exceptions (such as coal), rocks are composed of one or more minerals. Geologists classify rocks as either igneous, sedimentary, or metamorphic, depending on how they were formed.

Igneous rocks are formed from magma, the molten matter deep within the earth. There are two types of igneous rock. If magma rises toward the surface, it slowly cools and sometimes solidifies underground. The result is intrusive igneous rock. If magma reaches the earth's surface, it emerges from volcanoes or fissures (cracks) as lava. Lava cools rapidly aboveground, solidifying into extrusive igneous rock. Intrusive igneous rock, such as granite, can be identified by its large, clearly visible mineral grains (crystals). Because extrusive rock solidifies more quickly than intrusive igneous rock, it is characterized by tiny crystals. Basalt, with its fine texture, high density, and dark color, is the most common extrusive igneous rock, lying beneath the vast ocean floor. Pumice, another common extrusive igneous rock used in some abrasives, acquires its rough porous texture from the explosive release of gas that often accompanies volcanic eruptions.

What else makes up the earth's crust? Is the crust made of solid rock? Maybe the author will tell me.

I guess not. Okay, now the passage will tell me what minerals are, or maybe what minerals rocks are made of.

Nope, struck out again. But now I'm sure the passage is going to talk about igneous rocks, I remember that from getting the big picture.

I thought lava was the molten stuff in the earth. I wonder what the difference is.

What happens if it rises above the surface and cools aboveground is surely next. Maybe first I'll find out what causes magma to rise, or what makes it cool, or what causes it to solidify.

Guess not. Maybe the passage will give me an example of an intrusive igneous rock next.

Well, that answers one of my questions: magma is just underground lava.

Finally an example. Now the author will give me an example of extrusive igneous rock. I'm beginning to get the hang of this passage.

Does that mean most fissures and volcanoes are underwater? Maybe I'll find out what the most common extrusive igneous rock on land is.

And so on. That should be enough to give you the general idea. You don't need write anything for this step unless an important question occurs to you, which you can jot down in your notes or in the margin of your book.

You'll notice that my predictions were rarely "right." More often than not the author chose to talk about something I didn't expect. That's okay, especially in a subject I know nothing about. **The point of Question 4 is not to be right, but just to keep you engaged in the material and ask other questions, to make you an active participant rather than a bored and reluctant spectator.** Even if the passage is boring, playing with it in this way keeps you on your toes and interested.

ANSWERING QUESTION 4 IN CLASSES AND LECTURES

Of course, in classes and lectures this question becomes *What's the teacher going to say next?* Because you are passive during a lecture, it's important to take active steps to prevent your mind from wandering. Just as in reading, dialoguing keeps you focused in lectures.

When you read, you determine the pace at which you dialogue and absorb information. If you don't understand something, you can spend time puzzling it over. On the other hand, in class your teacher sets the pace. Don't get so involved in dialoguing that you fall behind the discussion. Still, you'll be surprised how many of your teacher's lecture you can anticipate. Try it.

Except for that minor difference, dialoguing while listening is the same as dialoguing while reading—you'll just be able to do less of it.

SUMMARY

Question 4 asks you to guess what the author is going to say next. Using grammatical and structural clues, you can "ask" the author questions that you expect the text to answer. Obviously you will not always be able to anticipate what direction the text will take. The point is not to be right all the time, but to stay involved so you are challenged to extract the important information.

Don't make a big deal of this question. Remember how quickly thoughts flash through your head when someone invites you out to a movie, thinking and dialoguing take far less time for you to do than for me to explain. With a little practice, you won't even have to think about the questioning process—it will arise naturally. In practically no time, asking and answering Question 4 will become an unconscious habit.

The next question takes us deeper still into the material, and is invaluable in helping you demystify your subject systematically. In time, it too will become an automatic response to new information.

Answering Question 5:
What Are the "Expert Questions"?

BECOME AN INSTANT EXPERT ON ANY SUBJECT!

Each subject raises a unique set of questions about itself that must be asked and answered systematically if you are to understand it. I call these the expert questions. The expert questions for geology include the following:

- *What is this made of?*
- *What are its chemical, physical, and textural properties?*
- *How can this be identified?*
- *What process causes this?*
- *What other processes tend to happen at the same time?*
- *Where is this usually found?*
- *What else is usually found with or near this?*
- *What processes can cause this to change, and in what ways?*
- *What can I tell about the history of this?*

These are not the questions you would ask while studying English or psychology or algebra, each of which has its own set of expert questions. These are the questions an expert in geology asks–if you want to understand a subject the way an expert does, you'll have to ask them, too.

These are fill-in-the-blank-type questions. To use them, simply substitute whatever term you're reading about for the word *this* in the list above.

Here are some examples from the rock passage:

General Expert Question	Specific Example
• *What is this made of?*	• What is limestone made of?
• *How can this be identified?*	• How can basalt be identified?
• *What process causes this?*	• What process causes volcanoes?
• *Where is this usually found?*	• Where is sedimentary rock usually found?
• *What can I tell about the history of this?*	• What can I tell about the history of slate?

Question 1:
 What's my purpose for reading this?

Question 2:
 What do I already know about this topic?

Question 3:
 What's the big picture here?

Question 4:
 What's the author going to say next?

Question 5:
 What are the "expert questions"?

Question 6:
 What questions does this information raise for me?

Question 7:
 What information is important here?

Question 8:
 How can I paraphrase and summarize this information?

Question 9:
 How can I organize this information?

Question 10:
 How can I picture this information?

Question 11:
 What's my hook for remembering this information?

Question 12:
 How does this information fit in with what I already know?

DETERMINING THE EXPERT QUESTIONS

The sooner you learn to figure out the expert questions, the sooner the subject will begin to make sense. But you won't find a list of them in your textbook. You'll have to work them out for yourself. You can do this by studying the introduction to your textbook and especially the chapter summary questions. **If a certain type of question recurs frequently throughout a textbook, it's probably an expert question.**

Here's how you do it. Scan the questions to see if you find any common phrases. If you ignore the specifics of each question, you will discover that certain *forms* of questions appear over and over. These general forms are the expert questions.

For example, the chapter summary to our rocks passage might include the following questions:

- *How can one determine whether igneous rock is intrusive or extrusive?*
- *How can sedimentary rock be identified?*
- *Metamorphic rock is characterized by what physical features?*

Despite the apparent differences, these questions are just different ways of asking how a rock can be identified.

THE ORIENTATION QUESTIONS

Besides the expert questions, you must be sure to answer another set of questions–the "orientation questions." I call them orientation questions because they help get you oriented to a subject. **They also happen to be the most popular test questions.**

Here they are.

- *What's the definition of this?*
- *What's an example of this?*
- *What are the different types of this?*
- *What is this related to?*
- *What can this be compared with?*

That's all, just five. Unlike the expert questions which are specific, the orientation questions are general and do not vary from subject to subject. As with the expert questions, you use these by substituting whatever you're reading about for the word *this.*

Here are some examples from the rocks passage:

General Orientation Question	Specific Example
• *What's the definition of this?* • *What are the different types of this?* • *What is this related to?*	• What's the definition of mineral? • What are the different types of igneous rock? • What is erosion related to?

KEEP THESE QUESTIONS IN MIND!

You'll be asking the expert and orientation questions repeatedly. You don't have to write them down, but do keep them in mind as you read. Sooner or later you'll have to answer them, too—they will very likely show up on your tests.

ANSWERING QUESTION 5 ON THE ROCKS PASSAGE

We could ask the expert and orientation questions about almost anything in the rocks passage, but the previous examples are sufficient to illustrate the process. Turn back to the passage (page 27) and try your hand at asking orientation and expert questions, or use some terms I've selected for you:

- magma   (for example, *What is magma made of?*)
- fissure   (for example, *What causes fissures?*)
- basalt   (for example, *How can basalt be identified?*)
- sediments   (for example, *Where are sediments usually found?*)
- fossils   (for example, *What can I tell about the history of fossils?*)
- weathering (for example, *What is weathering related to?*)

Once you've generated some questions, try to answer them!

ANSWERING QUESTION 5 IN CLASSES AND LECTURES

Keeping the expert and orientation questions in mind while you listen to your teacher is no different from keeping them in mind while you read. You just have to pace yourself more strictly so you can keep up with your teacher. Knowing the expert questions helps you anticipate what your teacher is going to say next (Question 4).

Question 4:
What's the author going to say next?

SUMMARY

Question 5 invites you to ask the questions that an expert would ask. Each subject has its own set of these expert questions, and the sooner you determine what they are, the better. Keep them in mind as you read; they'll allow you to pick out the information that is most important to understanding a specific subject.

The orientation questions are a bit different. There are only five, and they're the same for every subject. As the name suggests, these questions help you get oriented to a new topic. Keep them in mind along with the expert questions as you read.

The expert and orientation questions allow you to get to the meat of a subject and analyze it just like an expert. Whatever other questions you ask as you read, be sure you ask—and try to answer—them.

In the next chapter we'll discuss how you bring your personality into the dialoguing process. Personalizing the material like this makes it that much more alive and relevant to your experiences. All this adds up to a familiarity with the subject that you absolutely cannot have otherwise—even with something as dry and dense as rocks.

Answering Question 6:
What Questions Does This Information Raise for Me?

MAKING IT YOUR OWN

In the last chapter you learned to ask the expert and orientation questions. These questions are crucial, but they're also systematic. You simply plug in words and come up with "How can shale be identified?" or "Where is sedimentary rock usually found?" Since you're following a formula of sorts, your questions will be the same as everyone else's.

This chapter invites you to come up with questions that are uniquely your own. They are suggested by the material but are based on your background and interests, and hence appeal directly to your curiosity. Since no one has your interests, your knowledge, or your background, no one's questions will be the same as yours.

GET CURIOUS!

You can start by asking the six "journalist's questions":

- Who?
- What?
- Where?
- When?
- Why?
- How?

You may notice that some of these will not always apply to a given subject or topic. In geology, for example, only rarely will you ask the question *Who?* In history or English, on the other hand, you ask it frequently.

In general, questions beginning with the words *How* and *Why* force you to dig into the material and analyze it more deeply than do ones beginning with *Who, What, Where,* or *When*. Asking *why* the American Civil War was fought, say, is going to require more analysis than asking *when* or *where* it was fought.

WHAT MAKES A QUESTION GOOD?

It would be impossible to list every conceivable question you can devise; you are limited only by your imagination. Having said that, some questions are better than others. How can you tell if a question is "good"? **A good question tends to have more than one answer.**

Question 1:
What's my purpose for reading this?

Question 2:
What do I already know about this topic?

Question 3:
What's the big picture here?

Question 4:
What's the author going to say next?

Question 5:
What are the "expert questions"?

**Question 6:
What questions does this information raise for me?**

Question 7:
What information is important here?

Question 8:
How can I paraphrase and summarize this information?

Question 9:
How can I organize this information?

Question 10:
How can I picture this information?

Question 11:
What's my hook for remembering this information?

Question 12:
How does this information fit in with what I already know?

Here are four powerful questions you should include in your arsenal.

- **So what?**   How is this significant? What does it tell us about other things?
  (*What does the fact that fossils are found in sedimentary rock tell us?*)

- **Says who?**   Is this a fact or someone's opinion? How can this be verified? Does this depend on a particular point of view?
  (*How do we know that basalt lies underneath the ocean floor?*)

- **What if…?**   What would happen if…? What if I…?
  (*What would happen if magma stopped rising to the surface?*)

- **What does this remind me of?**   Where have I seen something like this before? What does that suggest about this?
  (*What does the rock cycle remind me of?*)

Each of these questions will help you understand whatever you are reading, particularly the last two.

GET CREATIVE WITH THE TWO MOST POWERFUL, IDEA-GENERATING QUESTIONS!

All thought is a feat of association: having what's in front of you bring up something in your mind that you almost didn't know you knew.

ROBERT FROST

When asking and answering the questions *What if…?* and *What does this remind me of?* you should loosen up and be as creative and even outrageous as you can. Don't restrict yourself to "logical" responses. Fantasize and analogize!

The question *What if…?* gets you wondering and fantasizing about the information. There are three common variations: *applying* the information as it is, *changing* it, and *personalizing* it.

- To apply information from our sample passage, you might ask, *What kind of rock would I expect to find if a volcano erupted underwater?* Only by applying and using information can you make it yours.

- To change information from our sample passage, you might ask, *What would happen to the rock cycle if magma stopped rising to the surface?* By changing and manipulating things, you better understand them as they are.

- To personalize the information from our sample passage, you might ask, *If I were a rock, what type would I be?* This seems like a silly question, but it really gets you involved in the material and helps you relate to it. Einstein developed his theory of relativity by asking questions like, *If I were traveling on a light beam and holding a mirror, would I be able to see myself?* (Albert was one rad cyberdude.)

The question *What does this remind me of?* gets you thinking in terms of analogies and metaphors, and starts the process of connecting the new information to what you already know. For example, the rock cycle might remind you of other cycles in nature, such as the water cycle (earth science) or the nitrogen cycle (biology). What you know about the rock cycle will help you understand these other cycles; what you know about these cycles, in turn, will help you understand the rock cycle.

What does this remind me of? **is the most important question in this entire book!** This question alone will lead to all the others. If you remember nothing else from this book, remember to ask it constantly.

DIG, DIG, DIG!

The goal is to see how many questions you can ask and how many different answers you can come up with for each. This is a never-ending process! Each question you think of will lead to an answer, which will suggest another question, which will lead to another answer, and so on. This is how you build understanding. It's also the way you stay interested in a subject.

You may wonder why we ask so many sophisticated questions of the material we're studying when teachers usually ask comparatively simple questions on tests. One of the key points of CyberLearning is this: the only way to learn and be interested in school is to do *more* than your teachers require. You're bored not because you're doing too much in school, you're bored because you're doing too *little*. **Remember Smart Student Principle #2: Merely listening to your teachers and completing their assignments is *never* enough.**

> *Thinking means connecting things, and stops if they cannot be connected.*
>
> GILBERT KEITH
> CHESTERTON

> ### EXERCISE #3
>
> *Instructions:* Before continuing, take out a sheet of scratch paper. Turn back to the rocks passage (page 27) and see how many questions you can generate as you read, as I did in the passage a few pages back. Feel free to refer to the expert and orientation questions (pages 67 and 69) for inspiration. Take as much time as you need, but don't stop until you've generated *at least* a dozen questions.

ANSWERING QUESTION 6 ON THE ROCKS PASSAGE

Here are *some* of the additional questions I came up with as I was reading the passage. I wrote these down so you could see them, but I would not have taken notes on all these questions. You'll notice that some are expert and orientation questions, but most are ones that just seemed interesting to me. Keep in mind that your questions will probably be different.

- What type of minerals are rocks made of?
- Is it possible to form man-made rocks?
- What types of rocks are found on the moon?
- What causes magma to rise? Does it have anything to with earthquakes?
- How long does it take magma to cool?
- Where do volcanoes tend to occur most often?
- How do sediments cement and compact together and harden?
- What causes sedimentary rock to accumulate in layers?
- What type of sedimentary rock does not form underwater?
- How do fossils get "into" sedimentary rock?
- Are fossils found in igneous and metamorphic rock?
- Where do we find metamorphic rock?
- How do sedimentary rocks, which are formed above ground, undergo metamorphism, which takes place below ground?
- Since marble is formed from limestone and limestone is formed from marine organisms, does that mean that marble is found only where water is or used to be?
- What would happen to the rock cycle if magma stopped rising?
- What type of rock is the hardest?
- How do we determine the age of a rock?
- What causes erosion and weathering?
- What type of rock is most/least subject to erosion? Why?
- Does erosion occur at the bottom of oceans?
- What kind of heat does it take to melt rocks?
- Is it possible to determine what different types of cycles a rock has gone through in its "lifetime".
- What do rocks tell us about the environment at the time they were formed?

I know this seems like a lot of questions for such a short passage, but remember that several questions can flash through your mind in a second. At first you'll have to read a passage several times to generate questions, but in time the expert and orientation questions will arise as naturally as your own.

DON'T FORGET TO ANSWER YOUR QUESTIONS

WHAT QUESTIONS DOES THIS INFORMATION RAISE FOR ME?

You may be remembering **Smart Student Principle #6: The point of a question is to get you to think—*not* simply to answer it.** You *should* think, but you should also try to answer your questions. The point of Principle #6 is that your thinking about a question shouldn't stop simply because you've found an answer; there may be *many* answers.

Answering questions is an integral part of dialoguing. **Once you've asked a question, don't wait to read the answer—guess what it will be!** You won't always be right, especially when a subject is new to you, but give it your best shot. If you guessed correctly, great. But even being *wrong* has its benefits: when you discover the correct answer, you'll be much more likely to remember it. In any event, continually guessing the answer to your questions keeps you involved in the material. It's also excellent practice for taking exams.

Dialoguing as you read is a lot like problem solving. Each question you ask is a problem, which you then set out to solve. Some of your questions will be answered by the text, but many will not be. You may have to do some hard thinking or turn to your supplementary information source.

CONSIDER YOUR QUESTIONS IN ORDER OF IMPORTANCE

Expert and orientation questions must be answered if you want to understand them and do well on tests (I trust you want to do both). Your other questions can range from the important to the wildly speculative. I've arranged a number of questions from my previous notes (page 74) in order of priority:

- *What type of minerals are rocks made of?*
  (Expert and orientation question; high priority; check my supplementary source of information or ask teacher.)

- *What causes magma to rise?*
  (Expert question; medium to high priority.)

- *What causes erosion and weathering?*
  (Expert question; medium to high priority.)

- *Are fossils found in igneous or metamorphic rocks?*
  (Expert question; not hard to find or figure out; medium to low priority.)

- *What would happen to the rock cycle if magma stopped rising?*
  (An interesting speculation and probably not that hard to figure out, but very low priority.)

- *What types of rocks are found on the moon?*
  (Related subject; very low priority.)

While it's important to raise as many questions as you can, you'll never have enough time to answer them all. Telling the difference between low- and high-priority questions requires some judgment, but with practice you'll get the knack. High-priority questions should be tackled immediately. You'll have to consult your supplementary information sources or ask your teacher. Low-priority questions should be pondered for a moment and then dropped, to be taken up another day if you have the time and inclination. Who knows? Maybe your curiosity will be so piqued you'll discover a new hobby or career.

ANSWERING QUESTION 6 IN CLASSES AND LECTURES

The basic principles behind this question are the same whether you're reading a book or listening to your teacher. Of course, keeping up with your teacher will severely limit the number of questions you can ask, and you'll have to wait until the class is over before you have time to work out any answers.

SUMMARY

This step is where you personalize the information and make it yours. You should have fun with your questions. *What does this remind me of?* invites you to analogize; *What if...?* invites you to fantasize. One question will suggest another, so go with the flow. Get curious about the material. The more questions you ask, the more the material becomes your own, so take your time to answer Question 6.

Dialoguing while you read gets you thinking and keeps you focused; your mind can't wander when you keep it busy formulating and answering questions. It makes you interested in what you read because anything the author says is in response to your questions. Finally, dialoguing gets you ready for exams since you're practicing exactly what you'll have to do—answer questions. It's going to be hard for your teacher to come up with questions you haven't already thought of. Analyzing them beforehand puts you way ahead of the game.

Try to answer your questions, too. Guess what the answer will be before seeing what the author will say. Even if you're wrong you'll be engaging the material. Some of your questions won't be answered at all, but that's okay (even if it is a little frustrating). You'll soon learn to judge which questions are high priority.

Knowing how to ask specific, probing questions is one of the most important skills you'll need in school. I promise that your ability to pose insightful questions will improve dramatically with practice.

Now that you've unleashed your simmering curiosity and personalized the material, it's time to decide what information you need to know. Question 7 is where you focus on the information of the greatest importance. But first, an intermission. (If you're in a groove with CyberLearning you can skip the intermission and return later.)

Question 7:
What information is important here?

Intermission:
Attitude Check #1

TAKE THIS QUIZ!

The first quiz you took, back on page 15, gave you a chance to evaluate your initial attitude about school and the learning process. You've been doing quite a bit of reading since then, so now is a good time to see how much your attitude has begun to change. (By the way, don't expect all the answers necessarily to be 0's again.)

ATTITUDE CHECK

Instructions: For each statement below, in the space provided indicate whether you agree (1) or disagree (0) with it. Choose the response that best reflects what you truly believe, not what you think is the "right" answer.

[ ] 1. If you listen to what your teachers say and faithfully complete all the work they assign, you will receive high grades.

[ ] 2. A person's grades say a lot about his or her basic intelligence.

[ ] 3. A person's grade in a course gives you a pretty good idea of how much he or she has learned.

[ ] 4. When deciding grades, teachers should give equal weight to how hard you try as well as how much you learn.

[ ] 5. Most teachers put their personal feelings aside and are reasonably objective about the grades they hand out.

[ ] 6. Grades are remarkably accurate predictors of a person's future success, both in school and after graduation.

[ ] 7. A grade is just one person's opinion of your work so there's not much point to working hard to get high marks when they don't really mean that much.

[ ] 8. Good grades improve your self-esteem; bad grades lower it.

The "answers" to this quiz follow the next brief discussion.

HOW SMART STUDENTS THINK ABOUT GRADES

You and your classmates are forced to compete for grades that become a part of your "permanent record." Your grade point average can affect where you go to college, where you go to graduate school, and even what kinds of jobs you get for years after you leave school.

Considering the impact grades can have on your life choices, it's remarkable how many misconceptions surround the grading process. Your grades are not a measure of how smart you are, or of how much you know. Nor should you expect to earn high grades merely by working hard. While studying five hours a night without understanding much may earn you the sympathy of a compassionate teacher, sympathy alone isn't going to get you an A; it might not even get you a C. The only thing hard work guarantees is fatigue.

And don't expect high grades as a reward for obeying your teachers—listening to what they say, reading what they assign, and generally doing what you're told. Following orders does not entitle you to high grades, though it's easy to see why many students believe this. Grades are a powerful tool that teachers often use to ensure your conformity by rewarding "good" behavior and punishing "bad" behavior with appropriate marks.

You may see grades as objective measures of your performance, but they are nothing more than a teacher's opinion of what you deserve. Each teacher determines what type of academic work receives credit and how much, whether partial credit is awarded for incomplete work, and where to set grade cutoffs.

Grading is a highly subjective process which is often based on arbitrary or even emotional considerations. To some extent, of course, grades do reflect how much you have learned. But they can also reflect, depending on the teacher, how hard you tried, how much you improved, how neatly you wrote or dressed, how interested you seemed, how often you participated in class, and how much your teacher liked you. Unfair? You bet. But now that you know, make this knowledge work for you.

Smart students realize that teachers often award grades more to the student than to his or her work. Judging from experience, I'd bet that half the grade a paper or exam receives is determined by the name at the top of it. If a teacher decides you are an A student, your work will receive A's; if your teacher decides you are a C student, your work will receive C's.

So work hard the first few weeks of term. It's important that you convince your teachers early on that you are a smart student whose work invariably deserves A's. Then, when you make mistakes—as even the smartest students will—your teacher will think they are the mistakes of an A student and interpret them accordingly. Teachers have been known, when grading a test, to "overlook" the mistakes or oversights of a top student while penalizing classmates for making the identical errors!

For the most part, teachers base your grades on how well you and your work live up to their expectations. The problem is that teachers do not always state what they expect from you. Indeed, many of their expectations are subconscious.

"But teachers usually tell us how they grade," you say. Sure, most teachers will tell you how they grade; that is, they'll tell you how they *think* they grade. Look, this should come as no surprise, but teachers are just people. Like the rest of us, they make mistakes, want approval, and wrestle with their insecurities.

Few teachers are aware how much their grading opinions are shaped by their prejudices and emotions. **Smart students are probably more aware of their teachers' personal biases and unstated expectations than the teachers are themselves!** Pay close attention to the little ways that teachers unknowingly reveal what they *really* expect of you. How they express themselves. The words they use. How they phrase questions in class. How they respond to questions from students. The clues are often subtle, but you'll spot them if you're alert.

After discovering all this about the grading process, you're probably more certain than ever that grades are unfair. Exactly! Now you're catching on! Who ever said school was fair?

"ANSWERS" TO ATTITUDE CHECK #1

Once again, the smart student's response to each of these questions would be a 0. Don't worry if your responses are different; your attitude will come around sooner or later.

After the preceding discussion, I'll just say a few words about each question:

1. If you listen to what your teachers say and faithfully complete all the work they assign, you will receive high grades.

    [0] Not only may you not get high grades, you may not even learn much. If you put a 1 on this one, you and I have a lot of work to do on your attitude. **Remember Smart Student Principle #2: Merely listening to your teachers and completing their assignments is *never* enough.**

2. A person's grades say a lot about his or her basic intelligence.

    [0] As we have discussed, your grades reflect dozens of things, intelligence perhaps *least* among them. There's nothing remotely objective or scientific about the grading process. Grades aren't IQ scores (which, by the way, reflect only an exceedingly narrow band "intelligence"). **Remember Smart Student Principle #4: Grades are just subjective opinions.**

3. A person's grade in a course gives you a pretty good idea of how much he or she has learned.

    [0] See the previous comment.

4. When deciding grades, teachers should give equal weight to how hard you try as well as how much you learn.

[0] How hard you work may influence how much a teacher likes you and that in turn may affect your grade, but there's nothing in the rule book that say teachers *should* consider how hard you work.

5. Most teachers put their personal feelings aside and are reasonably objective about the grades they hand out.

[0] Teachers are no more able to ignore their emotions than you are.

6. Grades are remarkably accurate predictors of a person's future success, both in school and after graduation.

[0] While your grades certainly affect your choices, they are not accurate predictors of anything. In fact, your high school grades are not even particularly good predictors of your college grades, let alone your future success in life. **Remember Smart Student Principle #4.**

7. A grade is just one person's opinion of your work so there's not much point to working hard to get high marks when they don't really mean that much.

[0] Grades *are* just opinions, but ones that can have a major impact on your options in school and after graduation. Your grades don't permanently determine your future success (see previous comment), but they definitely affect your initial career options. **Remember Smart Student Principle #12: School is a game, but it's a very important game.**

8. Good grades improve your self-esteem; bad grades lower it.

[0] This subtle question trips up many smart students-in-training. If grades are just subjective opinions—and they are—why should good grades change your self-esteem one way or another? Sure it's nice getting an A and it's a major bummer getting a C. But what grade you get should not change how you feel about yourself. Grades are just the way score is kept in the highly subjective and imperfect game of school. **Remember Smart Student Principle #10: How well you do in school reflects your attitude and your method, not your ability.**

Well, I guess all the smart student responses were 0's after all. But I'm sure you weren't fooled for long.

Okay, break's over. Let's get back to work on the Twelve Questions.

Answering Question 7:
What Information
Is Important Here?

LOOKING BACK

Questions 4 through 6 established a dialogue between you and the text. You've been reading like never before, asking questions and unleashing your natural curiosity. Now it's time to rein in the questions and information you've generated and begin the selection process.

DECIDING WHAT TO TAKE NOTES ON

While you're asking questions of the material as you read, you should be taking notes. Question 7 tells you *what* you need to take notes on, while Question 8 tells you *how* to take notes.

All you're doing at this stage is deciding what information in the material you're studying is important for your purposes. Don't worry if the material still seems confusing and you can't remember anything. Questions 9 through 12 will remedy that.

LISTEN UP: HOW THE 80-20 RULE, PARETO'S PRINCIPLE, AND ZIPF'S LAW CAN SAVE YOU A WHOLE *LOT* OF STUDY TIME!

About a century ago, an Italian economist named Vilfredo Pareto noticed that of any group of objects, a tiny fraction contributes most of the total value. If a company, say, sold five products, one would account for almost all the sales; if it had a hundred customers, the best twenty or so would make almost all the purchases. If you arranged the products or customers or whatever in order of importance, each additional one after the first would be less and less valuable. After a certain point the value of a new product or customer would become insignificant.

Half a century later, an American linguist named George Kingsley Zipf (who probably wore thick glasses as a kid and got teased a lot by his classmates) noticed something similar in language. If all the words in the English language are ranked in order of how frequently they are used, the most frequently used word *(the)* appears approximately twice as often as the second ranked word *(of)*, three times as frequently as the third ranked word *(and)*, ten times as frequently as the tenth ranked word *(I)*, and so on.

Since then, other researchers have made similar observations in many diverse fields. The underlying principle has been summed up in the 80-20 rule. This nifty rule of thumb states that 80 percent (four-fifths) of the total value, impact, or significance of any group of items will come from only 20 percent (one-fifth) of those items. The flip side, of course, is that the remaining 80 percent of the items contribute only 20 percent of the value.

If you look at any aspect of your daily life, you'll see what I mean. For example:

- If you own five pairs of shoes, you'll wear one of them 80 percent of the time.

- If you have thirty friends, you'll do 80 percent of your socializing with six of them.

- If there are twenty students in your class, four of them will hog 80 percent of the discussion time.

Don't get hung up on the mathematics; the numbers are just intended as rough guidelines. The point is this: Most of the value of any group of items is contributed by very few of those items. Concentrate your efforts on the few important things before bothering with the rest of the stuff—you may not need it at all!

HERE'S WHAT ALL THAT MEANS IN TERMS OF YOUR READING LOAD

The art of reasoning consists in getting hold of the subject at the right end, of seizing on the few general ideas that illuminate the whole, and of persistently organizing all subsidiary facts round them. Nobody can be a good reasoner unless by constant practice he has realized the importance of getting hold of the few big ideas and hanging on to them like grim death.

ALFRED NORTH
WHITEHEAD

Contrary to popular student belief (but probably not to yours), some facts and ideas in your textbook are more important than others. **Remember Smart Student Principle #3: Not everything you are assigned to read or asked to do is equally important.**

If you have fifty pages to read in your textbook this week, the 80-20 rule says that 80 percent of the important facts and ideas are going to be found in only 20 percent—count 'em: ten—of those pages. The other forty pages contain material that is less important for you to know and even irrelevant for your purposes.

In a sense, this is what outlines and study guides try to do for you—separate the important 20 percent you really need to know from the 80 percent of what is less important. That's why study guides are a lot thinner than textbooks, which try to present everything.

One major disadvantage of study guides, however, is that they don't let you select the important information for yourself. Using one forces you to rely on someone else's judgement about what is or is not important. As you know, the process of deciding what information you need or don't need is a key part of building understanding.

NO MORE GUILT ABOUT NOT READING EVERYTHING

By not overloading your brain, you're doing yourself a big favor. You may not realize this, but you can absorb only a limited volume of facts and ideas at any one time. **And the only way you can effectively absorb the relevant information is to ignore the irrelevant information.** (I figured you'd be glad to hear this.)

That's right—not only am I telling you it's okay to skip over material, I'm saying you'd better! You may feel uncomfortable with this suggestion. You may be afraid that if you don't try to read and learn every detail, you'll be missing something important. Or perhaps skipping over material makes you feel guilty, while reading each and every word makes you feel studious and conscientious, even if you don't understand much.

This attitude can get you in big trouble pronto. If we were to arrange the half-dozen ideas in a chapter in order of importance, we would get something like the following progression:

The Most Important Idea
2nd Most Important Idea
3rd Most Important Idea
4th Most Important Idea
5th Most Important Idea
6th Most Important Idea

And so on. As you can see, the importance of each idea drops off rapidly. Make sure you master the few important ideas before attempting to incorporate the lesser ideas. **Trying to digest and understand all the information in a textbook is not only a colossal waste of time, it's also an excellent way to become quickly and hopelessly confused!** If you want to understand what is going on in school, it is absolutely vital that you know how to tell the difference between:

- which information you should focus on;
- which information you should skim;
- which information you should ignore completely.

The following chart will give you a general idea of how to budget your study time:

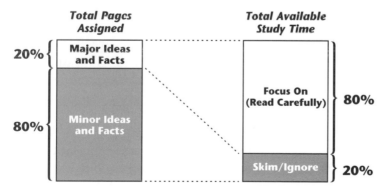

If, for example, you have one hour to read fifteen pages, you should spend roughly 80 percent of your time (forty-eight minutes) thinking about the most important 20 percent of the information (three pages).

THE TRICK, OF COURSE, IS KNOWING WHAT'S IMPORTANT AND WHAT'S NOT

It is not always clear whether something belongs to the important 20 percent (which you will take notes on) or the not-so-important 80 percent (which you will largely ignore); sometimes it's a judgment call. In the first few weeks of a course, everything will seem important (and since the main concepts of a course are usually covered then, everything may very well be important). But hang in there—as you become familiar with your course and your teacher, you'll get a handle on what you need to know and what you can safely ignore.

You should read at least a few paragraphs ahead to see whether something is important before backtracking to take notes on it. If you can't decide whether something sounds important, assume it is and jot it down in your notes. Later, as you learn more in the course, you'll be better able to judge whether you should keep it in your final notes or chuck it.

What's definitely important includes the following:

- **Any facts or ideas you need to answer the expert and orientation questions.** We covered this earlier.

- **Your thoughts, questions, and reactions.** Your *responses* to the material are sometimes more important than the material itself. Be on the lookout also for anything that surprises or confuses you. Such information points either to gaps in your understanding that you'll need to clear up, or to exceptions or contradictions that emphasize general rules.

- **Any key terms, concepts, or ideas.** Each subject has important terms that you should know. Textbooks typically call your attention to them with italics or bold print, or in glossaries. And as you know from the big picture (Question 3), each textbook chapter has only a handful of major ideas (though unfortunately you may have to wade through dozens of pages of complex text to extract them).

> Question 3:
> What's the big picture here?

Facts and details may or may not be important; it really depends. Most examples are included to support the main ideas and are not critical to your understanding if you can devise your own. As you will learn when we discuss Question 8, being able to come up with *your own* definitions and examples as well as to express ideas in your own words is a crucial smart student skill.

Finally, remember that what's important will depend on your *purpose.* A fact that is irrelevant if you are preparing for an exam might be essential if you are writing a research paper. **I'm not saying that what's important depends entirely on whether or not something will appear on a test, but it's certainly a major consideration.**

HERE ARE SOME CLUES

WHAT INFORMATION IS IMPORTANT HERE?

There are some fairly reliable signposts authors provide to tip off important ideas. Here are some places to look and some things to look for:

- **The beginning and the end.** Authors open and close with their most important ideas. You will find them at the beginning and the end of the book, of each chapter, of each section, and of each paragraph.

- **Anything emphasized graphically.** Anything in bold or italics is being stressed by the author for a reason. You can't rely solely on authors, however, because what they deem important may not be important for your purposes. Still, do not disregard the author's emphasis.

- **The gist of any chart or diagram.** Charts and diagrams are another form of graphic emphasis. The chart or diagram itself may not be important, but the idea it conveys probably is.

- **The chapter summary.** The whole point of a summary is to include only the most important information, but keep in mind that it represents the author's point of view, not yours. Don't rely on it blindly.

You may have noticed that these are the same places you look to get the big picture (Question 3). These aren't the only places you'll find the information you need, but they're the first ones to check.

Question 3:
What's the big picture here?

THE SCOOP ON SKIMMING AND "SPEED READING": IT'S ALL A MATTER OF SHIFTING GEARS

Skimming is an essential reading skill that is especially vital when you need to review masses of material to extract a few key ideas or facts. Skimming is scanning a text to decide what's important and what's not. Obviously, that means you must be able to tell the difference between the two.

Many students suppose that skimming means zipping through text, reading every fourth or fifth word and ignoring the rest. It doesn't. Imagine driving a race car on a long winding track. You cool it on the curves and then let her rip on the straightaways. While the physical clues are not as obvious, the principle is exactly the same with skimming. You are continually shifting gears, slowing down when you need to concentrate on the important ideas and speeding up when you get to patches of insignificant or irrelevant details.

Which brings me to speed reading. If you're thinking about taking a speed reading course, save your money. It's no great feat to read a book in an hour or two—if all you're concerned with is getting a general sense of the main ideas. Of course, sometimes that *is* all you want, but that's just getting the big picture. You already know how to do that.

The secret is not reading everything quickly, it's knowing what you should read slowly, what you should read quickly, and what you should ignore totally. You can read faster simply by not lingering over useless information. **Speed reading may enable you to read faster, but it will not significantly reduce the time it takes you to understand a given subject.** (They're not called "speed understanding" courses.)

This book shows you how to learn, and how to learn efficiently. But there's no getting around it: you still have to answer the Twelve Questions—some of them over and over—and that takes time. While you can gain a superficial understanding of something in a short period, there is absolutely no limit to how thoroughly and profoundly you can understand it if you put in the time. It's all a question of your priorities and how much time you're willing to invest.

ANSWERING QUESTION 7 ON THE ROCKS PASSAGE

You'll see what information I thought was important in the next chapter when I show you the notes I took (page 90).

ANSWERING QUESTION 7 IN CLASSES AND LECTURES

While not everything they say is important, most teachers do not waste much class time discussing things they consider trivial or superfluous. Pretty much everything the teacher says during a lecture is important for you, either for understanding the material or for anticipating what will be on the test. As you know, keeping up with your teacher means you won't have much time to decide whether something's important. So you'll be doing a lot less selecting during a lecture than while reading.

Pay special attention to the following:

- **The beginning and the end of the lecture.** Just as the first and last paragraphs of a chapter are very important, the first few minutes and the last few minutes are the most important of the entire lecture. Teachers often summarize their entire lecture during the first few minutes; in the last few minutes, major points are summed up, along with any important points there wasn't time to cover.

- **Anything that goes on the board.** Your teacher wants to be sure everyone's got it.

- **Anything your teacher repeats, emphasizes, or otherwise stresses.** Again, your teacher is obviously trying to drive home a message.

- **Your teacher's use of language.** Pay special attention to pet words or phrases that your teacher uses frequently. You'll want to incorporate them into your papers and test answers!

- **How your teacher responds to questions or comments from the class.** Don't take notes only on what your teacher says. Sometimes your classmates ask noteworthy questions or make insightful comments. Pay attention to how much time your teacher spends on the questions and how he or she answers them.

- **Your thoughts, reactions, and questions.** Note any thoughts or questions that occur to you that you'd like to think about later.

- **Anything the teacher says after a long pause, takes a long time to explain, or has difficulty expressing.** Be aware that if your teacher goes to the trouble of expressing something difficult—it is very important information that is likely to appear on a test.

- **Anything your teacher discusses that is not covered in your textbook, and especially when your teacher disagrees with the textbook.** When teachers offer you their personal views, listen carefully! This is the official word from the people who decide your grades.

- **Whether your teacher concentrates on details or tries to present the larger themes and the big picture.** This tells you what kind of test questions you can expect.

- **Whether your teacher keeps referring to material covered previously.** If so, there's a good chance your exam will be cumulative and include this older material.

- **Questions your teacher raises but does not answer.** These are known as rhetorical questions, and there's a very good chance your teacher will expect you to answer them on the next test.

- **Anything in handouts.** If your teacher goes to the trouble of preparing a handout, it's usually for a good reason. Read that handout carefully!

YOU'LL BE ASKING QUESTION 7 OVER AND OVER

You ask Question 7 the first time as you're reading something and taking notes. But each time you go through your notes during the semester, you ask it again. Many things that seemed important earlier in the term will seem less so as you learn more. **Instead of mindlessly rereading your old notes over and over, continue updating and condensing them.** Make it a game to see how much you can simplify your notes (and your life) each time you review them. In the coming chapters you'll see how much the simple process of reducing and condensing your notes as much as possible improves your understanding immeasurably.

Nothing in education is so astonishing as the amount of ignorance it accumulates in the form of inert facts.
HENRY BROOKS
ADAMS

SUMMARY

Focus on figuring out what the important information is among your reading material and then skim or ignore the rest! Remember the consequences of the 80-20 rule: 80 percent of the important information is contained in 20 percent of the assigned pages. Once you learn to pick out the important information, you'll be able to slash your reading time dramatically.

How do you know which information is important? It isn't always easy to tell in the beginning of a course, but you do have guidelines. Information that answers expert or orientation questions, for example, is always important. Moreover, authors and teachers provide a whole variety of clues to what information they think is important. With practice you should have no problem telling the difference between information you need to know and that which you should ignore.

Now that you know what you should be taking notes on, the next chapter will show you how to take those notes. There's a lot more to it than writing down everything you hear in class or read; or rather, a lot less.

Answering Question 8:
How Can I Paraphrase and Summarize This Information?

TAKING NOTES

The previous question dealt with *what* you should be taking notes on. Now we're going to cover *how* you should be taking those notes.

GET IT DOWN ON PAPER

While you are selecting the important information as you read, you should be taking notes. Some students, however, don't like taking notes. They would rather read, highlight, and reread their textbooks to death. But taking notes while you read will clarify and distill the text so that you can absorb it later. Isn't this more efficient than rereading the entire textbook?

The purpose of taking notes at this stage is not only to record the important information you've selected but also to keep you actively involved and thinking about the material. Taking notes helps you understand and remember the information by writing down physically what you've just encountered visually. Translating the text into notes with abbreviations and symbols further engages your visual sense. The more senses you call upon while reading, the more you involve your brain, and the more you understand and remember.

RULE #1: WHEN TAKING NOTES, USE YOUR OWN WORDS

Always try to paraphrase an author's words. It may be difficult to do much translating, especially in technical subjects like geology. Nonetheless, you must try using as many of your own words as possible. If you aren't using your own words but merely repeating what someone else has said, there's no guarantee you understand the information. (**Warning: when translating the author's words, make sure you don't change the meaning! Also, if the author continually uses certain terms or phrases, you'll want to note these buzz words down exactly.**)

RULE #2: USE AS FEW WORDS AS POSSIBLE

Squeeze, condense, and compress the information down to the fewest possible words. Doing this forces you to paraphrase the material (Rule #1). Condensing the material also forces you to think; again, the more you think, the more you understand and remember. Finally, once you've distilled information down to its essence, you'll have that much less to remember. (**Warning: don't use so few words that your notes don't make sense when you review them!**)

Question 1:
 What's my purpose for reading this?

Question 2:
 What do I already know about this topic?

Question 3:
 What's the big picture here?

Question 4:
 What's the author going to say next?

Question 5:
 What are the "expert questions"?

Question 6:
 What questions does this information raise for me?

Question 7:
 What information is important here?

Question 8:
 How can I paraphrase and summarize this information?

Question 9:
 How can I organize this information?

Question 10:
 How can I picture this information?

Question 11:
 What's my hook for remembering this information?

Question 12:
 How does this information fit in with what I already know?

HOW YOUR NOTES SHOULD LOOK

Here's how a smart student would have taken notes on our rocks passage, paraphrasing, summarizing, and abbreviating whenever possible.

Compare these notes with the ones you took (Exercise #2, page 26) and those Johnny took (pages 29 and 30). Which version would you rather study from?

rocks - formed from minerals (except coal)
        - 3 types: igneous, metamorphic, sedimentary

igneous rock - 1) intrusive, underground, magma (molten matter), cools slowly,
                 large grains (granite)
                              — fissures
              2) extrusive, above ground, lava — volcanoes, cools quickly, small
                 crystals (pumice, basalt)

sedimentary rock - sediments (particles) that form strata (layers)
                                         erosion
                   1) rocks broken by < weathering, later cement or compact
                      and harden (shale from mud/clay; sandstone)
                   2) remains a) animal: (dissolved, decomposed shells/skeletons
                                          of marine life) (limestone)
                             b) plant: (dissolved, decayed in swamps) (coal)
                   - usually forms underwater
                   - identified by - layers
                                   - particles of varying sizes
                                   - fossils

metamorphic rock - formed when rocks underground changed by great heat/pressure
                  - metamorphism, makes rocks rougher, denser, alters composition
                  - identified by - distorted structure
                                  - wavy bands
                  - shale becomes slate
                    limestone "   marble
                    granite   "   gneiss

rock cycle - any rock can change into one of the others

Question 9:
  How can I organize the information in my notes?

Question 10:
  How can I picture this information?

Question 12:
  How does this information fit in with what I already know?

This, however, is far from being our final set of notes. We still have to include our classroom notes on the passage, and Questions 9, 10, and 12 are *each* going to require extensive revisions.

TAKING NOTES ON YOUR READING: NUTS AND BOLTS

- **Don't take notes sentence by sentence.** Try dialoguing with at least a paragraph, and preferably a section, before deciding what is important. Once you've finished taking notes on that section, move on to the next and continue the process.

- **Turn away from the text and try to take notes from memory.** You'll probably have to peek back. This isn't so much to memorize the material as to force you to recall, think, and use your own words. It's also good practice for exams. Try reconstructing important diagrams and charts from memory, too. Treat this step like a game.

- **Organize your notes with a clear structure rather than simply making a list.** You'll be doing this in the next two steps (Questions 9 and 10), when you process your notes for understanding. Still, it's a good idea to give them some structure from the start to make the connections between ideas apparent.

Question 9:
 How can I organize this information?
Question 10:
 How can I picture this information?

- **Translate any diagrams, graphs, tables, and charts into words.** Figure out the main idea conveyed by the graphic element and express it in your own words. A picture may be worth a thousand words, most teachers expect prose responses to their questions instead of drawings.

- **Develop your own shorthand of symbols and abbreviations.** This saves time and begins shaping and transforming the information into something personal that you've had a hand in creating. And as we will discuss at length under Question 11, your mind is more attuned to graphic images than words; creating symbols out of the text helps your mind remember and understand.

Question 11:
 What's my hook for remembering this information?

- **Print rather than use script.** You'll work a lot faster. If you're used to script, you may find this hard to believe but with a little practice you'll see that your fastest *legible* script is not nearly as fast as your fastest legible printing; check it out. Also, you'll work a lot more neatly if you use ball-point pens or felt-tip markers rather than pencils, which smudge. Save fountain pens for your love letters; they slow you down and leak all over the place.

- **Use loose sheets of paper.** When you study you'll need to spread your notes out; you won't be able to do this if they're in a bound notebook. Lined paper is best, either from legal pads or those punched for 3-ring notebooks. Since you'll be using loose paper, it's a good idea to date and number your sheets, and to record the pages they refer to in your textbook.

TAKING NOTES ON YOUR READING: NUTS AND BOLTS (CONTINUED)

- **Write only on one side of each sheet.** Again, from time to time you'll need to spread out your notes to get the big picture. (I realize that you'll use twice as much paper, but you can recycle your paper at the end of the term.)

- **Don't recopy your notes.** This is a waste of time. You'll be rewriting them completely anyway, as you'll see shortly. (Yes, I know this seems like extra work, but it pays big dividends.)

- **Don't use a computer to type your notes.** Now that laptops are becoming affordable, some students are using them to take notes. Don't. You don't have the same freedom or involvement with a keyboard as you do with pen and paper. (I'm a great champion of computers for other purposes, however, like writing papers.)

Don't forget that you'll usually have class notes that cover much the same ground as the notes you took on your reading. Since you'll be combining these two sets of notes shortly, save any major revisions for that step.

TAKING NOTES IN CLASSES AND LECTURES

The same basic rules apply to taking classroom notes as taking reading notes. Again, keeping pace with your teacher will force some concessions in how you take notes, but the basic rules are the same.

Don't become a classroom stenographer. Attempting to take word-for-word notes makes it almost impossible to listen, let alone learn. Listening means hearing and understanding. Instead of furiously scribbling down every word your teacher utters, listen carefully to a few sentences before you write down only the most important points. Don't worry about falling behind; there will be natural breaks in the lecture when you can catch up. If you *do* fall behind or you find your attention has lapsed, leave some blank space and a couple of words so you can pick up the thread later. You can always get the missing notes from a friend after class.

TAKING CLASSROOM NOTES: NUTS AND BOLTS

In addition to the nuts and bolts on taking textbook notes, here are a few additional tips on taking lecture notes:

- **Be on the lookout for terms, buzz words, and pet phrases your teacher uses frequently.** It pays to drop a few of these into your papers and your exam responses.

- **If an idea or question occurs to you that you'd like to think about, jot it down in the margin with a capital *Q* for "question to think about later."**

- **If you aren't sure how to spell a word your teacher uses, put *sp?* after the word and verify the correct spelling later.**

- **If you missed the lecture entirely (and you should avoid this), borrow notes from a classmate as soon as you can.** Borrow from someone who—unlike you—takes down *everything* the teacher says compulsively. Then you can decide what's important and what's not.

COMBINING YOUR TEXTBOOK AND CLASS NOTES

Your textbook and classroom notes will not be identical. There will be things the author said that you thought were important but that your teacher didn't mention during class, and things your book didn't mention that your teacher spent a great deal of time discussing.

I don't need to remind you that what your teacher considers important should be given considerable weight. In any event, you'll need to combine your two sets of notes into one, removing duplicated material and incorporating anything new your teacher has added. **This is why some smart students take their textbook notes to class and then copy their class notes directly into the appropriate spots.** This technique works well if your teacher follows the textbook in a consistent way.

COMBINING YOUR TEXTBOOK AND CLASS NOTES ON THE ROCKS PASSAGE

I realize you don't have any class notes on the rocks passage–you'll have to borrow Johnny's. As I just noted, Johnny's extensive and meticulous notes serve your purposes quite well, effectively acting like a human tape recorder.

Here they are.

- rocks made from one or more minerals
- minerals: natural substances with definate physical and chemical properties
  - most are compounds (exeptions: carbon, iron oxygen)
  - 92 natural elements, 8 = 98% of all rock mass, 2 = 75%

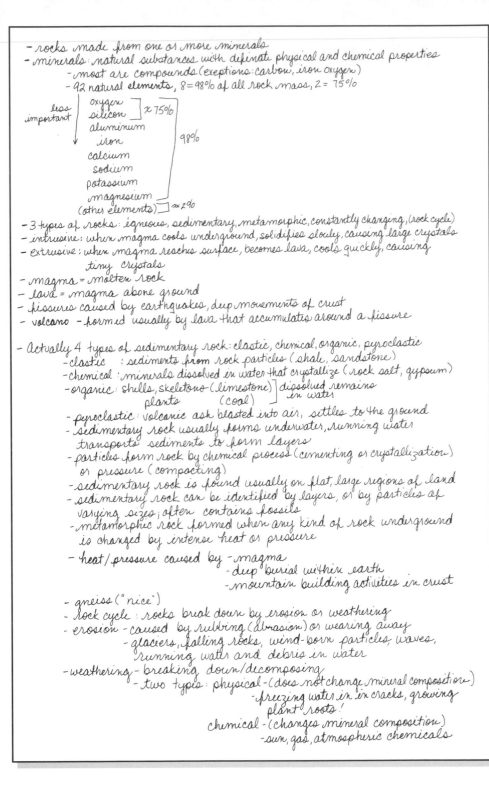

less important
- oxygen ⎱ ≈ 75%
- silicon ⎰
- aluminium
- iron ⎱ 98%
- calcium
- sodium
- potassium
- magnesium ⎰
- (other elements) ⎤ ≈ 2%

- 3 types of rocks: igneous, sedimentary, metamorphic, constantly changing, (rock cycle)
- intrusive: when magma cools underground, solidifies slowly, causing large crystals
- extrusive: when magma reaches surface, becomes lava, cools quickly, causing tiny crystals
- magma = molten rock
- lava = magma above ground
- fissures caused by earthquakes, deep movements of crust
- volcano - formed usually by lava that accumulates around a fissure

- Actually 4 types of sedimentary rock: clastic, chemical, organic, pyroclastic
  - clastic   : sediments from rock particles (shale, sandstone)
  - chemical : minerals dissolved in water that crystallize (rock salt, gypsum)
  - organic: shells, skeletons (limestone) ⎱ dissolved remains
    plants   (coal) ⎰ in water
  - pyroclastic: volcanic ash blasted into air, settles to the ground
  - sedimentary rock usually forms underwater, running water transports sediments to form layers
  - particles form rock by chemical process (cementing or crystallization) or pressure (compacting)
  - sedimentary rock is found usually on flat, large regions of land
  - sedimentary rock can be identified by layers, or by particles of varying sizes; often contains fossils
  - metamorphic rock formed when any kind of rock underground is changed by intense heat or pressure

  - heat/pressure caused by - magma
                            - deep burial within earth
                            - mountain building activities in crust

  - gneiss ("nice")
  - rock cycle: rocks break down by erosion or weathering
  - erosion - caused by rubbing (abrasion) or wearing away
            - glaciers, falling rocks, wind-born particles, waves, running water and debris in water
  - weathering - breaking down/decomposing
            - two types: physical - (does not change mineral composition)
                              - freezing water in in cracks, growing plant roots!
               chemical - (changes mineral composition)
                      - sun, gas, atmospheric chemicals

Before continuing, please complete the following exercise.

EXERCISE #4

Instructions: Compare *your* notes on the passage (Exercise #2, page 26) with Johnny's *class* notes (previous page). Some information will be the same but you'll notice that the class you "missed" covered some additional material. On Johnny's class notes above, circle or underline the new information "your teacher" provided.

Here's what you should have selected:

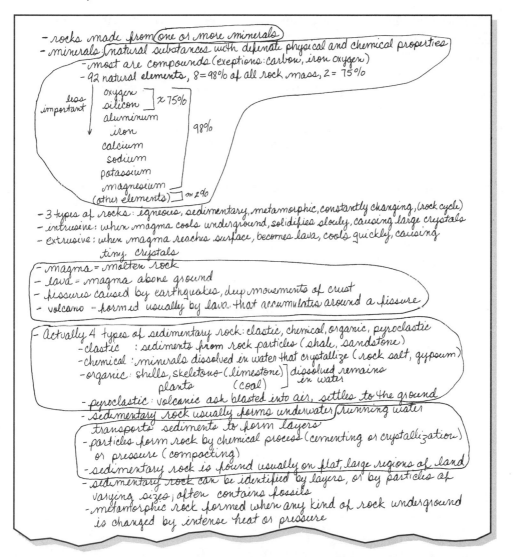

- rocks made from one or more minerals
- minerals: natural substances with definate physical and chemical properties
    - most are compounds (exeptions: carbon, iron oxygen)
    - 92 natural elements, 8 = 98% of all rock mass, 2 = 75%

| less important | oxygen silicon] ≈ 75% aluminium iron calcium sodium potassium magnesium (other elements)] ≈ 2% | 98% |

- 3 types of rocks: igneous, sedimentary, metamorphic, constantly changing, (rock cycle)
- intrusive: when magma cools underground, solidifies slowly, causing large crystals
- extrusive: when magma reaches surface, becomes lava, cools quickly, causing tiny crystals
- magma = molten rock
- lava = magma above ground
- fissures caused by earthquakes, deep movements of crust
- volcano - formed usually by lava that accumulates around a fissure
- Actually 4 types of sedimentary rock: clastic, chemical, organic, pyroclastic
    - clastic : sediments from rock particles (shale, sandstone)
    - chemical : minerals dissolved in water that crystallize (rock salt, gypsum)
    - organic: shells, skeletons-(limestone)] dissolved remains
            plants   (coal)   in water
    - pyroclastic: volcanic ash blasted into air, settles to the ground
- sedimentary rock usually forms underwater running water transports sediments to form layers
- particles form rock by chemical process (cementing or crystallization) or pressure (compacting)
- sedimentary rock is found usually on flat, large regions of land
- sedimentary rock can be identified by layers, or by particles of varying sizes; often contains fossils
- metamorphic rock formed when any kind of rock underground is changed by intense heat or pressure

95

> - heat/pressure caused by - magma
>   - deep burial within earth
>   - mountain building activities in crust
> - gneiss ("nice")
> - Rock cycle : rocks break down by erosion or weathering
> - erosion - caused by rubbing (abrasion) or wearing away
>   - glaciers, falling rocks, wind-born particles, waves, running water and debris in water
> - weathering - breaking down/decomposing
>   - two types : physical - (does not change mineral composition)
>   - freezing water in in cracks, growing plant roots!
>   chemical - (changes mineral composition)
>   - sun, gas, atmospheric chemicals

This new information is very important. As you know, any information your teacher provides that is not included in your textbook demands a high-priority ranking.

You now have to combine your classroom and textbook notes. Before continuing, please complete the following exercise.

EXERCISE #5

Instructions: On a separate sheet of paper, use what you've learned about paraphrasing and summarizing to update your original textbook notes (Exercise #2, page 26) with the additional information you've selected from Johnny's painstaking classroom notes.

Your combined textbook and classroom notes should look something like this:

-rocks (except coal) made of <u>minerals</u> (substances with definate physical/chemical properties)
- most minerals are compounds (exceptions: carbon, iron, oxygen)
- 92 natural elements; 8 = 98% of all rock mass

- oxygen ⎤ 75%
  silicon ⎦
  aluminum ⎤
  iron   ⎥
  calcium   ⎥ 23%
  sodium   ⎥
  potassium ⎥
  magnesium ⎦
  84 others ⎤ 2%

- 3 types of rocks: igneous, sedimentary, metamorphic (rock cycle)
- <u>igneous</u>:   1) <u>intrusive</u>   2) <u>extrusive</u>
           underground   above ground   emerges from ⎯⎯ <u>fissures</u> (caused by
           magma (molten rock)   lava (magma above g.)   earthquakes, deep
           rises, cools slowly   emerges, cools quickly   movements of crust
           large grains, crystals   tiny grains   <u>volcanoes</u> (usually
             (granite)   (basalt, pumice)   formed from lava
                                       accumulating around
                                       a fissure

- <u>sedimentary</u>: sediments (particles) that form strata (layers), usually transported by running water
        - particles usually formed from rocks under 1) erosion, 2) weathering
        - <u>erosion</u> (rubbing/abrasion) caused by: glaciers, falling rocks, running water +
          waves (+ debris), wind-born particles
        - <u>weathering</u> (breaking down, decomposing)
          1) physical (does not change mineral composition) freezing H_2O in cracks, plant roots
          2) chemical (changes   "   "   ) sun, gas, atmospheric chemicals
        - particles form rocks by 1) chemical process (cementing, crystallization)
                        2) physical process (compacting = pressure)
        - 4 types of sediments
          1) <u>clastic</u> - rock particles (shale, sandstone)
          2) <u>chemical</u> - minerals dissolved in water that crystallize (rock salt, gypsum)
          3) <u>organic</u> - a) shells/skeletons of marine organisms (limestone) ⎤ dissolved or
                      b) plants (coal)   ⎥ decomposed
                                        ⎦ in water
          4) <u>pyroclastic</u> - volcanic ash, blasted into air, settling to earth
         - identified by layers; particles of different sizes; fossils
         - usually found in large, flat regions

- <u>metamorphic</u>: rocks changed by great heat/pressure ⟸ magma
                                             deep burial
                                             mountain building

        - <u>metamorphism</u>: makes rocks rougher, denser; changes composition
        - identified by wavy bands; distorted structure
        - shale becomes slate
          limestone   "   marble
          granite   "   gneiss ("nice")

- <u>rock cycle</u>: any type of rock can become any other

By the way, even though you have combined your two sets of notes, don't throw out the originals; you may need to refer to them at another time.

SHOULD YOU MARK UP YOUR TEXTBOOK?

If you don't own your textbook, of course, this is not an issue. If you do own your textbook, whether you choose to mark it up depends on a few considerations.

In the first place, you shouldn't need to mark it up. Once you've taken out the important information in note form, you won't need to refer to a textbook much, if at all. (Also, if you're considering selling your textbook when you complete the course, a marked-up textbook is usually worth considerably less.) On the other hand, if your teacher refers to the textbook frequently during class discussions, annotating it before class is worth doing.

If you choose to mark up your textbook, doing it the old way (liberal highlighting and underlining) is a waste of time.

Question 7:
What information is
important here?

MARKING UP YOUR TEXTBOOK: NUTS AND BOLTS

If you're going to mark up your textbook—and many smart students *don't*—keep the following points in mind.

- **Throw away your highlighters!** Highlighted text is distracting and gives everything equal importance. Most students highlight mechanically; that is, without deciding first whether something is important (Question 7).

- **Avoid pens that smudge**. And don't go crazy with different colors; one or two are all you should need.

- **Read an entire paragraph before deciding what to underline.** The same principle that's behind waiting to take notes applies here, too.

- **Underline as few words as possible, not entire sentences.** Deciding precisely what words to underline requires almost as much thought as translating the author's words into your own when you take notes. For lengthy ideas, use vertical marks in the margin.

- **Don't forget to record your thoughts and questions in the margin.** Besides helping you formulate ideas, this will save you review time later.

- **Don't use a ruler.** Rulers force you to underline sentences without giving adequate thought to what you're reading.

IF YOU'RE GOING TO MARK UP YOUR TEXTBOOK
Here's how a smart student would have marked up a textbook.

HOW CAN I PARAPHRASE AND SUMMARIZE THIS INFORMATION?

ROCKS

Rocks are hard, natural masses of solid matter that make up the earth's crust. With a few exceptions (such as coal), rocks are composed of one or more minerals. Geologists classify rocks as either igneous, sedimentary, or metamorphic, depending on how they were formed. *how does it harden?*

Igneous rocks are formed from magma, the molten matter deep within the earth. There are two types of igneous rock. If magma rises toward the surface, it slowly cools and sometimes solidifies underground. The result is ① intrusive igneous rock. If magma reaches the earth's surface, it emerges from volcanoes or fissures (cracks) as lava. Lava cools rapidly aboveground, solidifying into ② extrusive igneous rock. Intrusive igneous rock, such as granite, can be identified by its large, clearly visible mineral grains (crystals). Because extrusive rock solidifies more quickly than intrusive igneous rock, it is characterized by tiny crystals. Basalt, with its fine texture, high density, and dark color, is the most common extrusive igneous rock, lying beneath the vast ocean floor. *how do shale, limestone get underground?* Pumice, another common extrusive igneous rock used in some abrasives, acquires its rough porous texture from the explosive release of gas that often accompanies volcanic eruptions.

Virtually all sedimentary rocks are formed when particles, known as sediments, accumulate in strata (layers). Most sediments are created when rocks of any kind are broken down by erosion or weathering. When these particles cement or compact together and harden, they form sedimentary rock. Shale, the most common sedimentary rock, is formed from mud and clay; sandstone, as its name suggests, is formed from sand. Some sediments, however, are created from animal or plant remains that have decayed or decomposed in water. Most limestone, for example, is formed from the minerals of decomposed shells or skeletons of marine organisms, while coal is formed from plants that have decayed in swamps. Sedimentary rock usually forms under water. It can frequently be identified by characteristic layers or by particles of different sizes, and often contains fossils.

Metamorphic rocks are formed when rocks of any type are changed by long periods of intense heat or pressure within the earth. *what causes* This process, known as metamorphism, alters the texture, structure, and mineral composition of the existing rock, usually making it rougher and more dense. Metamorphic rock can sometimes be identified by its distorted structure, or by wavy bands. When the sedimentary rock limestone undergoes metamorphism, it becomes marble. Shale, another sedimentary rock, becomes slate under metamorphism, while the igneous rock granite becomes gneiss.

As hard as they are, rocks do not last forever. Rocks above ground are continuously exposed to weathering and erosion. Over thousands or even millions of years, they are broken down and worn away to sediments, which can later form new sedimentary rocks. Rocks below ground can also change. Any rock subjected to *intrusive? how do Other types of rocks get below ground? how?* sufficient heat and pressure undergoes metamorphism and forms new metamorphic rock. And if the heat is great enough, any rock can be melted back into magma and later form new igneous rock. Thus, any type of rock can be transformed into one of the others. This dynamic, never-ending process of rock formation is known as the rock cycle.

Again, why don't you compare these notations with Johnny's (page 31) and the ones you made (Exercise #2, page 26). Which ones most effectively highlight the important points in the rocks passage?

SUMMARY

Taking notes is an important step toward understanding the material. Simply copying doesn't work; you need to process the information in your mind and in your own words. Structure and organize the material; use a personal shorthand; take notes on at least a paragraph at a time; paraphrase whenever possible. To do all this, you'll need to think deeply about what you're reading. Remember: the more active your mind is while you read, the more you'll understand and remember later.

You should approach classroom notes in the same basic way—don't scribble down everything, but find the points that are most important. As you begin to revise your notes (something you'll be doing a lot), you should combine your classroom and textbook notes. Question 8 is only the beginning. As you will see shortly, studying should consist not of rereading your notes, but of continually reshaping and revising them. And you revise them by asking the CyberLearning questions over and over (especially Questions 8 through 12).

Don't be put off by the prospect of revising "perfectly good" notes. It's neither repetitive nor boring because you'll be uncovering new information as you do it. I know it sounds like work (and it is!), but it will save you an incredible amount of time down the road.

Once you take notes on a section or chapter, you should not need to reread the chapter ever again. You might need to refer to it for certain facts or diagrams, but you've already extracted the important information it contains. From here on out you are communicating with the information completely in your own language and on your own terms. Each new set of notes brings you closer to understanding and mastering the subject.

Question 8:
  How can I paraphrase and summarize this information?

Question 9:
  How can I organize this information?

Question 10:
  How can I picture this information?

Question 11:
  What's my hook for remembering this information?

Question 12:
  How does this information fit in with what I already know?

Answering Question 9:
How Can I Organize This Information?

PUT ASIDE YOUR TEXTBOOK

Now that you have finished taking notes on your textbook (in our case, on the passage), you will not need to look at it again; you can answer the remaining questions (9–12) using only your notes. Already you're more independent by being less tied to a grindingly dull textbook and more plugged into a language you understand—your own!

By the way, since we combined our classroom and textbook notes, we will no longer need to distinguish between the two sets in our discussion of the CyberLearning method.

GROUPING AND REGROUPING

Organizing information means collecting information into groups or categories so that you can see different patterns, connections, and relationships. Just as each subject asks different questions, each subject organizes information differently. Sociology and psychology, for example, both examine human behavior, but each defines and organizes and categorizes it differently.

Further, any body of information can be organized and reorganized in a number of ways, depending on your purposes and what questions you are trying to answer. Each organization will reveal a different aspect of the material while hiding others. Though some methods of organization are more useful than others, there is no "best" way to organize information.

Our sample passage, for example, divides rocks into three categories: igneous, sedimentary, and metamorphic. This organizes the different types of rocks depending on *how* they were formed. Why not categorize rocks depending on *where* they were formed?

Here's what you're looking for when trying to answer this question.

- **In how many different ways can the various pieces of information be compared?** Rocks can be compared by looking at how they were formed, where they were formed, what they were formed from, and so on. **You should try reorganizing the information in as many ways as possible.** You're looking for new groupings that make some kind of sense or reveal new connections. This isn't a logical process, so experiment—you never know what you'll discover. **The important thing is that you *try* to reorganize the material, even if you end up not being able to do it.**

- **What items are similar in some way?** Collect them into a group and name it. That name is the group's "heading" or "category," and should indicate what the items have in common. (Try to keep the number of groups to a manageable number—preferably fewer than ten—so the information does not become too complicated for you to use or remember.)

- **What items are different?** Separate them into different categories. (I'll show you some examples shortly.)

- **What items depend on each other?** Link them so you see and remember the connection. (Again, I'll show you some examples shortly.)

- **How do the different items compare in terms of the expert and orientation questions?** One of the purposes of organizing information is to help you answer questions on it. Since the most important questions are the expert and orientation questions, you will find it helpful to create one table or chart that ensures you answer them. (For a discussion of these questions, see the chapter covering Question 5 that begins on page 67.)

Question 5:
What are the "expert questions"?

Before we see how a smart student would go about answering this question on the rocks passage, complete the following exercise.

EXERCISE #6

Instructions: Looking over your latest set of complete notes (Exercise #5, page 96), consider the different ways rocks were compared (other than the obvious groupings of igneous, sedimentary, and metamorphic). See how many different groupings you can come up with in the space below. (Hint: Remember the expert questions: for example, *What process causes this?* or *What's this made of?*)

ORGANIZING AND REORGANIZING INFORMATION IN THE ROCKS PASSAGE

Here are the six organizational schemes I came up with:

① Rocks formed below ground
  - intrusive igneous
  - metamorphic

Rocks formed above ground
  - extrusive igneous
  - sedimentary

② Rocks formed using heat or pressure
  - igneous
  - metamorphic
  - pyroclastic sedimentary

Rocks formed without heat or pressure
  - clastic sedimentary
  - chemical sedimentary
  - organic sedimentary

③ Rocks formed without water
  - igneous
  - metamorphic
  - pyroclastic sedimentary

Rocks formed with water
  - clastic sedimentary
  - chemical sedimentary
  - organic sedimentary

④ "Organic" Rocks
  - organic sedimentary

"InOrganic" Rocks
  - All others

⑤ Rocks not formed from other rocks
  - organic sedimentary
  - chemical sedimentary

Rocks formed from other rocks
  - igneous
  - metamorphic
  - clastic sedimentary
  - pyroclastic sedimentary

⑥ Fossil-bearing rocks
  - clastic sedimentary
  - organic sedimentary

Non-fossil-bearing rocks
  - All others

And so on. Perhaps you thought up other ways to organize the information.

You can continue this process of breaking the material down and creating categories as long as you'd like. **I know this seems time-consuming, but looking over the different categories will give you new insights and understanding.** For example, the first two groupings suggest that rocks require heat, pressure, or water to form; the last grouping suggests that fossils form only near water. I have absolutely no idea what use I'll be able to get out of these new insights, but I now have a better understanding of rock formation. I also have the pleasure of having made a discovery.

This process is a lot like shuffling and reshuffling cards to see if you have a good hand. It's okay that many—perhaps most—of your groupings will not give you any significant insights into the material. But these groupings are still worthwhile. To understand why information is organized the way it is, you must explore other ways of organizing it. **Building understanding is largely a matter of trial and error.**

LINKING INFORMATION IN THE ROCKS PASSAGE

An integral part of answering this question is hunting for links between isolated bits of information. Before continuing, please complete the following exercise.

EXERCISE #7

Instructions: Again looking over your latest set of notes (Exercise #5, page 97), on another sheet of scratch paper list any facts or ideas that can be linked. (Hint: Look for processes, or for anything mentioned in more than one context.)

Here are the links I found:

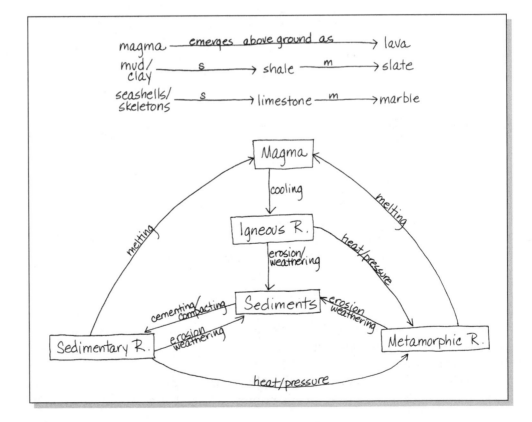

ORGANIZING THE PASSAGE INFORMATION TO ANSWER THE EXPERT AND ORIENTATION QUESTIONS

HOW CAN I ORGANIZE THIS INFORMATION?

Although this step is basically unstructured, you should approach the expert and orientation questions systematically so you're sure you've answered them. Creating a table or chart allows you to do just that.

EXERCISE #8

Instructions: I prepared the blank table below to organize my answers to some of the expert and orientation questions. Before looking at my completed table, which follows, try to fill it in yourself. You'll probably need to copy it onto a larger sheet of paper, since I had to reduce my notes so they could squeeze onto this page. By the way, completing this table from memory is an *excellent* way to rehearse for exams, but feel free to consult your notes when necessary. (You may not have enough information to complete the table, and some of the boxes may be irrelevant.)

---

	example	made of	identified by	caused by	where found	found near
volcano						
fissure						
intrusive igneous						
extrusive igneous						
clastic sedimentary						
chemical sedimentary						
organic sedimentary						
pyroclastic sedimentary						
sediments						
strata						
metamorphic						
erosion						
weathering						

Here's how I completed the chart:

	example	made of	identified by	caused by	where found	found near
volcano	NR	lava piled up around fissure	NR	earthquakes, crustal movements	NR	NR?
fissure	NR	NR	NR	"	NR	NR?
intrusive igneous	granite	solidified magma	large crystals	", cooling	underground	volcanoes
extrusive igneous	pumice, basalt	solidified lava	tiny crystals	", cooling	above ground	volcanoes
clastic sedimentary	shale, sandstone	rock particles	fossils, layers	cementing, compacting	above ground, underwater	large flat regions
chemical sedimentary	rock salt, gypsum	minerals	fossils?, layers?	crystallization	"	"
organic sedimentary	limestone, coal	animal, plant remains	fossils?, layers?	compacting?, crystallization?, cementing?	"	"
pyroclastic sedimentary	?	volcanic ash	fossils?, layers?	volcanic ash settling to ground	above ground	", volcanoes
sediments	NR	rocks, animal remains, ash, crystallized minerals	NR	erosion, weathering, crystallization	above ground, also underwater	NR
strata	NR	sediments	NR	water transporting	underwater	NR
metamorphic	slate, marble, gneiss	rocks	rough, dense, wavy bands; distorted structure	magma, deep burial, mountain-building	underground	mountains
erosion	falling rocks, glaciers, water, wind-born particles	NR	NR	wearing away	NR	NR
weathering	sun, gas, atmospheric, freezing h₂0, plant roots	NR	NR	physical or chemical	NR	NR

Again, I realize this table may be hard to read but I had to reduce it to fit onto this page. The question marks stand for information I need to collect, though all of it may not necessarily appear on a test. The "NR" stands for "not relevant."

That does it for Question 9.

SUMMARY

There is no one right way to organize a subject. The key to Question 9 is experimentation. Each method of organization you try reveals different aspects of the information, so try anything you can think of. How many ways can you group the information? Which items can you link? What insights do the expert questions reveal when organized?

This experimenting and organizing may sound like more work, but it leads to true understanding and saves time later. Becoming engaged with the material in this way prevents you from merely "looking at" it and remaining mystified. It's also excellent test-taking practice!

Organizing the information is just one more step in mastering your subject. If you do it thoroughly, you greatly reduce the risk of being caught unprepared by "surprise attacks" on exams. What's more, this step, like the others you've been completing, will reveal any deficiencies in your understanding well before the test!

Onward. With Question 10 we personalize our notes still further.

Answering Question 10:
How Can I Picture This Information?

PUTTING YOUR PERSONAL STAMP ON THE MATERIAL

Question 8 asks you to paraphrase and summarize the important information you are extracting from your reading. In other words, it asks you to translate the material into your own words, abbreviations, and symbols. In so doing you are remaking the material into something you've created and furthering your understanding of it.

Question 10 continues the distillation process by asking you to translate as much of the material as possible into pictures.

A PICTURE IS WORTH A THOUSAND WORDS

You're not just "being creative" here. Representing information as pictures is a critical step in building understanding. Information has form and structure; to understand information, you must "see" this form. Representing it graphically is an excellent way to do this.

Although we like to think that the human race has progressed a lot since the days when our main concern would have been hunting for prey while outrunning larger and faster predators, our brains haven't changed much.

Your primitive brain is quite good at handling pictures, and it's not bad at handling words that create pictures. Graphic words like *elephant* or *milk shake* don't give it much trouble, but when confronted with abstractions like *democracy* or *magnetism* or *free will,* your brain is not sure what to do. If you want your caveman brain to process and understand abstract words and concepts, you have to help it as much as possible by translating them into concrete visual images. Even the act of designing a picture or diagram will improve your understanding of information and help etch it on your brain.

THERE'S NO ONE WAY TO DO THIS

Just as you can organize information in different ways, you can represent it graphically in different ways, too. Here are some points to keep in mind:

- **Have some scratch paper handy.** Before committing your pictures to your notes, experiment with the information and with different types of diagrams to see what works best for you.

Question 1:
What's my purpose for reading this?

Question 2:
What do I already know about this topic?

Question 3:
What's the big picture here?

Question 4:
What's the author going to say next?

Question 5:
What are the "expert questions"?

Question 6:
What questions does this information raise for me?

Question 7:
What information is important here?

Question 8:
How can I paraphrase and summarize this information?

Question 9:
How can I organize this information?

**Question 10:
How can I picture this information?**

Question 11:
What's my hook for remembering this information?

Question 12:
How does this information fit in with what I already know?

*The words or
language, as they are
written or spoken, do
not seem to play any
role in my mechanism
of thought.... The
physical entities which
seem to serve as
elements in thought
are certain signs and
more or less clear
images.... The
above–mentioned
elements are, in any
case, of visual and
some of muscular type.
Conventional words
or other signs have
to be sought for
laboriously only in the
secondary stage.*

ALBERT EINSTEIN

- **Use different techniques to emphasize the relationships and relative importance of the various ideas you are trying to capture.** Vary the size, shape, lettering, and even color of your diagrams.

- **Be creative in designing your diagram, but not *too* creative.** Keep it simple enough to reconstruct from memory. Tables, graphs, and basic geometric figures are best; complicated diagrams hide the underlying organization of the information. If your picture or diagram is too "artistic," you will have trouble remembering or using it when you are taking an exam. You don't want your visuals more complex than the ideas they are trying to simplify!

- **The traditional outline—with its letters, numbers, and Roman numerals—is too verbal and linear, and not graphic enough.** It may be helpful when writing a paper, but it is ineffective as a visual means of representing information.

- **Don't rely on the pictures or diagrams provided by your teacher or textbook.** Your brain relates to pictures you devise much better than to those devised by someone else.

- **You won't be able to make everything visual, but try anyway.** You'd be surprised how much you can represent graphically if you put your mind to it. I'll bet you could even take those abstract words I mentioned earlier (*democracy, magnetism, free will*) and come up with symbols or pictures to represent them. As with all the CyberLearning questions, making the effort is the important thing.

YOUR ALMOST-FINAL NOTES FROM THE ROCKS PASSAGE

In a moment you will see my lean and mean, picture-rich version of notes. But before continuing, please complete the following exercise.

EXERCISE #9

Instructions: Return to your latest version of notes (Exercise #6, page 102). Rewrite them completely, this time translating as much of the information to pictures as possible.

Here's what a smart student's notes might look like after answering Question 10. How do yours compare? Your diagrams will probably be very different from these; no two smart students picture information in the same way. Still, these notes will give you some idea of how far a smart student can take the process.

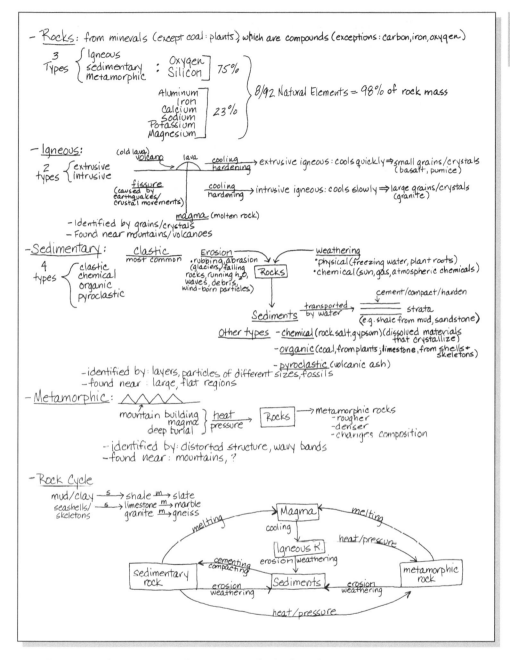

- <u>Rocks</u>: from minerals (except coal: plants) which are compounds (exceptions: carbon, iron, oxygen)
  3 Types { Igneous / sedimentary / metamorphic } : Oxygen / Silicon] 75%
  Aluminum / Iron / Calcium / Sodium / Potassium / Magnesium] 23% } 8/92 Natural Elements = 98% of rock mass

- <u>Igneous</u>:
  2 types { extrusive / intrusive }
  (old lava) <u>volcano</u> → lava → <u>cooling hardening</u> → extrusive igneous: cools quickly ⇒ small grains/crystals (basalt, pumice)
  <u>fissure</u> (caused by earthquakes/crustal movements) → <u>cooling hardening</u> → intrusive igneous: cools slowly ⇒ large grains/crystals (granite)
  <u>magma</u> (molten rock)
  - Identified by grains/crystals
  - Found near mountains/volcanoes

- <u>Sedimentary</u>:
  4 types { clastic / chemical / organic / pyroclastic }
  <u>Clastic</u> most common
  <u>Erosion</u> • rubbing, abrasion (glaciers, falling rocks, running h₂0, waves, debris, wind-born particles)
  <u>weathering</u> • physical (freezing water, plant roots) • chemical (sun, gas, atmospheric chemicals)
  Rocks
  Sediments — <u>transported by water</u> → cement/compact/harden — strata (e.g. shale from mud, sandstone)
  <u>Other types</u> — chemical (rock salt, gypsum) (dissolved materials that crystallize)
  — <u>organic</u> (coal, from plants; limestone, from shells + skeletons)
  — <u>pyroclastic</u> (volcanic ash)
  - identified by: layers, particles of different sizes, fossils
  - found near: large, flat regions

- <u>Metamorphic</u>:
  mountain building / magma / deep burial } <u>heat pressure</u> → Rocks → metamorphic rocks - rougher - denser - changes composition
  - identified by: distorted structure, wavy bands
  - found near: mountains, ?

- <u>Rock Cycle</u>
  mud/clay —s→ shale —m→ slate
  seashells/skeletons —s→ limestone —m→ marble
  granite —m→ gneiss

  Magma — cooling → Igneous R. — erosion/weathering → Sediments
  melting / melting / heat/pressure
  sedimentary rock — cementing compacting / erosion weathering
  metamorphic rock — erosion weathering / heat/pressure

You'll notice that I created some symbols for the process, and some rough pictures to go along with the identifying characteristics. You'll also note that I departed from the linear structure of my original notes.

If you glance back at the original notes we took back in Question 7, you may be surprised at how far they've evolved. But we're not finished. I called this our almost-final version because in Question 12 we will be condensing these notes one step further (yes, even more).

Question 7:
  What information is important here?
Question 12:
  How does this information fit in with what I already know?

SUMMARY

Does drawing pictures sound like fun? Well, it should be. But devising pictures is also one of the best ways to make information stick because your mind absorbs and understands images better than it does words. As you go through your notes, represent visually anything you can. Use shapes, lines, lettering, and even color to capture your ideas. I guarantee you'll find your pictures much easier to remember than your words.

Answering Question 11:
What's My Hook for Remembering This Information?

CONGRATULATIONS

You should be feeling much more confident in your understanding of rocks. Imagine for a moment that rather than applying the past ten questions, I had simply instructed you to reread the passage and your notes as often as you thought necessary. Do you think your understanding would be anywhere near what it is now? More to the point, do you think learning the material the old way (constantly rereading) would have been as interesting? Of course not.

As you've been adding to your knowledge, both of rocks and of the smart student approach, you may have noticed that something is missing: anxiety. By following these steps, asking and answering the questions, you have eliminated the panic that comes from studying without specific goals in mind.

Now let's move on to the next step—devising hooks.

YOU'VE MEMORIZED MORE THAN YOU REALIZE

Until now, the CyberLearning questions have focused your efforts on *understanding* important major ideas and concepts rather than on *memorizing* minor facts and details. We delayed memorizing not because facts and details are unimportant, but because it's hard to remember material you don't understand. By answering the first ten CyberLearning questions you've developed a solid grasp of the material. You now have a framework that will help you remember the details.

By the way, the work you put into building that framework has also planted most of the information firmly in your long-term memory. And you thought you were just asking questions, organizing information, and drawing pictures!

YOU DON'T HAVE TO MEMORIZE EVERYTHING

How much and what kind of memorizing you must do varies from course to course. Some subjects require less memorizing than others. Philosophy has fewer facts to remember than, say, biology. What's more, some teachers place greater emphasis on remembering information. A course where your grade is determined by tests requires far more memorizing than does one where your grade is determined by papers. For that matter, preparing for a short-response, fill-in-the-blank test will require more memorizing than a multiple-choice test (where *recognizing* the answer is as good as remembering it).

Question 1:
What's my purpose for reading this?

Question 2:
What do I already know about this topic?

Question 3:
What's the big picture here?

Question 4:
What's the author going to say next?

Question 5:
What are the "expert questions"?

Question 6:
What questions does this information raise for me?

Question 7:
What information is important here?

Question 8:
How can I paraphrase and summarize this information?

Question 9:
How can I organize this information?

Question 10:
How can I picture this information?

Question 11:
What's my hook for remembering this information?

Question 12:
How does this information fit in with what I already know?

111

WHATEVER WORKS, WORKS

As you've seen, building understanding of information requires asking a specific series of questions, the CyberLearning questions. While they answer those questions differently, all smart students ask the same ones whether they are aware of it or not.

Memorization techniques are another matter. Each smart student has developed personal favorites, depending on what needs to be memorized. Despite their differences, however, all memorization techniques are based on the same underlying principles. Don't worry if a technique seems silly or illogical; the only thing that matters is whether it aids your memory.

HAVING SAID THAT, HERE'S WHAT *DOESN'T* WORK

Memorizing traditionally entails repeating information so many times that you can't help but remember it, even if you don't understand it. By saying or seeing something often enough, you hope your brain will somehow absorb the information. Unfortunately, passive repetition is one of the least effective ways to memorize. It's also the most boring.

THERE'S NOTHING WRONG WITH YOUR MEMORY

Many people complain that they have a "bad" memory the way they might complain about having weak eyesight. But memory is not a sense, and you are not born and stuck with yours. Memorizing is a skill that can be developed and improved like any other.

You can do this by using specific techniques that people have used for thousands of years. These techniques, or "tricks," do not improve your memory; rather, they improve how you use it. Assuming your brain functions normally, you can learn to memorize better. This chapter shows you how.

YOUR BRAIN NEEDS A HOOK

As I pointed out in the previous chapter, your brain evolved to ensure your physical survival, which, unlike your academic survival, did not depend on stockpiling mountains of information. Nonetheless, your caveman brain has an awesome capacity for processing and storing certain *types* of information.

If you're having trouble remembering something, it's because you aren't presenting it to your brain in a way it can handle efficiently. The trick is to find a way to hook that information to things your brain can store and recall easily. In a way, the hard-to-remember information piggybacks on the easy-to-remember information.

Early elementary school teachers realize this, which is why they introduce new words next to a visual representation. While a student recognizes the shape and color of an apple, he or she is recognizing the length and shape of the word alongside.

THE FOUR HOOKS

While your brain has a very difficult time with abstract ideas or isolated facts, it stores four things very well:

- pictures
- patterns
- rhymes
- stories

If you find a way to link an isolated fact or an abstract idea (hard-to-remember things) with something you already know or with a picture, a pattern, a rhyme, or a story (easy-to-remember things), memorizing becomes a snap!

WHAT'S MY HOOK FOR REMEMBERING THIS INFORMATION?

THE GREEKS HAD A WORD FOR IT

Mnemonics (nih–MAHN–iks) is derived from the Greek word for memory (amnesia is derived from the same word). Mnemonics is just a ten-dollar word for techniques that help you remember things. A mnemonic is nothing more than a memory hook.

Mnemonics have been around for thousands of years. Orators in ancient Greece used them to memorize epic poems tens of thousands of words long. Modern memory experts use them to perform circus stunts like memorizing entire phone books of small towns. Impressive, though you have to wonder why they couldn't put their time and ability to better use.

Which brings us to the chief drawback of mnemonics: they are simply gimmicks. True, devising a mnemonic does force you to engage the material actively. And mnemonics come in handy when you have masses of information to memorize, like a foreign language vocabulary or historical dates. But use them as a last resort. While they help you remember information, they do not help you understand it.

ALL YOU NEED TO KNOW ABOUT MEMORIZING: THE TEN KEYS

We have already discussed some basic principles of memorizing. In all there are ten keys that form the basis of our four–step approach to memorizing, which you will be learning shortly. (As always, you don't have to memorize this list; I've numbered the points so that we could refer to them.)

Key #1: Try to understand it first.

Key #2: Create a hook—a picture, a pattern, a rhyme, or a story.

Key #3: Link it.

Key #4: Don't bite off more than you can chew, and chew that bite thoroughly before taking another.

Key #5: Get emotionally involved.

Key #6: Engage as many senses as possible.

Key #7: Smell the roses.

Key #8: Sleep on it.

Key #9: Use it or lose it.

Key #10: Quiz yourself periodically.

KEY #1: TRY TO UNDERSTAND IT FIRST

It's not by chance that memorizing comes at the tail end of the CyberLearning questions. Information that is organized, logical, or that otherwise makes sense to you is more easily memorized than information that isn't. Indeed, if something makes logical sense, if it's connected to what you already know, you'll rarely need to memorize it; it's isolated facts and disconnected ideas that are troublesome.

Think of your memory as a filing system that stores information for future access. An efficient filing system must be organized so you'll know "where to look" when you're trying to remember something. (You'll also recall from Question 9 that information needs to be organized to be readily understood.)

Question 9:
How can I organize this information?

If you can't organize information in a meaningful way, organize it in any way you can. If this sounds pointless, it's not. Again, even if you can't find a way to organize the information, having tried keeps you involved and working with the material, and this helps you remember it. In fact, there's less to memorize. Once you've grouped information, for example, the principle that unites that information is less to remember and vastly simpler to retrieve than all the individual facts.

Once you understand information, you can often reconstruct it when you can't remember it. Try the following exercise:

> **EXERCISE #10**
>
> *Instructions:* In what year did Abraham Lincoln deliver the Gettysburg Address? (Hint: If you can remember the date of the American Revolution as well as the first line of the Gettysburg Address, you can reconstruct the date it was delivered.)

RECONSTRUCTING FORGOTTEN INFORMATION

Let's say you don't remember the date Lincoln wrote the Gettysburg Address (I didn't), but you *do* recall that it begins, "Four score and seven years ago..." That's eighty-seven years. If you add 87 to 1776 (the date Lincoln's referring to, and one you *do* remember), you get 1863. Voilà! You've reconstructed a fact you'd forgotten—or perhaps a fact you'd never known!

When memorizing information, continually ask yourself how you would reconstruct an item if you forgot it. This resourceful tactic forces you to think and make connections, and comes in handy on tests when you can't remember something.

KEY #2: CREATE A HOOK—A PICTURE, A PATTERN, A RHYME, OR A STORY

There is compelling evidence that the left hemisphere (half) of your brain stores information differently from the right. The left side of your brain apparently deals in words, numbers, parts, and logic, while the right is more attuned to pictures, wholes, patterns, rhythms, and emotions. In school we tend to rely too much on our left brain. You will remember more if you engage your right brain by visualizing what you are trying to learn, by finding rhymes or patterns in it, and creating stories that engage your emotions.

The following points about hooks are worth noting:

- **Hooks work best when you have devised them yourself.**

- **Don't rely on one; they work best in combination.**

- **While a hook that makes logical sense is better than one that doesn't, *any* hook that helps you remember information is doing the job.**

KEY #3: LINK IT

Information linked with something you already know, or with a hook (Key #2), becomes easily memorized. Linking new information with old is part of understanding it (Key #1), but if you can't find logical connections, any connection will help. **In fact, if the link is not logical, make it crazy—the wilder, wackier, and more bizarre it is, the easier it will be to remember!**

Let's say you're trying to memorize that water at sea level boils at 212 degrees Fahrenheit, and these happen to be the digits of your telephone area code. Link these two facts using a hook (Key #2). You could imagine throwing your telephone into a boiling ocean. It's not a logical connection, but by linking the new information to something you already know and incorporating a memorable hook, you're more likely to remember it. Abstract numbers like 2–1–2 do not make much impact on our caveman brains; images like tossing a phone into a boiling ocean do.

KEY #4: DON'T BITE OFF MORE THAN YOU CAN CHEW, AND CHEW THAT BITE THOROUGHLY BEFORE TAKING ANOTHER

You have not one but two types of memory—short-term and long-term. Short-term memory lasts half a minute or so, while long-term memory can last decades.

New information is more or less automatically stored in short-term memory without any effort on your part. For example, when you call an operator and ask for a phone number you are about to dial, it gets stored in short-term memory. If you don't make an active effort to remember the number, you will probably forget it soon after you've dialed it because your brain quickly "decides" it is unimportant and promptly discards it. **To be sure you can remember a piece of information for more than a few moments, you must make vigorous efforts to transfer it to long-term memory.** Creating a hook (Key #2) and using the information (Key #9) are excellent ways to do this.

Before information can be stored in your long-term memory, however, it must be placed in short-term memory. Now, the interesting thing about short-term memory is that it has an extremely limited capacity.

George A. Miller, a linguist and psychologist, discovered that the brain can store only seven pieces of information, give or take a couple, before it "overloads." If you take in more than seven bits at one time, some will get discarded (that is, forgotten) before they are processed and stored into long-term memory. It's kind of like a game of musical chairs with only seven seats; once you go beyond that, some information gets "erased."

Of course, you don't have to count facts as you're memorizing them. The rule here is simply to memorize a manageable number of items at one time before taking in new information.

KEY #5: GET EMOTIONALLY INVOLVED

You remember information more easily if it arouses or emotionally affects you. Personalize the information. It isn't always easy, but try to relate the material in your courses to things that matter to you. Hooks that are funny, outlandish, dramatic, or even racy are easier to remember than those that hold no interest.

KEY #6: ENGAGE AS MANY SENSES AS POSSIBLE

The more senses you use when memorizing information, the more likely you are to remember it. For memorizing information you use three primary senses, each of which has its own memory.

- visual (seeing)
- auditory (hearing)
- kinesthetic (muscular or body awareness)

The first two senses are commonly used, but don't overlook your kinesthetic memory. If you turn back to the quote by Einstein on page 108, the "muscular" elements he was referring to were his kinesthetic intelligence! I know that sounds fantastic, but if you've ever forgotten a phone number only to be surprised that your fingers "knew" which phone buttons to push, your kinesthetic memory came to your rescue.

Everyone has his or her own unique learning style, which includes how you prefer using your senses. Learn to manipulate information to take advantage of your "best" sense, which may depend on what you are trying to memorize. Certain types of information you will remember visually, while others you will remember with your auditory memory. Oddly enough, I remembered math formulas on tests by "hearing" them and verbal information by "seeing" it.

No matter which of your senses is dominant, it's best to use all three simultaneously. Repeating a fact out loud as you write it engages your visual, auditory, and kinesthetic memories. Practice even when you aren't studying. You'll be surprised what a good memory you suddenly have!

KEY #7: SMELL THE ROSES

When you are memorizing information, look up from time to time and take mental notes of your surroundings: the wallpaper, the tree outside your window, the coffee stain on the rug. The memory of your surroundings at the time will get stored with the information you are learning. If you can't remember something, recalling the environment in which you learned it can help prod your memory. How many times has a simple smell—coffee brewing, a sea breeze—transported you back to an episode you thought you'd forgotten?

While you are studying, from time to time close your eyes for brief breaks and "take in" the way your body feels. This will help your brain link your kinesthetic sensations (Key #6) with the information you're trying to memorize.

Listening to soft background music while you study may also help you remember better. Music, like smells, can bring back long-forgotten memories. I mean *soft* background music, not heavy metal. Since you may find any music distracting—for that matter any noise at all—experiment to see if music works for you, and if so, what type works best.

KEY #8: SLEEP ON IT

For some reason that is still a mystery to psychologists and other scientists who study how your mind works, your brain apparently processes and stores information while you sleep. If you review information you are trying to learn just before you go to sleep, you will find that you remember quite a bit of it when you wake up. Stay in bed for a few minutes before getting up and see how much you can recall.

KEY #9: USE IT OR LOSE IT

Information that you do not use is forgotten a lot more quickly than information you do use. Using the information does not mean passively repeating it over and over. It means accessing it, thinking about it, and applying it in various ways. And this is just what the CyberLearning questions force you to do.

KEY #10: QUIZ YOURSELF PERIODICALLY

Quiz yourself every so often by actively recalling the information. Information that is recalled frequently becomes easily recalled when you really need it (on tests). Don't get frustrated if it doesn't pop up immediately; that's what your hooks are for.

Don't confuse recognizing information with being able to recall it. This is another of the many pitfalls of the read-highlight-reread approach to studying. When reviewing their notes, many students fool themselves into thinking that because they remember having seen the material before, they can remember the material. But there's a big, big difference between the two. Recognizing someone you've been introduced to before, for instance, does not mean you'll be able to remember that person's name. Be sure you can recall the information without looking at your notes for clues. And don't move on until you have created some sort of sense-memory hook for calling it back up when you need it.

Another popular error you should be aware of is the danger of quizzing yourself immediately after learning new information. If you test yourself within a minute or two of having learned something, you're only checking your short-term memory. The problem, as you know, is that short-term memory evaporates quickly (Key #4). Just because you can remember something a minute after you have learned it does not mean you'll be able to remember it on an exam next week.

Remember that most forgetting occurs soon after you've been exposed to new information. Instead of quizzing yourself immediately after acquiring new information, use it immediately (Key #9) and then quiz yourself in a day or two. After that, you can space out review sessions from once a week to once a month to once every few months. The more you spread the work out, the better.

Don't make too big a deal of quizzing yourself. Short, frequent sessions are better than long, infrequent ones. **Quiz yourself in spare moments you'd otherwise waste—doing your laundry, standing in line at the deli, waiting for someone to get off a public phone.** This is a good use of "down time" that you should try to incorporate into your daily routine. You'll learn about getting more out of your day in *How Smart Students Manage Their Time* (page 247).

PUTTING IT ALL TOGETHER: THE FOUR STEPS TO MEMORIZING

We can sum up the ten keys in a four-step approach to memorizing information:

Step 1: Decide whether the information makes sense or can be reconstructed from what you already know.

Step 2: Play around with the information until some outstanding feature suggests a hook (picture, pattern, rhyme, story) that helps you remember it.

Step 3: Actively engage as many senses as possible (visual, auditory, kinesthetic) to reinforce the link between your hook and the material you're memorizing.

Step 4: Use the information and practice recalling it as the days and weeks go by.

If you look back over the previous ten CyberLearning questions, you'll notice that they helped you retain what you were reading by forcing you to use and recall the information.

ANSWERING QUESTION 11 ON THE ROCKS PASSAGE

Devising hooks for all the information in the rocks passage would be a little tedious for our purposes, so instead I'll select some examples. Before continuing, please complete the following exercise.

EXERCISE #11

Instructions: I selected the following facts and ideas from our combined notes on the sample passage. For each selection, decide whether you can remember it "logically," and if not, what kind of hook (picture, pattern, rhyme, or story) you will link it to.

---

1. Igneous rock is formed from molten rock, sedimentary rock is formed from broken rocks that accumulate in layers, and metamorphic rock is formed from rock that has undergone change.

2. In order of importance, the following elements make up almost all rock: oxygen, silicon, aluminum, iron, calcium, sodium, potassium, magnesium.

3. Basalt lies beneath the ocean floors.

4. Limestone is formed from the shells and skeletons of marine organisms, and can in turn form marble.

5. Erosion is caused by glaciers, falling rocks, wind-borne particles, and water in motion.

WORKING THROUGH EXERCISE #11

Again, there is no right or wrong way to memorize information, only general rules. Your hooks for memorizing this material will undoubtedly be different from mine. Whatever does the job for you is fine, though following the ten keys will ensure that you do it as efficiently as possible.

1. Igneous reminds me of the word *ignite* (they are in fact related words), so that's my hook for remembering that it is formed from molten matter. I already knew that sediments were particles, so sedimentary rock is easy to remember. Metamorphic rock reminded me of metamorphosis, which I remember from biology is the process of changing structure; that's my hook for remembering the third type.

2. These elements are all familiar to me so all I need is a hook to remember the order. If I take the first letter (or two, in the case of silicon and sodium), I can make up the following "mini-story": "Oranges sipped and in canned soda pleases many." It's easier for me to picture and remember this silly "story" than those eight unrelated elements, which I can easily reconstruct once I have the first initial to work with.

3. I imagined myself pouring salt into a bay—producing bay salt (basalt).

4. For this one I imagined a small lime as the round shell of a marine organism that can be used as a marble if it hardens.

5. I imagined myself walking along on a windy winter day when dust gets in my eyes, causing me to slip on a piece of ice and fall into a puddle. Another silly story that allows me to link four otherwise unrelated actions (moving glaciers, falling rocks, wind-borne particles, and water in motion).

Your hooks will be different from mine. It doesn't matter, as long as they help you remember the information.

SUMMARY

Practice, practice, practice. In no time at all devising hooks will be a snap for you and forgetting information will be a thing of the past. People who complain that they have "bad" memories probably just aren't using their memories well. The worst way to memorize something is to repeat it over and over and over. This approach is passive, it's boring, and—guess what—it doesn't work too well. Your brain simply doesn't like to absorb information that way.

In this chapter, you've read about ten keys to effective memorization—techniques to coax your brain into retaining information. If these techniques seem more like a bag of tricks, well, they are. But when it comes to memorizing, you've got to go with what works. The fact is, if you can link some bit of information to a picture, create a pattern of it, say it in a rhyme, or tell it in a story, you've probably locked it into your long-term memory.

Eleven down; just one CyberLearning question to go.

Answering Question 12:
How Does This Information Fit in with What I Already Know?

THE *BIG*, BIG PICTURE

Question 3 asks you for the big picture of the material you are studying. This big picture provides you with a perspective so that you can see how all the different pieces of information fit together. Now that you have a firm grip on the material (having answered the first eleven questions), the last question asks you to take another few steps back. You need to see how the new information fits in with what you already know about other subjects as well as this subject.

DON'T SIMPLY ACCUMULATE YOUR NOTES

I'm sure you know by now that accumulating notes from class to class, just adding today's onto yesterday's and then rereading the notes a few days before a test, is not an effective way to learn. At the end of each week, if not each assignment, you need to combine and consolidate your notes. As I pointed out under Question 7, a lot of information that seemed important earlier in the term can now be weeded out. **In fact, at a certain point in the term the total volume of notes you study from should actually begin to decline!** Your accumulated notes during a fifteen-week course should look something like this.

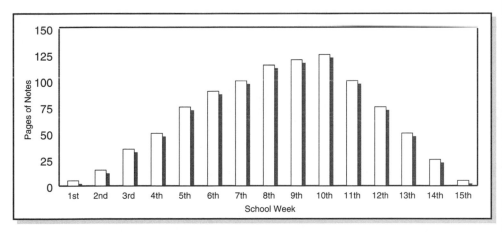

Isn't this a beautifully engineered and symmetric system? You begin and end the term with a single page of notes. Yes, I know that sounds incredible, and yet this chapter will show you how to do just that.

Of course, you shouldn't throw away your original notes; you may need to refer to them for a specific fact or detail. Nonetheless, the notes you'll be working with and revising from week to week should begin to contract as your understanding grows.

THAT'S RIGHT, A SINGLE PAGE

This summary sheet combines your notes from all your lectures and reading assignments into one digestible overview of the entire course. Your aim is to find a way to boil down all your course information to a single sheet of paper! You'll have to write small, and the sheet of paper may be somewhat larger than standard size, but you *can* do this. **It's important to get it down to one sheet because the process forces you to select only the most important information to include, and so that you can see at a glance how all the ideas in the course are interrelated.**

CREATING YOUR INITIAL SUMMARY SHEET

Of course, the summary sheet doesn't happen at once. You begin compiling your summary sheet the first week of a course. This is basically a rough outline of the subject's major topics—most courses have fewer than a dozen. You can discover these topics in the introductory lecture, the course description in the school catalog, your textbook's introduction or table of contents, the course syllabus or outline, or a general encyclopedia article. Copy each of these ideas down on a single sheet of paper, leaving room between the various headings. This list is your initial summary sheet.

1. The Changing Crust

2. Rocks:

3. The Soil Layer

4. Erosion and Weathering

5. Streams and Rivers

6. The Oceans

7. Ice and Glaciers

8. The History of the Earth

Let's say that in the first week of class, from the teacher's syllabus you were able to piece together the following initial summary sheet (here reduced so it can fit on the page).

Think of your summary sheet as the frame of a tall building that you will fill in, floor by floor, in the following weeks. Each new topic gets boiled down to the minimum possible facts and ideas, then inserted into the proper place on this sheet.

As you cover each new topic, you insert your condensed notes into this summary sheet. **You'll have to write small since your eventual aim is to squeeze an entire course onto one sheet of paper!** Notice, in looking over the bare-bones summary sheet, that what you have learned about rocks (Rocks) will change what you learned previously (The Changing Crust). **This means you'll have to revise your summary sheet notes on material you've already covered.**

If you look over the summary sheet, you'll also notice that we've touched on several upcoming topics: The Soil Layer, Erosion and Weathering, Streams and Rivers, and The Oceans (and possibly The History of the Earth). As you cover these topics, you'll be connecting them to what you know about rocks.

What you have learned about rocks will change your understanding of what you know about other topics in geology. In our case, since we haven't studied other topics in geology, we can only imagine how we would connect what we now know about rocks with what we know about other things. You do this by updating your summary sheet with each new topic you cover.

Here's how I reduced all the information contained in the almost-final notes on rocks so that it would squeeze into the summary sheet. (Once again, don't worry if you can't read every word; the point is simply to give you and idea how your summary sheet should look.)

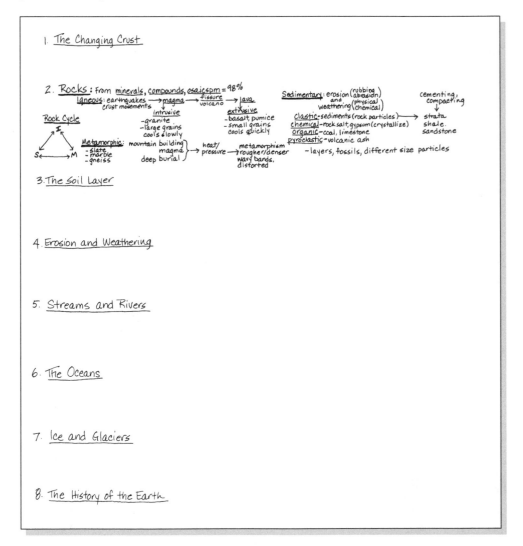

Notice that my summary sheet omits a lot of the information contained in my condensed notes. **Once you feel confident that a piece of information is safely stored in long-term memory, the tiniest reminder on your summary sheet will be enough to recall it entirely.** (Actually, this summary sheet isn't quite accurate since it doesn't reflect the notes I "took" previously on "The Changing Crust.")

HOW DOES THIS INFORMATION FIT IN WITH WHAT I ALREADY KNOW?

UPDATE YOUR UNDERSTANDING EVERY FEW DAYS

Repeat this process as soon as possible after every lecture or reading assignment, adding each new topic to your summary sheet. Each class will give you more information you'll need to include, so at some point your summary sheet may expand beyond a single page. As your understanding develops, however, you will continually devise better ways to represent the information and reduce your summary sheet to a single page.

Again, I know this constant updating of your notes sounds ambitious, but it's better than rereading your notes, and by the end of term you'll be glad you made the effort.

SHIFT YOUR PERSPECTIVE FROM TIME TO TIME

Incorporating each new topic into your summary sheet forces you to keep the big, big picture sharply in focus. As you revise your notes, go back and forth between examining the details of that week's topic and the overall structure of the course. As we discussed in Question 3, you need to understand the material at both levels. Returning to the analogy of constructing a building; once you complete a floor, you step back and take a look at the building as a whole before starting work on the next floor.

Question 3: What's the big picture here?

YOUR UNDERSTANDING OF *OTHER* SUBJECTS SHOULD CHANGE, TOO

Question 12 is much broader than the topic or subject you happen to be studying. **It asks you to examine how your understanding of other things has changed, too.** Your newfound knowledge of rocks should directly enhance your understanding of geography, chemistry, astronomy, ecology, biology, and botany, not to mention other subjects.

For example, my understanding of ancient Greek and Roman architecture (about as meager as my knowledge of geology) was enhanced by learning about the sedimentary rock, marble. Discovering that marble is formed from limestone, which in turn is made from shells and skeletons of marine organisms, explained why these two cultures so close to the ocean were able to use such vast quantities of it.

SUMMARY

Yes, you can reduce an entire semester's notes in a subject to a single page. Remember that dense, boring passage on rocks? Questions 1 through 11 invited you to explore this material in many different ways. Now Question 12 invites you to reduce all the information you've generated to a fraction of a page.

Your accumulated knowledge and understanding of the material makes this possible. Not only do you know what is and isn't important, you can now represent complex ideas with just a few well-selected words. As you go through the semester, you'll find that you can squeeze each new topic onto your summary sheet, revising it as new patterns and relationships emerge. Further, you'll be able to relate what you learn to knowledge outside the course, building your understanding of the really big picture—the world at large.

You should have an extremely solid grasp of the rock material. In fact, you probably know more now about rocks than next week's history exam! Don't worry, the method will work in that class, too.

In the next chapter we'll look back over the complete process and review the Twelve Questions before seeing how we can modify our approach to handle any subject.

The Twelve Questions:
A Recap

LOOKING BACK TO SEE HOW FAR YOU'VE COME

Answering the CyberLearning questions has forced you to transform your notes considerably. You paraphrased and summarized the important information you had selected from the rocks passage, and then you combined those notes with your classroom notes on the same material (Question 8). Next you explored the information in your notes for new ways to organize it (Question 9). You then took your combined notes and translated as much as you could into graphic form (Question 10). Finally, you condensed this almost-final set of notes to squeeze it into your summary sheet (Question 12). Again, these steps are not as distinct in actual practice as our discussion might suggest.

We've covered a lot of ground so it would be a good idea to summarize the major points of the Twelve Questions. First, the questions:

Before you begin reading, answer the following question:

    1.   What's my purpose for reading this?

After you read the title, answer the following question:

    2.   What do I already know about this topic?

Skim the material and answer the following question:

    3.   What's the big picture?

Return to the beginning. This time read more closely, sentence by sentence, as if you were chopping your way through a dense jungle. As you do so, ask yourself the following questions:

    4.   What's the author going to say next?

    5.   What are the "expert questions?"

    6.   What questions does this information raise for me?

While you read to find the answer to the previous three questions, you must decide what information is important and how to take notes on it. You do this by answering the following two questions:

    7.   What information is important here?

    8.   How can I paraphrase and summarize this information?

Question 1:
What's my purpose for reading this?

Question 2:
What do I already know about this topic?

Question 3:
What's the big picture here?

Question 4:
What's the author going to say next?

Question 5:
What are the "expert questions"?

Question 6:
What questions does this information raise for me?

Question 7:
What information is important here?

Question 8:
How can I paraphrase and summarize this information?

Question 9:
How can I organize this information?

Question 10:
How can I picture this information?

Question 11:
What's my hook for remembering this information?

Question 12:
How does this information fit in with what I already know?

After you finish reading, you can put aside your textbook and turn to your notes. As you explore and revise your notes, answer the following questions:

9. How can I organize this information?

10. How can I picture this information?

11. What's my hook for remembering this information?

After you complete your analysis of the current topic, answer the following question:

12. How does this information fit in with what I know?

Here are the major points about CyberLearning to keep in mind:

- **Not all these questions, or the other questions you raise, are equally important.** Depending on the material you are studying and your purpose for reading, some of these questions can be skipped entirely while others will need to be investigated in great detail. Don't worry—you'll learn how to tell the difference easily.

- **You won't always be able to answer the questions you raise; the important thing is that you *make the effort*.**

- **The question order is approximate only; some questions overlap naturally and can be combined.** When you get the hang of the process you'll easily be able to paraphrase information (Question 8), organize it (Question 9), picture it (Question 10), and devise a hook (Question 11) simultaneously.

- **Depending on the particular subject you are studying, you may have to modify the Twelve Questions slightly.** We'll be covering this topic shortly.

- **Although the Twelve Questions form a complete process, you ask them not once but continually.** There is no limit to how many times you can ask these questions of the same material. As the following diagram illustrates, CyberLearning is a dynamic, ongoing process.

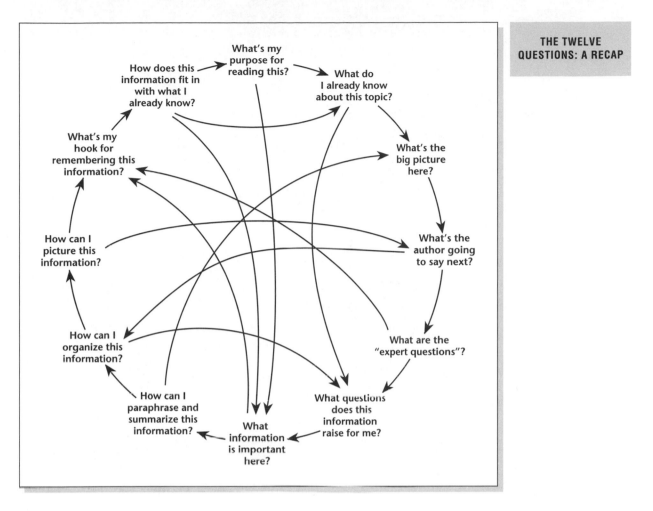

A short while ago, the Twelve Questions may as well have been Greek to you. It was new, unknown, abstract, and probably a little intimidating. Now the Twelve Question approach is yours. Make the most of it, rely on it, and it will never let you down.

Don't forget to practice this technique. Knowing the CyberLearning Method won't help you if you don't use it.

WHAT'S COMING UP NEXT

The next chapter is an intermission on what it means to understand something. Now that you have a firm grasp of the CyberLearning method, you'll be able to appreciate what the rigorous Twelve Questions were building toward. After that you'll learn how to modify our basic approach to handle just about any subject you are studying. Skip ahead to *Part IV: How Smart Students Get Their Grades* if you're anxious to see how smart students rehearse for exams. You've already done a lot of the preparation, but you still need to rehearse the test-taking process.

Intermission:
What Does It Mean to Understand Something?

WHY UNDERSTANDING IS SO IMPORTANT

You may be wondering why we go to such lengths to understand a subject if all you're usually required to do on tests is repeat what the teacher or textbook said.

Well, you have a point. Most tests do *not* require a profound understanding of subject matter. If you are good at memorizing or cramming, you can probably ace exams covering information you scarcely understand and won't remember beyond test day.

So why bother with answering the Twelve Questions? Why bother developing understanding? There are four good reasons why you go to the trouble:

- First, although you can get by in school simply by cramming meaningless facts, memorizing material is difficult if you don't understand it—a little like phonetically memorizing a speech in a foreign language. Moreover, as your education advances, an increasing emphasis *is* placed on understanding.

- Second, your school experience will be more satisfying and rewarding if you try to understand rather than merely memorize. The same CyberLearning steps you take to understand information will also prevent boredom. **Remember Smart Student Principle #8: Subjects do not always seem interesting and relevant, but being actively engaged in learning them is better than being passively bored and not learning them.**

- Third, you'll feel better about yourself if you're taking active steps to understand a subject rather than resisting it and remaining ignorant. **Remember Smart Student Principle #9: Few things are as potentially difficult, frustrating, or frightening as genuine learning, yet *nothing* is so rewarding and empowering.**

- Fourth, the ability to understand information is a crucial life skill. You can get through school without understanding much, but you'll be in big trouble professionally *and* personally once you graduate and enter the real world.

A COMMONLY MISUNDERSTOOD WORD

For most students, learning in class means sitting back and listening while the teacher "teaches." The same word learning is also used in completely different contexts. Learning the multiplication table, for example, means memorizing it. But learning biology or trigonometry or American history involves a lot more brain work than memorizing facts, formulas, and dates.

For smart students, learning is the process by which you build understanding of a subject. What does it mean, then, to understand something?

A SIMPLE TEST

An education is not how much you have memorized, or even how much you know. It's being able to tell the difference between what you do know and what you don't.

ANATOLE FRANCE

Consider the following statements:

- *Sunlight causes photosynthesis in plants.*
- *Peru exports copper.*
- *The painter Claude Monet was an Impressionist.*
- *The American Civil War was the outcome of a constitutional crisis.*

Merely knowing these facts and being able to spit them back on tests is not the same thing as understanding them.

If you don't know the difference between understanding something and not understanding it, it's very easy to fool yourself into thinking you do when you don't. If you've ever taken an essay test on material you *thought* you understood only to find out the hard way that you didn't, you know what I'm talking about.

It's important to know what *not* understanding something feels like, so you can begin to take active steps to correct the situation. **And as a simple test, we can say that you don't understand a concept until, at the very least, you can**

- **define it in your own words;**
- **give your own examples of it;**
- **explain its relationship to other concepts.**

As you know, these orientation questions just barely scratch the surface; developing understanding is a never-ending process.

UNDERSTANDING DOESN'T JUST HAPPEN

What is the hardest task in the world? To think.

RALPH WALDO
EMERSON

The world does not make sense; you're the one who gives it structure and meaning. Knowledge and information do not exist for you apart from what *you* do to shape that information and connect it to what you already know. Information is not something that you find but something you create. Understanding is not something that can be given to you, but something you must build for yourself.

Understanding does not come from simply reading your textbook or listening to your teacher. Learning is not automatic. Simply being exposed to complex information and ideas will not make those ideas magically "sink into your brain."

Learning is an active process, which involves asking and answering questions constantly. As you do this, you begin to make connections between the new information you are learning and what you already know. To create understanding, you must also bring something to the information by shaping it and organizing it into something that is your creation.

WHAT DOES IT MEAN TO UNDERSTAND SOMETHING?

Let's consider one of the preceding statements—*Peru exports copper.* You begin the learning process by systematically asking questions about each term *(Peru, exporting,* and *copper):*

- *How much copper does Peru export?*
- *What other nations export copper?*
- *Which nations import copper?*
- *What else does Peru export?*

And so on. You then answer these and other questions, organize the resulting information, and connect it to other things you know. Every new idea is built in this way, and they build on one another. As you gain an understanding of a new idea, your understanding of other ideas will grow, too.

NOBODY'S GOING TO DO THIS FOR YOU

One reason most students find school difficult is that they never think in terms of their specific responsibilities. If I asked them to describe their job in school, they would probably say something like this: listen to what the teacher has to say and do what the teacher asks us to do. These students are ignoring **Smart Student Principle #2: Merely listening to your teachers and completing their assignments is *never* enough**.

Teachers can't pour facts into your head, and they certainly can't create understanding. When you become a smart student, you'll see your "job" differently. **Teachers don't teach you—you teach yourself.**

There are probably times when you sit back and expect your teacher to do all the teaching. Then it's your teacher's problem if you don't learn, right?

Wrong!

It's your problem. You're the one who lives with the consequences of your education, not your teacher. If you want to learn, *you* have to do most of the work, not your teacher.

YOU'D BETTER GET USED TO IT: LEARNING IS THE PROCESS OF OVERCOMING CONFUSION

While giving a lecture on quantum mechanics, the famous physicist Niels Bohr told a scientist in the audience that if he wasn't confused and bewildered by the presentation, he hadn't been paying attention. I think he could have said the same thing about the initial stages of learning anything new. **If your brain isn't a little shaken up by something new, you missed the point.**

On the other hand, I want to oppose the idea that the school has to teach directly that special knowledge and those accomplishments that one has to use directly later in life. The development of general ability for independent thinking and judgment should always be placed foremost, not the acquisition of special knowledge. If a person masters the fundamentals of his subject and has learned to think and work independently, he will surely find his way and besides will better adapt himself to progress and changes than the person whose training consists principally in the acquiring of detailed knowledge.

ALBERT EINSTEIN

Confusion is a natural part of learning, but it's also a frustrating and discouraging part—and frightening. **Yet if you aren't a little scared while you're learning something new, you aren't learning as much as you could.**

I said "a little scared," not panicked. But that's what many students wind up becoming. Shortly after they begin reading, they become confused. Not realizing that this is the first step in understanding anything, they become upset, which gradually blossoms into a full-blown panic. In desperation they figure that if they don't understand what they're reading, at least they can memorize it. But trying to memorize something you don't understand will interfere with your later understanding.

So don't panic if you don't understand a new topic. In fact, if you think you do understand a new topic after reading it once, you're cutting short the learning process. Remember that you have twelve CyberLearning questions to answer. Believe me, how quickly you learn a subject has very little to do with how well you eventually come to understand it. Smart students frequently learn more slowly than their classmates in the early part of a course, but they catch up quickly and pass them in the final stretch.

THE LEARNING PROCESS TAKES TIME

Some people will never learn anything for this reason: because they understand everything too soon.

ALEXANDER POPE

Learning a subject is a multi-stage process. The first stage is simply to *follow* the main ideas, definitions, and direction of the lecture or textbook. You then build your understanding by asking questions of the material to discover how its new facts and ideas relate to one another and to what you already know. Gradually, you organize those concepts into a structure that has meaning for you.

You may have been told that you should "read for understanding." In a sense, this advice is impossible to follow. There is simply no way you are going to understand a complex textbook as you read it. As you have seen, you must have several encounters of different sorts with material before you can even begin to understand it.

The process of learning a new topic is like storming a fort. You will have to stage several attacks before you can knock down the wall separating you from a subject. It's not a smooth process. You can go for several weeks in a state of utter confusion about a topic and then suddenly, one day, eureka! Everything comes together and you say, "Oh, *now* I understand it!" Understanding one topic may depend on your understanding several related ones, and only when you grasp them do you finally come to grips with the topic you've been struggling with.

THINK OF LEARNING SOMETHING AS SOLVING A COMPLICATED JIGSAW PUZZLE

Developing understanding is lot like putting together a puzzle—it takes time, patience, and hard work. You don't construct the puzzle all at once. A lot of it is hit and miss. You sift through all the pieces, then start to work on the edges first—an outline of the big picture—since the straight-edged pieces are easy to find.

Eventually, as you continually refer to the box cover to keep the big picture in mind, you find a few pieces that fit together. So you concentrate on that part of the puzzle for a while. Be patient. Sooner or later you get stuck because some pieces are missing. So you go to work on another part of the puzzle while you keep your eyes out for the missing piece you need. Gradually the puzzle takes shape, and sections connect. As this happens, your progress accelerates. Finally you put together the entire puzzle. It's yours.

Learning a subject is much like that.

BUT YOU NEVER *COMPLETELY* UNDERSTAND ANYTHING

Considering what "understanding" something means to most people, you'd think you either have it or you don't. But understanding something isn't black and white, like whether you own a dog. Smart students realize that building understanding is a continuing process that can deepen as far as they take it. By probing, asking more questions, and making more connections, there is no limit to how profoundly you can understand a subject. It really comes down to how much time you can (and want to) give it and what your other priorities are.

NINE THINGS YOU CAN DO WHEN YOU'RE CONFUSED WHILE READING

Not understanding something is frustrating but try not to let it upset you; as you now know, confusion is a natural part of the learning process. Remember also that not everything in every course is relevant to your purposes, and even if you wanted to understand everything in every course, there's simply not enough time.

Having said that, there are steps you can take that will clear away some roadblocks to your understanding. Since your confusion can have a number of causes, you may have to try more than one of the following suggestions:

1. **Look it up.** The most obvious confusion occurs when you don't understand what a word means or the terminology is misleading. For simple concepts, this can be corrected by finding the definition in a dictionary or encyclopedia. It will also help you to note its pronunciation so you can "pronounce" it in your head as you read. But for more advanced concepts, understanding involves more than knowing the definition. It is unlikely that you will understand what "photosynthesis" means, for instance, simply by looking up its definition. But sometimes a definition will have to do while you wait for other pieces of the puzzle to fall in place.

2. **Return to your road map—the big picture.** Sometimes the details of a topic can make you lose sight of the main ideas.

3. **Jump immediately to the end.** If you don't see where the author's discussion is leading, you may have lost the big picture, but sometimes simply seeing the conclusion or summary is all you need.

No student knows his subject: the most he knows is where and how to find out the things he does not know.
WOODROW WILSON

Question 11:
What's my hook for remembering this information?

4. **Find another source of information.** As I pointed out in the Intermission beginning on page 59, a textbook or a teacher provides you with only one point of view. Sometimes all you need is a different perspective. See page 60 for guidelines on choosing a supplementary information source.

5. **Find an example.** If a topic becomes too abstract, examples are almost always more enlightening than explanations. If one example doesn't help, find another.

6. **Retrace your steps.** Teachers and authors sometimes skip steps in their presentations or omit "obvious" points. If you don't see the connection between something that is said and what follows, go back to the last point you *did* understand and trace where you lost the thread.

7. **Sleep on it.** As you know from our discussion of Question 11, your brain processes information when you're asleep. Take the problem material to bed with you and review it one last time before turning out the lights. You have now "planted" the problem in your brain. When you wake up the next morning, don't get out of bed immediately; you want to remain in that dreamlike mental state as long as possible before fully waking up. Without "trying too hard," casually look over the material again. You'll often find that your confusion has mysteriously cleared up overnight without your doing anything! Be sure you immediately write down your early-morning insight or it will vanish as quickly and as surely as your memory of last night's dreams.

8. **Teach someone.** A great way to clarify something that confuses you is by explaining it to someone, preferably someone who knows less about the topic than you do. To be clear you'll be forced to stick to the essential points, and the questions your "student" asks will stimulate your own thinking. You'll frequently find that midway through your explanation you've cleared up your own confusion. (Savvy parents use this method to help their children with homework.)

9. **Ask for help.** I put this last for a reason: you'll learn more if you try working things out on your own first. If you're completely stymied, ask someone (a classmate or your teacher) for a hint or an example rather than a complete explanation. This will give you a chance to work out the rest for yourself. (Better yet, explain your difficulty to the person, as in the previous suggestion. Trying to articulate your confusion often clears it up!)

If none of these tips does the trick, don't spend any more time—you don't have all the pieces of the puzzle. Skip what you're stuck on and see if you can make sense of the rest of the section before returning to what's stumping you. If that fails, switch to a completely different subject and return to what's confusing you in the next day or two. (*Do* put off till tomorrow what you can't possibly do today.) Be patient. As you continually revise and update your summary study notes, the "missing information" will emerge.

WHAT'S COMING UP

In the next three chapters, I'll cover the various types of subjects and how to apply the CyberLearning method in each.

How Smart Students
Approach
Different
Subjects

PART III

Not All Subjects Are Alike:
Modifying the CyberLearning Method

THE DIFFERENT TYPES OF SUBJECTS

Until now we have used a geology passage to illustrate how smart students learn. You've probably been wondering whether you can use the same CyberLearning approach to learn English, psychology, and algebra. Yes, although you'll have to modify it slightly. Once you've mastered the Twelve Questions, you'll have little difficulty adapting them to your different courses.

If you were to look among courses in your school catalog, you would probably find subjects divided into the following basic areas:

- humanities: art history, film criticism, literature, music theory, philosophy
- social sciences: anthropology, economics, geography, history, law, psychology
- natural sciences: biology, chemistry, earth science, physics
- mathematics: algebra, calculus, computer science, logic (and so on)
- business courses: management, insurance, accounting (and so on)
- foreign languages: French, Spanish, Japanese (and so on)
- performing arts: music, film, dance, theater

There's nothing wrong with grouping similar classes according to subject matter like this. **But smart students are also keenly interested in the type of thinking and studying a course demands.** So smart students classify subjects differently. The following exercise will help you understand how and why smart students do this.

EXERCISE #12

Instructions: Before you continue, please skim through the following four lists of courses. Write a plus [+] next to the ones you are good in or really enjoy (these are probably the same) and write a minus [−] next to the ones you hate or find extremely difficult (again, probably the same). Just mark the courses you feel strongly about one way or the other. The courses are listed alphabetically. If you feel strongly about one that you don't find listed, find the column with the closest match and write it in.

Type I	Type II	Type III	Type IV
[ ] anthropology	[ ] art history	[ ] accounting	[ ] creative writing
[ ] astronomy	[ ] dance theory	[ ] chemistry	[ ] dance (performing)
[ ] biology	[ ] English	[ ] computer science	[ ] debate
[ ] civilization	[ ] film criticism	[ ] economics	[ ] foreign languages
[ ] earth science	[ ] literature	[ ] engineering	[ ] music (performing)
[ ] education	[ ] philosophy	[ ] finance	[ ] painting
[ ] geography	[ ] theology	[ ] logic	[ ] theater
[ ] government		[ ] mathematics	
[ ] history		[ ] physics	
[ ] law			
[ ] management			
[ ] marketing			
[ ] political science			
[ ] psychology			
[ ] sociology			

HERE'S WHAT YOU SHOULD NOTICE

NOT ALL SUBJECTS
ARE ALIKE

Unless you have a talent for learning all subjects, you'll find that the courses you really like (or dislike) will tend to fall into one or two of the types above because each type requires different learning objectives.

- In Type I subjects, your primary task is to acquire and understand organized bodies of *information.*

- In Type II subjects, your primary task is to acquire and understand *interpretation techniques.* Each of these subjects deals with a different form of communication, which the interpretation techniques enable you to identify and respond to critically.

- In Type III subjects, you are also learning information, but your primary task is to acquire and understand various *problem-solving techniques.*

- In Type IV subjects, your primary task is not so much to understand as it is to create, perform, or communicate.

There is of course a great deal of overlap between this classification scheme. For example economics, a Type III subject, has some elements of Type I subjects. And law, a Type I subject, has much in common with the Type II subjects.

Despite the broad classifications, you'll find that you tend to gravitate toward one or two types and avoid the others. The point of these lists is simply that even though the subjects are different, the kind of thinking and studying involved in each type is similar. Don't worry about remembering these lists; but refer to them when you're considering what classes to take (see *How Smart Students Choose Their Courses and Teachers* on page 255).

WHAT THAT MEANS FOR THE CYBERLEARNING METHOD

You may have noticed that the geology passage I used to illustrate the Twelve Questions is a Type I subject. In the next two chapters you will learn how to modify our basic approach to handle the Type II and Type III subjects.

Type IV subjects, in which you are creating, performing, or communicating, fall outside the scope of this book. Learning to write poetry or to paint, for example, requires a very different set of skills from those required to learn trigonometry.

How Smart Students Learn Interpretation Techniques

THE TYPE II SUBJECTS

You will recall from our discussion in the last chapter that Type II subjects are those in which you are expected to identify, analyze, and respond critically to different forms of communication. You are also acquainting yourself with artistic traditions that span centuries. Again, Type II subjects include the following:

- art history
- dance
- English
- film criticism
- literature
- philosophy
- theology

Each deals with a specific art form with the exception of the last two. Philosophy and theology may seem out of place in this group, but as with the other Type II subjects they require you to analyze and respond to communication; specifically, *arguments*. You will find, for example, that literature and art deal with many of the same themes as do philosophy and theology.

Unlike Type I and Type III subjects, here you are concerned with not just *what* is being said, but *how* that message is being said. Also, with these subjects your personal response to what is being said forms an integral part of your academic experience to a far greater degree than with any of the other types of subjects. One of the things you're learning to do is appreciate and respond to an art form.

This chapter is an introduction to applying the CyberLearning method to Type II classes, using literature—specifically *Romeo and Juliet*—as an illustrative example. We'd need volumes to cover how to read literature critically. Again, once you understand the basic Twelve Question approach, you'll know how to modify it to deal with the particular subject you're taking.

READING FOR SCHOOL VERSUS READING FOR FUN

One of the frustrations of reading literature in school is that you can't simply "enjoy" the story or play. Your teacher expects you to analyze and criticize it, and somehow that takes a lot of the fun out of it. Always keep in mind that all literature is written in the first place to be enjoyed, not to be analyzed by English professors or high school students.

Another problem is that some types of literature are intended not to be read but to be *experienced.* Playwrights write plays to be *seen;* poets write poems to be *heard.* It is far easier to watch *Romeo and Juliet* performed on stage than to read it.

You should note two important points:

- Your teacher is less interested in the story line or plot than in the *way* the story is told and what the plot means. Your teacher may ask short-answer questions in class or on tests to make sure the class has read the work, but you are old enough now to move beyond the "and then…" level of junior high book reports and really get into the motivations and lessons of the story.

- You will have to read a work more than once before you begin to "get it." I mean this! The first time, you read it is for the general story line. This is the time to relax and enjoy the work. The second time, you'll be reading to pick up individual scenes, characters, and other details. It may take a third reading before you pick up the symbolism and other nuances.

THE SAME TWELVE QUESTIONS—WITH A TWIST

You'll find that for Type II courses our basic CyberLearning approach requires only slight modifications. **The only major change is that you'll be reading the original source material several times instead of continually revising your notes.** Since *how* the author is saying it is just as important as *what* the author is saying, you'll need to refer to the original work more and your notes less.

So let's see how we would apply the Twelve Questions to literature, using Shakespeare's *Romeo and Juliet* as our example.

QUESTION 1: WHAT'S MY PURPOSE FOR READING THIS?

In literature classes there is usually a good deal of class discussion, so you need to be prepared to participate. Your purpose for reading includes not only analyzing the work but also formulating a reasoned opinion about it. Literature classes also require a lot of writing; tests are generally essay exams.

QUESTION 2: WHAT DO I ALREADY KNOW ABOUT THIS TOPIC?

This includes not only what you know about the work but also what you know about the author and the period he or she was writing about. So for *Romeo and Juliet* you'd jot down what you know about the play, what you know about Shakespeare and his other plays, and perhaps what you know about the historical setting (sixteenth-century Italy).

QUESTION 3: WHAT'S THE BIG PICTURE HERE?

The big picture for a story or play consists of five basic elements:

- *What is the basic story line? (What are the major scenes or plot elements?)*
- *Who are the major characters and what are their relationships?*
- *What is the point of view? (Who's telling the story?)*
- *What is the setting?*
- *What is the primary theme or message? (What is the moral?)*

It shouldn't be too hard to discover these things; they are often revealed in the editor's introduction. (The primary theme or message may not be easy to discern at first, but it's not essential at this point.)

QUESTION 4: WHAT'S THE AUTHOR GOING TO SAY NEXT?

One of the responsibilities of a fiction author is to keep you wondering what will happen next in the story. Sometimes the author will use literary devices to *foreshadow* future events. Anticipating what will happen next is a natural part of reading a story, not of reading a geology passage or something even more abstract.

QUESTION 5: WHAT ARE THE "EXPERT QUESTIONS"?

Another distinguishing characteristic of Type II subjects is their large number of expert questions. Philosophy, for example, is almost exclusively about the art of asking questions. Literature has literally *dozens* of expert questions; compare that with geology, which had fewer than one dozen.

The following are some of the more important expert questions for literature. I've grouped them into categories (and here and there provided answers).

Expert Questions About Character

- *Who is the major character? Who are the hero and heroine?* Romeo and Juliet.
- *Who are the other major characters?* Nurse, Mercutio, and Friar Laurence.
- *What role does each play? What is the relationship between characters?* Juliet, for example, is Capulet's daughter, her nurse's friend, Romeo's wife, and Paris's betrothed.
- *What does each want?* Romeo wants Juliet. Juliet wants Romeo. Friar Laurence wants to help the young lovers, and thereby conciliate the feuding families. Mercutio wants to enjoy life and live it fully.
- *What does each one truly need?* Romeo, for one, needs to cool his jets.

- *What is the character and personality of each like? Is it three-dimensional? By what traits can each be identified? Does this personality contrast with that of any other characters?*

- *What obstacles stand in the way of each?* Romeo is confronted by external obstacles (the family feud, the prince's law against feuding, a not-too-bright adviser in the form of Friar Laurence), as well as internal obstacles (his youth, his inexperience, his recklessness, his infatuation).

- *How much choice does each character have? What are each one's obligations to friends, family, and society at large?* Romeo feels bound by friendship to avenge Mercutio's death by killing Tybalt. This duty conflicts with his duty to society, and Romeo is banished.

- *What are the stakes? What risks are each character willing to take?* Romeo and Juliet are clearly willing to die for each other, while members of the feuding families are apparently willing to die for honor.

- *How does each character change throughout the play? What does each learn?* Romeo, Juliet, Paris, Tybalt, and Mercutio all die tragically. The survivors learn by their tragic deaths.

- *How do we learn about each character (their actions, their dialogue, their thoughts)?*

- *Who are the minor characters? What are their roles?* One of the minor characters is Paris. His role is to act as Romeo's rival for Juliet.

Expert Questions About Plot

- *What is the initial event that sets the major character in pursuit of his or her goal?* Romeo, thinking himself lovesick for Rosaline, nonetheless falls madly in love with Juliet at first sight.

- *What are the major plot points? How are these events tied together?* (See my plot diagram on page 152.)

- *Is the story told in chronological order? If not, why not?*

- *How do the obstacles facing the major characters increase in intensity?*

- *What are the subplots? How do they relate to the main plot?*

- *Are the major events in the plot inevitable? What is the role played by destiny? What is the role played by chance?* It is only by chance that Romeo does not receive news of the harebrained scheme hatched by Friar Laurence to feign Juliet's death.

- *What are the major conflicts in the story?* On the most basic level, love versus hate; the individual versus his family.

- *Do any characters have a complete reversal of fortune?*

Expert Questions About Setting

- *Where does the story take place? Is this setting important to the story?* A feud between two families requires the setting of a small town or city. The conflict would lack its dramatic intensity if it took place in a large city like Rome.

- *When does the story takes place? Is this time important?*

Expert Questions About Point of View

- *From whose point of view is the story told? Why?*

- *How does this point of view affect what we know about the story and the characters?*

- *What do we know that the characters don't?* Well, for example, we know about Friar Laurence's scheme to feign Juliet's death. The fact that Romeo doesn't know about the scheme leads to the play's tragic ending.

Expert Questions About Theme

- *What is the major theme? What other themes does the author raise?* The major theme usually involves something like the nature of happiness, the relationship of the individual to others, the importance of duty, the relationship of the individual to nature and God, the existence of free will, and so on.

- *What is the overall moral or message of the story?* That love blinds, that hate blinds, that youth is impetuous, that the innocent suffer.

Expert Questions About Style

- *When does the author convey information directly (as through description and narration), and when indirectly (as through symbols, metaphors, irony, allegory, parable, subtext)?*

- *What is the author's choice of words? Sentence structure?*

- *What images or symbols recur in the work?* The play is full of references to light and darkness.

- *What contrasts occur in the book? What parallels?* Mercutio's unsentimental and expansive character contrasts sharply with Romeo's brooding and lovesick one.

Expert Questions About the Work as a Whole

- *Did you find the characters interesting and believable? Did you "relate" to any?*

- *What does this work tell us about the time in which it was written? About the time it depicted? About our time?*

Everything's got a moral, if only you can find it.
LEWIS CARROLL
Alice in Wonderland

By Order of the Author:
Persons attempting to find a motive in this narrative will be prosecuted; persons attempting to find a moral in it will be banished; persons attempting to find a plot in it will be shot.
MARK TWAIN
Huckleberry Finn

- *Into which major genre does this story fall (comedy, satire, tragedy, and so on)? How representative is it of this genre?* This play is typically classified as a tragedy, but there are also numerous comic element.

- *What is the significance of the title?* Perhaps it indicates the isolation of the two lovers from everyone else.

- *Why did the author choose this medium for the story?*

Expert Questions About the Author

- *How does this work compare with or relate to others by the same author?* We could find some interesting comparisons between the way Othello's love and Romeo's love both lead to death.

- *How have other authors dealt with similar themes?*

- *Does the author identify with any of the characters?*

- *How much was the author influenced by his times?*

- *What other authors or works of art have influenced him? Which in turn has he influenced?* Shakespeare's *Romeo and Juliet* became the modern classic *West Side Story*. (*West Side Story* would make an excellent supplementary information source for modern readers who have difficulty relating to Shakespeare's story set in the sixteenth-century. It was a hit Broadway musical that later became an award-winning movie; it's available on video.)

- *What distinguishing characteristics of this writer's work would enable you to identify other works by him or her?*

QUESTION 6: WHAT QUESTIONS DOES THIS INFORMATION RAISE FOR ME?

This question is actually tied up with the previous one since one of the functions of the literature expert questions is to draw out your personal response.

QUESTION 7: WHAT INFORMATION IS IMPORTANT HERE?

Anything that will help you answer the expert questions. There is nothing special to mention about this question.

QUESTION 8: HOW CAN I PARAPHRASE AND SUMMARIZE THIS INFORMATION?

You'll be referring to the original work more often than your notes, so it's especially important that you adopt a method of marking up your book. Unlike Type I and Type III subjects, those in this group emphasize *how* the author is saying what he's saying. So you'll want *exact quotes* of important lines of dialogue, *not* paraphrases. "Yo, Juliet!" loses a lot of Shakespeare's lyrical "But soft! What light through yonder window breaks."

QUESTION 9: HOW CAN I ORGANIZE THIS INFORMATION?

You can arrange several of the major elements of a play into groups: the characters, the symbols, the scenes, the points of view. Organizing information is especially helpful in helping you answer the theme questions.

Let's consider the characters. Here are a few groupings I came up with, starting with the most obvious:

---

① **Capulets or Pro-Capulets**
    Juliet (suicide)
    The Nurse
    Tybalt (slain)
    Capulet
    Lady Capulet
    Paris (slain)

Montagues or Pro-Montagues
    Romeo (suicide)
    Mercutio (slain)
    Benvolio
    Montague
    Lady Montague (dies of grief)

Neutral Parties
    Friar Lawrence
    Prince Escalus

Other
    Rosaline

---

② **Youth**
    Romeo (s)
    Juliet (s)
    Tybalt (s)
    Benvolio
    Mercutio (s)
    Paris (s)

Experience
    Nurse
    Friar Lawrence
    Prince Escalus
    Montague
    Lady Montague (d)
    Capulet
    Lady Capulet

---

③ **Lovers/Suitors**
    Romeo (s)
    Juliet (s)
    Paris (s)

Others
    Everyone else

Of course, there are other possible variations.

If you look over my groupings, you'll discover some interesting things. For example, the number of Capulets and Montagues that expire by the end of the play is equally balanced. The second grouping reveals that all the deaths but one occur among "youth" rather than "experience." Finally, we see clearly that all three lovers and suitors die. Each of these observations is worth making on an exam or in a paper.

QUESTION 10: HOW CAN I PICTURE THIS INFORMATION?

Yes, it is possible to picture character relationships and plots on paper. Here's how I drew the "plot line" of Romeo and Juliet.

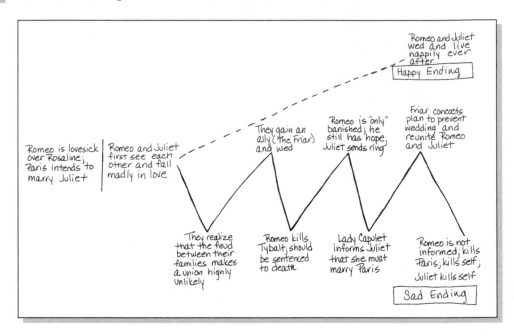

I've used a rising line to indicate actions moving towards Romeo's and Juliet's ideal goal. The ideal movement (without conflicts or setbacks) is indicated by the dotted line. This diagram also captures the main plot points (turning points of the story).

Here's how I pictured the various characters and their relationships.

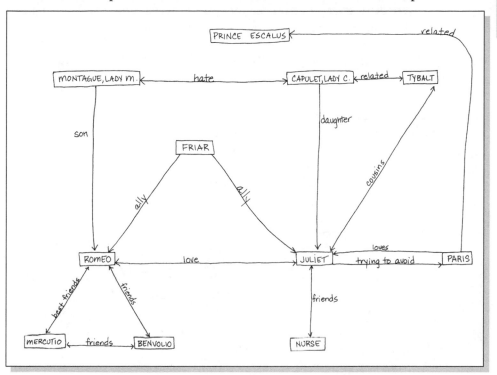

Notice how various themes and patterns are made apparent by this diagram.

Combine this step with Question 3: *What's the Big Picture?* **The first time you read the play, create a sheet with these two diagrams so you can refer to it as you read the play a second time.** Having the big picture in this diagram form will help you follow the action.

QUESTION 11: WHAT'S MY HOOK FOR REMEMBERING THIS INFORMATION?

Memorizing information is less important in literature classes for several reasons: one, because literature is all about telling stories, which is already a hook your brain has little trouble remembering; two, because there's less information that needs to be memorized; and finally, because literature classes emphasize papers and/or essay tests, both of which require less memorization than, say, a short-response test in biology.

By the way, a very common type of test question in Type II subjects asks you to identify characters solely on the basis of some lines of dialogue (*Which character said, "Tempt not a desperate man"?*) or to identify a particular scene on the basis of a short descriptive quote. This doesn't mean you should try to memorize every line in a play. Once you get to know the characters, it shouldn't be hard to figure out which character would say what (For example, Which male characters were desperate?). And once you grasp how the plot points are all tied together, it shouldn't be hard to identify a particular scene.

QUESTION 12: HOW DOES THIS INFORMATION FIT IN WITH WHAT I ALREADY KNOW?

How has your understanding of Shakespeare changed after reading *Romeo and Juliet*? How has your understanding of the nature of love changed? What have you learned about human nature and society that you can apply in other areas? **Question 12 is a very important question in literature and other Type II subjects.**

And that rounds out our survey of the CyberLearning method as it applies to literature and other Type II subjects.

SUMMARY

Type II courses are less fact-oriented than something like geology, a Type I course. Instead of stressing facts, these courses focus on interpretation, argument, and personal response. Even so, smart students use the same Twelve Questions to tackle Shakespeare that we used to get through the rocks passage.

It does take some minor modifications. Most important, you'll be continually referring back to the text rather than reworking your notes. Remember that in Shakespeare the language itself matters, not just the ideas. There are also a lot more expert questions in Type II subjects.

On the whole, though, you'll find that your basic approach is not fundamentally different. If you've mastered the Twelve Questions, using them to come to grips with a Type II subject should be a breeze. Notice that it only took me half a dozen pages and a few pictures to not only ask and answer the Twelve Questions, but to explain them as well.

How Smart Students
Learn Problem-Solving Techniques

THE TYPE III SUBJECTS

In the chapter *Not All Subjects Are Alike* (page 141), I introduced you to a new classification of subjects. **This chapter introduces how to apply the CyberLearning method to Type III subjects in general, and mathematics in particular.** You'll learn the eight primary causes of difficulty with this subject and what you can do to correct them. You'll discover that there is a lot more to learning mathematics than memorizing formulas. Even if you're a math genius, you'll discover new ways of learning the subject and improving your problem–solving ability. With the CyberLearning method you'll be able to personalize and reshape an alien subject into something that is truly your own.

You may have noticed that the common denominator of these subjects, which include

- accounting
- chemistry
- computer science
- economics
- engineering
- finance
- logic
- mathematics
- physics

is a heavy emphasis on mathematics, which is itself a Type III subject. In these subjects the primary emphasis is on learning techniques that enable you to solve problems. In general, there is far less information to acquire in these courses than in Type I or Type II courses, and the language is not so much one of words as it is one of numbers and symbols.

Many students are turned off by the abstract, almost alien, nature of these subjects. "When am I ever going to use the quadratic formula in real life?" is the typical complaint. Some students shake their heads wistfully when they receive their latest test results: "I'm good at other subjects, but I'm just no good at math." They almost seem proud of the fact.

IMITATE FIRST, UNDERSTAND LATER

The entire thrust of CyberLearning has been to stress the importance of understanding information. You also know, however, that understanding is a continuing process that can take weeks or even months. With mathematics it can take *years.*

Again, even if you're an outstanding math student, you will often be frustrated that you don't understand a certain formula or problem-solving technique. Let's say you read a section of your textbook on a particular technique. You follow the steps in the solution process. You can even duplicate those steps to solve similar problems yourself. But *why* the technique works is a complete mystery.

If you can at least understand *what* you're doing, eventually you'll understand *why* a technique or formula works, too. But while you're taking a course, the important thing is that you be able to use the technique to solve problems so you can ace your tests.

I mention all this because many students completely stress out when they don't understand why a technique works. "I *never* would have thought of doing that," they say in despair. And because they panic, they "shut down" and don't even try to follow the individual steps. Simply recognize that virtually all of the initial learning process for math involves nothing more than closely observing the precise steps in a given technique, and then imitating or duplicating those steps on similar sorts of problems.

If you've taken geometry, for example, you learned that the area of a circle of radius *r* equals

$$\pi r^2$$

and that

$$2\pi r$$

gives you the circumference. I think you'll admit that as formulas go these are relatively simple; you probably encountered them briefly as early as seventh or eighth grade. And yet unless you've taken calculus, you don't understand *why* these formulas work. You just take them on faith and use them, and that's fine.

The next time your teacher or textbook uses a formula you don't quite understand, don't think there's something wrong with you. There's a very good chance that *nobody* in your class understands it. The smart students just realize that the important thing is to follow the steps and that understanding will develop.

Okay then, let's take a look at why mathematics is so difficult.

SEVEN REASONS THAT MAKE MATH SEEM MORE DIFFICULT THAN IT REALLY IS

Thus, mathematics may be defined as the subject in which we never know what we are talking about, nor whether what we are saying is true.
BERTRAND RUSSELL

If you're having any difficulty with mathematics, it's for any one of the following reasons. Study this list carefully and determine which items most apply to any trouble you may be having in math.

1. **You're not aware of how to build understanding of mathematical concepts.** Understanding takes time and won't be achieved just by reading your book. From time to time you must put your book aside and see if you can reconstruct the solution to problems. Your being able to "follow" a solution does not mean you'll be able to solve similar problems on your own, any more than watching a dance means you'll be able to perform it yourself.

2. **You're not aware of how much guessing, approximating, trial and error, and out-and-out "playing around" goes on in mathematics.** Textbooks present mathematics as so logical and scientific that sometimes you can feel a little foolish not understanding concepts that seem to be so straightforward. And yet much of the mathematics you're studying took some of the greatest minds this planet has ever seen entire lifetimes to develop and work out. Even then it took maybe a generation or two before other leading mathematicians "saw the light." So don't worry if it takes you a term or two to get the hang of trig or probability or calculus. Mathematics is a logical subject but the process of understanding it is not!

3. **You don't like the abstract nature of mathematics.** Mathematics begins with concrete specifics and ends in abstractions. One of the points Bertrand Russell, the great philosopher and mathematician, makes in the later quote is not that mathematicians don't know what they're talking about. He's saying that mathematical statements can refer to anything. For example, the statement

$$x + x = 2x$$

is true whether x stands for umbrellas, bottle caps, or parrots. Likewise, the formula for the volume of a sphere is

$$4\pi r^2$$

whether you're talking about a marble or a bowling ball. Make the subject concrete. Instead of picking points on a number line, think of dropping pennies on a ruler; instead of the slope of a line, think of a ski slope; instead of a cube, think of a television set. Use your own examples; do whatever it takes to make the subject more real and tangible. This suggestion is nothing more than Question 10: *How can I picture this information?*

4. **You're uncomfortable or unfamiliar with the language of mathematics.** The language of numbers and symbols takes some getting used to. For example, if you're studying algebra it is assumed that you understand that the letters

$$a, b, \text{ and } c$$

typically stand for constants while the letters

$$x, y, \text{ and } z$$

indicate variables. Moreover, the letters

$$i \text{ and } e$$

usually stand for two special numbers. There's no reason for using these particular letters other than that they are the notations or

What is algebra, exactly? Is it those three-cornered things?
J. M. BARRIE

"conventions" that mathematicians have agreed upon over the centuries. It is a convention, for example, that

$$ab$$

means

$$a \text{ times } b$$

rather than something else. Sometimes these conventions can be quite subtle. For instance, the trigonometric expressions

$$\cos^2 x$$

and

$$\cos x^2$$

do not mean the same thing; nor do

$$2 \cos x$$

and

$$\cos 2x.$$

If you're not paying close attention you can overlook these nuances. **Make sure you familiarize yourself with the notations and conventions your teacher and textbook are using.** Although most are generally accepted, you will see slight variations from textbook to textbook and teacher to teacher.

5. **You're relying on faulty or erroneous "rules."** I once worked with a young student, for example, who had been told that the "rule" for adding a positive and negative number was to subtract one number from the other, with the result taking the sign of the "bigger" number. I'm not sure where he got this rule, but I'll bet he didn't work it out on his own. It does work when you're subtracting numbers, but being the bright student he was, he thought he could generalize the rule (an excellent mathematical habit, as you will see). So his problem then came when he moved on to *multiplying* positive and negative numbers because he thought the same rule applied—the product takes the sign of the bigger number. **Using faulty "rules" is one of the principal causes of math errors. If you ever find yourself saying, "Isn't there a rule that says…," you're falling into this trap. These misunderstandings often begin by a careless use of language, sometimes on the part of a teacher.** For example, many students have been taught that you cancel factors common to numerators and denominators. There is, however, no such operation as "canceling." Because students have heard this rule, however, they begin to confuse it with cross—multiplying, another rule.

6. **You're missing some of the building blocks.** Math is what teachers call a "sequential" subject, meaning that each topic builds on the previous one. You need to understand arithmetic before you can tackle basic algebra, basic algebra before geometry, geometry and advanced algebra before trigonometry, and trigonometry before calculus. It's quite possible, for instance, that the trouble you're having in trig is caused by gaps in your understanding of basic arithmetic. These gaps can go undetected for years, especially if you did well in courses that failed to cover certain key concepts. If you're a little shaky on some fundamental concepts, you don't necessarily have to drop the course you're now taking. It does mean, however, that you'll have to brush up on those topics.

7. **You haven't taken physics.** Mathematics did not develop as an abstract subject. It was developed to solve practical problems. Geometry, for example, literally means "measuring the earth" and was developed to help land surveyors in ancient Greece and Egypt. Most of the advances in mathematics have come from trying to solve problems in other areas, most notably those presented by astronomy and physics. Once you get beyond basic arithmetic, you'll find that many math textbooks use illustrative examples drawn from physics, but if you haven't taken physics, you're not going to find the examples all that illustrative. Even though physics is rarely mentioned as a requirement for math classes, you're at a serious disadvantage if you haven't taken it.

LEARNING TO EXPLORE MATHEMATICAL CONCEPTS: THE EXPERT QUESTIONS

Although mathematical concepts take a while to "sink in," there are steps you can take that will help this process along. While the more problems you solve the better for your understanding, merely solving problems over and over is not by itself an efficient way to build understanding of mathematical concepts, any more than rereading is an efficient way to understand written text.

The study of mathematics is apt to commence in disappointment.
ALFRED NORTH
WHITEHEAD

I must point out that the following questions govern the way you *learn* how to solve problems, not the way you will actually go about solving problems on tests. You'll be using a different set of expert questions to solve problem. We'll get to those shortly.

Here are the expert questions you should be asking as you're solving a problem or learning a new mathematical concept:

- *What would I guess the answer or result should be?*
- *What is each step of the solution accomplishing?*
- *What's the pattern here?*
- *If this changes, what else will change?*

- *What happens at "the extremes"?*
- *Can I generalize this result?*
- *What are the "special cases"?*
- *How can this question be rephrased?*
- *What are the essential features of this problem?*
- *What other types of problems or techniques does this remind me of?*
- *How many different ways can I solve this problem?*
- *Can I derive the formula?*
- *How can I make this concept more tangible?*

We'll be applying these questions to the following two sample textbook passages, one from algebra and one from geometry. Please read them as you would normally approach a math textbook:

Work Problems

A common type of word problem is the "work problem." Here are three examples:

Example 1: If Bob can do $\frac{1}{4}$ of a certain job in an hour, how many hours does it take him to complete the entire job?

Solution: $1 \div \frac{1}{4} = 4$ hours

Example 2: If Brenda can do a certain job in 3 hours and Bill can do the same job in 6 hours, how many hours will it take them to complete the job if they work together?

Solution: Each hour Brenda does $\frac{1}{3}$ of the job.

Each hour Bill does $\frac{1}{6}$ of the job.

Each hour Brenda and Bill do $\frac{1}{3} + \frac{1}{6} = \frac{1}{2}$ of the job.

Therefore it will take them $1 \div \frac{1}{2} = 2$ hours to complete.

Example 3: Assuming all men work at the same rate, if it takes a team of 3 men 12 days to complete a certain job, how many would it take a team of 4 men to complete the same job?

Solution: If 3 men can do the job in 12 days, it would take 1 man three times as long, or 36 days, to complete the job. If it takes 1 man 36 days to complete the job, it would take 4 men one fourth as long, or 9 days, to complete the job.

Pythagorean Theorem

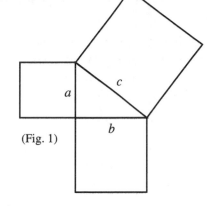

In a right-angled triangle, the square on the hypotenuse is equal to the sum of the squares on the other two sides: $a^2 + b^2 = c^2$ (Fig. 1).

We can use this relationship to calculate the length of any side of a right triangle given the lengths of the other two.

(Fig. 1)

Example 1:

In the figure above, if $a = 3$ and $b = 4$, then $c = ?$

Solution:

$$a^2 + b^2 = c^2$$
$$3^2 + 4^2 = c^2$$
$$9 + 16 = c^2$$
$$25 = c^2$$
$$c = 5$$

Example 2:

In the figure above, if $a = 2$ and $b = 1$, then $c = ?$

Solution:

$$a^2 + b^2 = c^2$$
$$2^2 + 1^2 = c^2$$
$$4 + 1 = c^2$$
$$5 = c^2$$
$$c = \sqrt{5}$$

The numbers (3, 4, 5) form what is known as a *Pythagorean Triple* because each side of the triangle is an integer length. Two other common Triples are (5, 12, 13) and (7, 24, 25).

Two other special cases of the Pythagorean theorem worth noting are the "30–60–90" and "45–45–90" (*isosceles right*) triangles (Fig. 2). The sides of these triangles always form the following relationships:

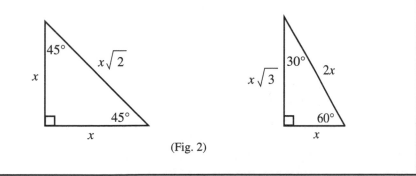

(Fig. 2)

Okay, let's see how to use the expert questions on the sample passages.

WHAT WOULD I GUESS THE ANSWER OR RESULT SHOULD BE?

When trying to solve a math problem, most students try to approach the result logically. **But before you solve any problem, you should always begin by guessing the result.** What does common sense suggest the answer should be? What is your best estimate?

This step is analogous to trying to answer your questions while reading before the author tells you. It's too bad guessing has such a bad reputation in school. Guessing is a *highly* sophisticated art. And yet people think guessing means trying to avoid thought. In fact, the opposite is the case. I'll lay down the following proposition for you to mull over. **All thinking is the process of making successively better guesses.** I don't just mean thinking about math, I mean thinking about anything. All learning is based on this concept, too.

Anyway, let's take a look at the second algebra example and see if we can guess the result. If Brenda can do the job in 3 hours working alone, our first guess is that working with Bill the total time must be *less* than 3 hours. Now, let's take two Brendas. Two Brendas would work twice as fast as one, and take half as long to complete the job: 1.5 hours. Since Bill is slower than Brenda, the answer must be *more* than 1.5 hours. Conversely, if two Bills were working, they would take 3 hours, so the answer must be less than that (although by coincidence we already knew that).

Guessing allows you to see if your solution makes sense. Some students "solve" this problem by relying on a "rule" that suggests taking the average of the two times, or 4.5 hours. If they had guessed the result before they placed blind faith in their method they would have known they were way off base.

WHAT IS EACH SOLUTION STEP ACCOMPLISHING?

It's important that you follow each solution step, even if you don't know why a particular step is necessary. Looking again at the second algebra example, you would note the following solution steps:

1. calculate the reciprocal of each person's individual time;
2. calculate the sum of these two reciprocals;
3. calculate the reciprocal of that sum.

It helps to say each step out loud as you're writing it down—a great memory hook!

If you can state what each step is doing, that's enough for now. Of course, if you have the time you should also try to understand *why* each step was necessary, but don't dwell on it too long.

WHAT'S THE PATTERN HERE?

This is a background question you should be asking all the time as you ask the other questions. Patterns, you'll recall, are one of the memory hooks. **What's**

more important, the search for patterns is one of the great goals of mathematics. Patterns suggest connections and often give clues to formulas.

IF THIS CHANGES, WHAT ELSE WILL CHANGE?

Our old friend: the *What if...?* question. Let's look at the Pythagorean theorem. It tells us that for any right-angled triangle, the square on the hypotenuse equals the sum of the squares of the other two sides. Well, let's change the rules. What would the relationship of the respective squares be if we *decreased* the right angle? If we *increased* it? (Guess the result!)

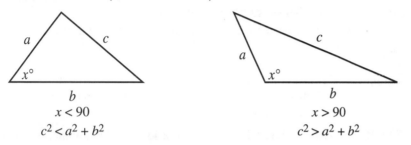

$x < 90$
$c^2 < a^2 + b^2$

$x > 90$
$c^2 > a^2 + b^2$

WHAT HAPPENS AT "THE EXTREMES"?

Try making one of the variables as large or as small as possible and see what happens. I did this earlier when I imagined two Brendas and two Bills. The time it would take two Brendas is the fast extreme; two Bills, the slow extreme. Extremes set boundaries to possible answers and help you estimate solutions quickly.

CAN I GENERALIZE THIS RESULT?

Generalizing a concept or a technique means seeing if it is true in more general cases. The Pythagorean theorem, for example, allows us to determine the length of the diagonal of a rectangle:

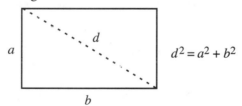

$d^2 = a^2 + b^2$

A rectangle has two dimensions. Does the Pythagorean theorem apply in three dimensions? You bet! We can use it to determine the diagonal of a box:

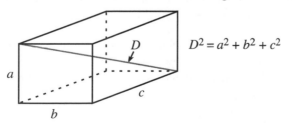

$D^2 = a^2 + b^2 + c^2$

WHAT ARE THE "SPECIAL CASES"?

You will often come across special cases when learning a concept or a technique. A square, for example, is a special rectangle. An isosceles triangle is a special triangle. The textbook passage on the Pythagorean theorem pointed out several such special cases. **Special cases are almost always worth memorizing separately.**

HOW CAN THIS QUESTION BE REPHRASED?

Don't just solve the problems as given in your textbook. **Devise other ways of asking them; your teacher certainly will on exams!**

In our second algebra example, the problem could have been phrased like this:

Example: If Brenda can do a certain job in 3 hours working alone, and in 2 hours working with Bill, in how many hours could Bill complete the job working alone?

Solution: Every 6 hours Brenda can do 2 jobs working alone, or 3 jobs working with Bill. So every 6 hours Bill completes 1 job.

If you don't practice rephrasing questions while studying, you might not recognize this example as identical to the one in the textbook.

Here's a more difficult variation:

Example: Brenda can do a certain job in 3 hours while Bill can do it in 6. If Brenda works for 1 hour alone and is then joined by Bill, how many hours will it take them to complete the *remaining* part of the job?

Solution: In the first hour, Brenda completes one–third of the job, which leaves two–thirds remaining. Since we know it takes Brenda and Bill 2 hours to complete an entire job, this remaining part will take them two–thirds as long, or $1\frac{1}{3}$ hours.

WHAT ARE THE ESSENTIAL FEATURES OF THIS PROBLEM?

You must be able to recognize a problem in different guises. The work problems, for instance, involve a job being done in a fixed amount of time. It is *not* an essential feature of the problem that the job be accomplished by people. Here's an equivalent (what mathematicians call *isomorphic*) problem:

Example: A sink has two drains, a large one that can empty it alone in 10 minutes and a small one that can empty it alone in 15 minutes. How many minutes will it take the sink to empty completely if both drains are open?

Solution: Every minute, the large drain empties $\frac{1}{10}$ of the sink while the small tank empties $\frac{1}{15}$ of the sink. Together, they empty $\frac{1}{10} + \frac{1}{15} = \frac{1}{6}$ of the tank every minute. At this rate, it will take 6 minutes to empty the tank.

WHAT OTHER TYPES OF PROBLEMS OR TECHNIQUES DOES THIS REMIND ME OF?

Another old friend: the *What does this remind me of?* question. The Pythagorean theorem might remind you of other theorems involving the sides of a triangle, such as the one that states that the sum of any two sides of a triangle is always greater than the third side.

HOW MANY DIFFERENT WAYS CAN I SOLVE THIS PROBLEM?

Once you solve a problem, don't skip immediately to the next one. See if you can approach it from other angles. Here's another solution to the second algebra example:

Solution: If Brenda can do the job in 3 hours, she can do 2 jobs in 6 hours. So working together, Brenda and Bill could complete 3 jobs in 6 hours, or 1 job in 2 hours.

The more ways you know how to solve a problem, the better you understand the concept (and the less likely you'll find yourself stuck on a test question).

CAN I DERIVE THE FORMULA?

Not all teachers require their students to be able to derive formulas, but knowing how improves your understanding immensely. Here's a simple geometric proof of the Pythagorean theorem by placing one square inside a larger one.

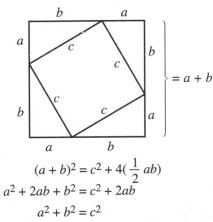

$$(a + b)^2 = c^2 + 4(\tfrac{1}{2} ab)$$
$$a^2 + 2ab + b^2 = c^2 + 2ab$$
$$a^2 + b^2 = c^2$$

(the area of the largest square equals the sum of the areas of the small square and the 4 triangles)

I think you'll agree that this diagram and proof help you understand the Pythagorean theorem.

HOW CAN I MAKE THIS CONCEPT MORE TANGIBLE?

Keep in mind that while mathematical concepts are often presented to you as abstractions, they originally hatched in a mathematician's brain in a very tangible form.

Looking at the Pythagorean theorem, instead of a hypotenuse and two sides of a triangle, picture yourself cutting diagonally across a field. That's one way to make it tangible. Come up with your own ways.

THE OTHER ELEVEN CYBERLEARNING QUESTIONS

By this point you should be familiar enough with CyberLearning's Twelve Question approach that I need not work through them another time. Other than the expert questions, there are only a few significant differences in the application of the Twelve Questions to Type III subjects.

- **Instead of revising your notes continually, spend most of your time solving *different* types of problems.** Solving the same problems over and over is not an efficient way to develop understanding.

- **Getting the big picture is more difficult.** Getting the big picture is more important in Type I subjects, where you have masses of information to digest.

- **You won't need to paraphrase or summarize the author's words that often.** In fact, as a general rule you should copy down each step of a solution exactly as it appears. As I noted earlier, learning problem-solving techniques in the early stages involves a great deal of imitation.

- **There is considerably less information to organize.** Mathematics and other Type III subjects, you'll recall, require you to learn problem-solving techniques rather than information. Of course, to the extent that you can organize techniques or formulas, your understanding will improve.

Other than the points noted above, everything you have learned about the Twelve Questions in previous chapters applies equally well to learning mathematics.

HOW TO READ A MATH TEXTBOOK: NUTS AND BOLTS

Here are some other tips to help you get the most out of your textbook.

- **Before you begin solving any problems, make sure you're familiar with the notation system and the definition of all the terms being used.**

HOW TO READ A MATH TEXTBOOK: NUTS AND BOLTS (CONTINUED)

- **Solve lots and lots of problems, and do one type at a time.** Practicing this way helps you see some of the underlying features and patterns of a concept or technique, and helps you develop a feel for it.

- **Remember that in the beginning, all you're doing is following the steps in your textbook and trying to imitate them.**

- **Do each step on paper, not in your head.** Even when you thoroughly understand a technique, you should force yourself to write down every step on paper. A concert pianist still practices the scales. This habit helps you focus and gets your mind in a problem-solving groove.

- **Get in the habit of reading *very* carefully; most "careless" errors are caused by misreading the problem rather than computational mistakes.** If this means putting your finger down on the page to make sure you're taking in each word, do it!

- **If you don't follow the solution to a problem, it's likely that the author has omitted some steps.** Prepare a list of problems you can't work out to discuss with your teacher.

- **A supplementary source of information is a must.** In mathematics you're learning not just problem-solving techniques but also to recognize on what sorts of problems and in what types of situations they apply. The greater variety of problems you solve using a given technique, the better you will understand that technique. A book written by a different author will provide you with questions from a different perspective. Find an information source that has lots of examples with step-by-step solutions, and preferably includes proofs or derivations for formulas. Be aware that a different author will sometimes use a different notation system, so be sure you familiarize yourself with it. (For more, see the discussion beginning on page 60.)

Now that you know how you should learn problem-solving techniques, let's see how you actually solve problems on tests.

SOLVING MATH PROBLEMS

There's really no great secret to solving math problems. We're all natural problem solvers; our brains are wired that way—we can't help ourselves. Math is presented as an abstract subject, but the basic principles of solving a math problem are no different from solving any other problem you're faced with.

The first step is to size up the problem. *What does this problem remind me of?* is an expert question that should get you pointed in the right direction. Then ask yourself, *What do I already know?* Write down all the information (the "givens" and the unknown) and any equations that suggest themselves. *How can I picture this?* tells you to draw a picture of the information.

If you're taking a test, don't waste too much time trying to solve the problem "the right way." Some students just stare at a math problem as if they expect the solution to pop out at them. The solution does sometimes pop out, but you've got to make some attempt.

Imagine yourself trying to open a lock with several keys. You don't just stare at the lock. You make your best guess about which key will fit and then you try it. If it doesn't work, you try another key. And you keep repeating this process as long as it takes before you arrive at a solution. Remember: all thinking is the process of making successively better guesses.

CLASSES AND LECTURES IN TYPE III SUBJECTS

The relationship of class lectures to the textbook is quite high in math and other Type III subjects. Be sure you read your textbook and come prepared with a list of problems you've been unable to solve. If you've done your homework and don't understand your teacher's presentation, it is quite likely that your teacher is inadvertently omitting steps from the solution. Simply ask your teacher to explain *what* each step is more explicitly.

SUMMARY

Most students hate math more than any other subject. There are many complaints: can't follow, don't think in algebraic symbols, won't ever use any of it in real life. If you think you're "not good" at math, you're just approaching it in the wrong way. By using CyberLearning, you can conquer math as you would any other subject. **Remember Smart Student Principle #10: How well you do in school reflects your attitude and your method, not your ability.**

The first step toward succeeding in math classes is to overcome the blocks that make math seem tougher than it really is. I've explained eight such blocks in this chapter, some of which you're sure to relate to. Although formidable, all of them can be beaten.

From here, the key is simply asking the right expert questions: What's the pattern here? What happens at the extremes? Can I generalize the result? Can I derive the formula? And so on. Remember that, as with other Type III subjects, you're not so much trying to gather and organize information as to master techniques. The expert questions, along with plenty of practice, will enable you to do just that.

It's been a while since we last checked up on your attitude. Is your pen ready?

Intermission:
Attitude Check #2

TAKE THIS QUIZ!
Time for another attitude check.

ATTITUDE CHECK

Instructions: For each statement below, in the space provided indicate whether you agree (1) or disagree (0) with it. Again, choose the response that best reflects what you truly believe.

[ ] 1. After answering a question or problem when you're studying, you frequently spend time trying to see how many *other* answers or solutions you can come up with.

[ ] 2. Most questions and problems have "right" answers and a "right" way to solve them.

[ ] 3. When you've been struggling to answer a difficult question, you would prefer to find the solution on your own rather than look it up or have someone tell you.

[ ] 4. When studying you frequently get nervous when you don't know the answer to a question.

[ ] 5. On essay tests, you are usually one of the last persons in the room to begin writing your answer.

[ ] 6. You are often afraid of making mistakes on tests.

[ ] 7. On multiple-choice tests like the SAT, if you spend time on a question and are still unsure of the answer, you'd rather "play it safe" and leave the question blank than guess and risk getting it wrong.

[ ] 8. If your answer to a question or problem is incorrect, you don't feel good about yourself.

The "answers" to this quiz follow a brief discussion.

HOW SMART STUDENTS THINK ABOUT QUESTIONS AND ANSWERS
It is much more important to know what questions to ask when you are studying a subject than to be able to answer them. In fact, it's also more difficult

because devising intelligent questions requires more thinking than answering them. Once you know what questions to ask (the hard part), finding the answers is usually a matter of simple research (the easy part). **More than understanding them, the process of *formulating* questions is what generates understanding.** Most if not all the major advances in knowledge over the centuries have taken place because someone asked a question nobody had ever thought of.

One of school's many unfortunate lessons is reversing the importance of questions and answers. Teachers convince students that the answer, not the question, is the important thing. The result is that school produces masses of *answer-focused* students, with profoundly negative consequences for them.

Answer-focused students see unanswered questions or problems as threats, to be disposed of as quickly as possible by finding an answer—any answer. All they want to know is the "right answers" to questions or the "right ways" to solve problems, and then to memorize those solutions as quickly as possible. Because they are so desperate for answers, they lunge at the first one that occurs to them. They like things black and white, and it's uncomfortable for them to consider that a question might have more than one answer.

Smart students, on the other hand, are *question-focused*. It's not that they don't care about answers; they do, but they know that understanding involves a lot more than finding a pat answer. Questions and problems are seen as challenges, not threats. Smart students get really bugged when they don't understand something, but they don't lose their patience—they *stalk* answers by exploring the question or problem from many angles. They probe, they ponder, they reflect. It's too bad you don't get more time to do this in class or on tests.

Smart students distrust obvious answers, especially the first ones that occur to them. If they have found one way to solve a problem, they will look for yet another way to solve it. They're not threatened by considering different points of view. Because their self-esteem does not depend on "being right," smart students tend to be open-minded and truly willing to learn. **One of the fundamental differences between smart students and their classmates is that smart students are willing to question their own opinions and conclusions.**

HOW SMART STUDENTS THINK ABOUT THEIR MISTAKES

Learning almost anything involves continually making and correcting mistakes. Imagine you're learning how to sink baskets from the free-throw line. You make an attempt. It falls short. Your mistake tells you to push the ball a little harder the next time. Your next shot hits the rim, but too far to the left. Another error, another chance to improve. You've got to adjust your aim a little to the right.

And so on. Mistakes provide important feedback; they're a necessary part of the learning process. **If you want to get better at doing or learning something, you have to be willing to risk that you might be wrong, that you might make a mistake, that you might have to change your thinking.** After all, nobody calls it the "trial and success" method.

There are basically two attitudes toward risks and mistakes: playing to win, or playing not to lose. These seem to reflect the same attitude, but they are in fact quite different. Most students, including many who have done fairly well at school, are unwilling to take chances. They feel they're doing fine with their current methods and are not about to jeopardize their success by trying a new approach. They play to avoid loss, to avoid being wrong or making a mistake. Because they think how well they do reflects on their ability, they take mistakes as a reflection of their personal worth. Such students don't like to think about their mistakes, so they rarely learn from them.

Smart students play to win, even if that means "losing" occasionally. They take risks because they see the risks differently. Unlike their classmates, smart students don't like to make mistakes, but they are willing to make them. A mistake simply means that their method or approach is lacking, not their ability. Smart students learn from their mistakes because their ego is not threatened by them. They are constantly sharpening their skills, constantly on the lookout for better methods, better ideas, better perspectives.

Get over your fear of mistakes.

"ANSWERS" TO ATTITUDE CHECK #2

Smart student responses are in brackets. You should begin to see some change in your attitude by now. If not, keep working at it! There are more *Attitude Checks* later in the book to see how you're coming along.

1. After answering a question or problem when you're studying, you frequently spend time trying to see how many other answers or solutions you can come up with.

    [1] Exploring a question does not necessarily end after you have answered or it. Coming up with alternative answers to a problem that is already "solved" may seem like a waste of time to many students but this is how smart students build their understanding. **Remember Smart Student Principle #6: The point of a question is to get you to think—*not* simply to answer it.**

2. Most questions and problems have "right" answers and a "right" way to solve them.

    [0] For most important questions, there is no such thing as a right answer or a right way to solve it. The answer to a question frequently depends on your point of view. One of the myths that school perpetuates is that most questions have simple answers or solutions. But most important questions in life do not have simple answers; and as you now know, most of the important questions in school don't, either.

3. When you've been struggling to answer a difficult question, you would prefer to find the solution on your own rather than look it up or have someone tell you.

[1] Smart students are independent, confident in their thoughts and beliefs. They are skeptical of accepting other opinions, even those expressed by their teachers or their textbooks. Smart students enjoy working things out and solving problems on their own and get frustrated when they're not allowed to do that. They don't like being told what to think or what to do. **Remember Smart Student Principle #7: You're in school to learn to think for yourself, not to repeat what your textbooks and teachers tell you.**

4. When studying you frequently get nervous when you don't know the answer to a question.

[0] Of course it's unpleasant not knowing the answer to a question, but that's not a reason to get nervous. You're rarely in a situation when you need to answer a question immediately. Even on a test there are over a dozen things you can do when you don't know the answer to a question (see page 190). **Remember Smart Student Principle #6.**

5. On essay tests, you are usually one of the last persons in the room to begin writing your answer.

[1] Smart students take their time to consider questions thoroughly and plan their answers. (You'll learn all about writing essays and taking tests in later chapters.)

6. You are often afraid of making mistakes on tests.

[0] There's a subtle difference between not wanting to make a mistake and being afraid to make one. Smart students try to avoid mistakes but realize that if they're going to learn anything or improve, mistakes are inevitable. **Remember Smart Student Principle #5: Making mistakes (and occasionally appearing foolish) is the price you pay for learning and improving.**

7. On multiple-choice tests like the SAT, if you spend time on a question and are still unsure of the answer, you'd rather "play it safe" and leave the question blank than guess and risk getting it wrong.

[0] Leaving a blank is not "playing it safe." Smart students strive to achieve high scores, which is a very different goal from trying to avoid low ones. If you truly don't want to make any mistakes, don't answer any questions! How well do you think you'd do then? One more time: Remember Smart Student Principle #5.

8. If your answer to a question or problem is incorrect, you don't feel good about yourself.

[0] Getting a question wrong doesn't mean you're not intelligent or that anything is wrong with you. What it does mean is that something is wrong with your method or attitude and that you'll have to reevaluate your thinking. **Remember Smart Student Principle #10: How well you do in school reflects your attitude and your method, not your ability.**

Okay, intermission's over. Back to work. You know how smart students achieve optimum learning. In the next few chapters I'll show you how they achieve maximum grades.

How Smart Students
Get Their
Grades

PART IV

How Smart Students
Rehearse for Tests

THIS CHAPTER IS JUST FINE-TUNING

The CyberLearning questions not only help you understand your subjects, they also help you prepare for exams. In this chapter we'll tie together everything you've learned. Now it's time to make sure you know the material and can use it on a test.

YOU ARE REHEARSING FOR A PERFORMANCE!

Taking an exam is a complex, challenging performance. Your teacher asks you a series of questions. Your job is to understand them, retrieve the relevant information from your memory, and organize responses that convince your teacher you deserve an A. And you have to do all this under time pressure.

The trouble with passive words like *review* or *study* or *prepare* for a test is that they don't emphasize what exactly you need to do. **Most of the time students spend studying for exams in the traditional way is wasted because they aren't practicing what they'll have to do on the test.** Rereading the textbook highlightings and classroom notes are not skills tested on exams and will not improve your ability to answer questions.

To rehearse for a performance, you must practice. Rehearsing for a test means practicing what you'll be doing on a test—recalling information, organizing it, and applying it to answers. **The principle of the rehearsal approach is to duplicate as many of the conditions and tasks you will be facing in the exam room as possible.**

THE REHEARSAL PROCESS

Get ready to study less, but learn and remember more! You'll be spending less time reading and more time thinking about the material, reciting it, and applying what you know to answer questions. Brace yourself. While active rehearsal-style studying is highly efficient and saves time, it's also more intense and demanding than what you're used to. But the payoff is far greater.

You'll need your notes, your summary sheet, your previous exams, and plenty of scratch paper. Although you shouldn't need to refer to your official or supplementary textbook, have them handy anyway.

Here are the seven rehearsal steps.

Step 1: Size up the exam.

Step 2: Get an overview of the course.

Step 3: Review your previous exams.

Step 4: Review your original notes.

Step 5: Make sure you can answer the expert and orientation questions.

Step 6: Condense your summary sheet one final time.

Step 7: Reconstruct your summary sheet from memory.

You can spread these steps over a number of study sessions. Depending on the type of exam you are taking, some steps may be more important than others.

STEP 1: SIZE UP THE EXAM

Knowing what you're up against lets you focus your study efforts. Sizing up the exam means more than finding out what material will be covered. You also have to know what kind of questions will be asked and what kind of answers your teacher expects. These factors affect what and how you will rehearse.

By the end of the first few weeks of the term, you should have a pretty good idea about the kind of exams you will take. As you saw in chapters 3 and 4, the kinds of questions you will be asked influence what information you need to select from lectures or your textbook.

Regardless of the course, here's what you should know before you take an exam:

- **Are the questions primarily from the lectures, textbook, or outside readings?** Is the teacher fond of springing "trick" questions taken from new sources?

- **Is it cumulative?** Note that cumulative exams stress the more recent material over what has already been covered on previous tests. A cumulative final, for example, will usually be more heavily weighted toward the last third of the course.

- **Do the questions focus on main themes, details, or both?** Finals tend to be less detail-oriented and cover the main themes of the course.

- **Do the questions require factual or analytic answers?** Does your teacher expect a regurgitation of the facts and ideas from the textbook and lectures, or original analysis?

- **Will it give you a choice of questions?** If so, you should concentrate your review on fewer topics.

- **What information will it provide?** In a science course, for instance, will your teacher provide formulas?

- **What level of expertise does it require?** For example, in a math course, will you be expected to derive proofs?

- **What types of questions will it include: essay, short-answer, multiple choice?**

- **Will it be a "special" type of exam like a take-home or open-book?** Incidentally, just because an exam is open book doesn't mean you should study any less for it.

- **Will someone other than your teacher be writing or grading it?** In college, for example, you may be facing a test written by the chair of the department and graded by your professor's teaching assistant. If so, your professor may be a less reliable source of information concerning test content.

- **Does your teacher (or the person grading the exam) have any strongly held values, viewpoints, or opinions?** If so, you'll need to keep these in mind when you express your own. You shouldn't be afraid to express a conflicting opinion, but don't unwittingly antagonize the person deciding your grade.

Here's how you can get that information.

- **"Ask" your teacher.** This is going to require a lot of tact and discretion on your part. The way not to ask your teacher is to blurt out direct questions like, "What's going to be on the exam?" Instead, try something like "What are the most important concepts I need to review."

- **Review your previous exams.**

- **Review copies of the teacher's old exams.** Check with students who have already taken the class, or see whether old exams are on file. Many college libraries, departments, and fraternities and sororities keep files of old exams that you can have access to. If you can't find copies of exams for that class, see if you can find your teacher's old exams from a different class. These will still give you some idea what to expect.

- **Ask someone who has already taken the course what the exams are like.** Better yet, see if he or she still has copies of the exams. But don't expect the questions to be identical—teachers aren't fools. And if they are the same you'd be cheating, something smart students never do and never need to do. You're looking for the general test parameters (which is perfectly fair game), *not* the exact questions (which is definitely unfair).

- **Look over your lecture notes carefully for clues.** Most teachers feel guilty if they test you on something they didn't mention in class.

- **Consider attending a review session.** Some teachers give optional pre-test review sessions to answer any last minute questions. I strongly recommend that you attend them, even if they seem like a waste of time. It's a good idea to come prepared with a list of any last-minute questions that you'd like answered.

- **Skim anything your teacher has written.** If you're in college, your teacher has probably written articles or books. If these haven't been assigned in class, you'll find it worth your time to look up one or two. Anything written by your teacher can be an invaluable source of potential test questions as well as your teacher's viewpoints and opinions. Of course, if you've been paying attention in class, you should have a solid handle on this information anyway.

Predicting exam questions is actually a lot of fun—treat it like a game. I'm not saying that you should know *only* what's on the exam, but you'd better be sure you know *at least* that.

STEP 2: GET AN OVERVIEW OF THE COURSE

This is a return to the big, big picture. What were the main terms, facts, concepts, themes, problems, questions, or issues stressed in class? Before you immerse yourself reviewing the details of the course, get an overview of the course structure.

Remember the 80-20 rule as it applies to studying: 20 percent of the facts and ideas covered in your course will account for 80 percent of the test questions. Don't worry about the details at this point.

STEP 3: REVIEW YOUR PREVIOUS EXAMS

Answer some of the questions briefly to see how much you've learned since the last test. Some of your answers should be different now that your understanding has evolved. Review your teacher's comments, too. You'll find a list of other things to look for on page 185 in the next chapter, *How Smart Students Take Tests.*

STEP 4: REVIEW YOUR ORIGINAL NOTES

Although most of your studying will be done from your summary sheet, you should skim through your original notes. Often something that did not appear important enough to include in your summary sheet will become important later in the course. Your teacher may have stressed something whose significance you did not appreciate at first.

STEP 5: MAKE SURE YOU CAN ANSWER THE EXPERT AND ORIENTATION QUESTIONS

When you're learning, the important thing is asking as many questions as possible, whether or not you can answer them all. When you're rehearsing for a test, the time has come to ask *and* answer questions, with a specific focus on the types of questions your teacher is likely to ask: the expert and orientation questions.

This step should be as much like a game as possible. Answer questions (or solve problems) topic by topic. Make sure you master one concept or technique before moving on to another.

Start with any copies of old exams you've been lucky enough to find. Don't simply look over these tests—answer the questions! You needn't write them out completely; outline answers are fine.

Outside textbooks (such as your supplementary information source) are another excellent source of questions. As I mentioned in the *Intermission* on page 59, each textbook author has a different point of view. You really know your stuff when you can answer questions written from another point of view. Simply look up the relevant sections and quiz yourself on questions at the end of the chapter.

The index of your textbook is another place to look. The larger the listing, the more important the category. Be sure you check out the glossary for the important terms and concepts you need to know. You should be able to define each one in your own words and provide your own examples. Don't forget to verify the spelling of the terms, too.

By the way, it helps to acquire a detailed expertise in one or two specific areas of the course. Try to go into a little more depth in these areas by doing extra research. You can often work this expertise into your answers even when it isn't strictly relevant to the question being asked. The impression you're hoping to create in your teacher's mind is that you're an expert in everything.

STEP 6: CONDENSE YOUR SUMMARY SHEET ONE FINAL TIME

The last time you updated your summary sheet should have been no more than a few days before. Even if you haven't learned anything new, take a new sheet of paper and condense your summary sheet one last time—writing it down helps you engrave your brain cells with the information. Keep working over the information until you find a way to squeeze it all onto one sheet.

As you know, it's important to keep your final summary sheet down to no more than one page so you can see everything at a glance. (If you absolutely can't squeeze your notes onto one summary sheet, use two. Then tape them together and reduce them to one on a copier. I realize I seem to be making a big deal of this single-sheet concept but yes, it's that crucial.)

STEP 7: RECONSTRUCT YOUR SUMMARY SHEET FROM MEMORY

You've condensed your summary sheet. Now, turn it over, clear off your desk, take a sheet of scratch paper, and reconstruct your summary sheet from memory! Do your best—but unless you have a photographic memory, you won't be able to do it on the first try. **As soon as you get stuck, review your summary sheet,** picture it in your mind, and start reconstructing it again—from scratch. Repeat this step as many times as it takes; your aim is 100 percent accuracy.

Once you can reproduce your summary sheet entirely, stop. Your rehearsal is over.

WHEN YOU HAVE FINISHED REHEARSING

Do not watch TV, do not talk on the phone, do not read the newspaper. **Go to sleep immediately!** Your brain processes and stores the last information it receives that day, so you don't want to disturb all the work you've done. (Of course, if the test you'll be taking is no big deal and you are confident of your mastery of the material, relax.)

WHERE SHOULD YOU REHEARSE?

While quizzing yourself during spare moments in odd places is an excellent warm-up, the final rehearsal process should duplicate as many of the test conditions as possible.

That means you'll need a place of quiet, even if you prefer doing your everyday studying while listening to background music. You won't, after all, be taking the test with background music. Your prior studying was to build understanding; at this point you want to be sure you use that understanding in a test situation.

And unless you plan on taking your exam sitting on a sofa, do your rehearsing at a desk or table. It should be large enough to spread out your work. Clear away anything you don't need.

Your chair should be hard—one that allows you to study in the same aggressive body posture you'll be in while taking the test. The slight muscular tension the chair helps you maintain will keep you alert.

SHOULD YOU REHEARSE ALONE?

It depends on your learning style. Study groups or study partners do have their advantages in the first five rehearsal steps, especially in sizing up the exam and in asking and answering questions. The last two steps, however—condensing and reconstructing your summary sheet—should be done alone.

HANDLING PRETEST JITTERS

Depend upon it, Sir, when a man knows he is to be hanged in a fortnight, it concentrates his mind wonderfully.

SAMUEL JOHNSON

It is natural—even beneficial—to be nervous before a test. Provided you are not completely panicked, a little nervousness improves mental clarity and your ability to concentrate. In fact, a state of total relaxation is exactly what you don't want at this time. Keep in mind that you'll be taking the test while nervous and under pressure. Since your rehearsal should simulate as many of the conditions as possible, a tense and alert emotional state is not a bad thing.

YOUR REHEARSAL TIMETABLE: COUNTING DOWN

When should you start rehearsing for an upcoming exam? Again, you have been preparing all along. Depending on how much material you have to cover, the high-intensity rehearsal for most courses can start anywhere from one to five days before the exam. When you start also depends on your learning style and under how much pressure you prefer to study.

You want to concentrate active rehearsing as close to the exam as possible, without waiting until the last minute. **If you have only one day to rehearse, do it the day before the exam, not seven days before.** Starting rehearsal too far in advance gives you more time to forget the material and become unfocused. Athletes know the crucial importance of timing their "taper" for the championship game. Rehearsing is like tapering: beginning too early is almost as bad as beginning too late.

The day before, check out the exam site if it's a room you're unfamiliar with. For an important exam you might even try to do some of your rehearsing in the test room.

The night before a major exam is very important. It is not a good idea to see a movie or go partying no matter how confident you feel. Do some rehearsing, especially just before you go to sleep.

Get your usual amount of sleep. Sleeping is study time (unless you do it during class), since your brain does a lot of information processing at night. Your summary sheet should be the last thing you look at before you turn out the lights.

Don't neglect taking the proper steps the morning of the exam. Review your summary sheet casually. Practice visualizing it in your head but don't try to reconstruct it on paper. In fact, don't try any serious last-minute quizzing or you'll risk becoming flustered or confused.

But if there are any last-minute facts or formulas that you haven't memorized, jam these into short-term memory an hour or two before the exam. Of course, the first thing you do when the test begins is write that information down before your short-term memory evaporates! And remember that your short-term memory is a limited storage-bin—about seven pieces of information per load—so try to store as much as you can into the larger and more sustainable long-term memory bank.

A FEW WORDS ABOUT THE FINE ARTS OF CRAMMING AND PULLING ALL-NIGHTERS

Let's get real here—many smart students have made a career of cramming.

Don't get me wrong. They go through the Twelve Questions rigorously, so it's not like they've never seen the material until the night before the exam. Rather they've found that cramming helps them focus on the essential issues; details are a luxury they simply don't have time for. They also find that they rehearse for and take tests better in that heightened state of awareness that adrenaline produces. In short, they like the rush.

If cramming works for you, stick with it. You can't argue with success.

Which brings me to all-nighters. You'd better know your limits—pulling one takes enormous endurance and concentration. Still, smart students pumped up on adrenaline have been known to stay up for days on end during final exam periods. It can be done in a pinch, and if it works for you there's no reason you shouldn't. But as a way of life it can be exhausting.

A FINAL MESSAGE: EXPECT THE UNEXPECTED!

Be ready to improvise on your exams if necessary. If you've followed the Twelve Questions to the best of your ability, you'll be as prepared as you're capable of being; that's all you or anyone can expect of you. **Part of mentally preparing for tests is realizing that you can never be *completely* prepared.**

SUMMARY

The key word here is "rehearse." It means that your test preparation should mimic as closely as possible what you'll be doing when you actually sit down in the exam room.

The seven-step rehearsal process emphasizes this rigorous approach to preparation. The first step is to anticipate what the exam will be like: what the format will be, what material will be covered, what type of answers your teacher will expect, and so on. In a later rehearsal step, you'll find and answer as many expert questions as you can. Doing this, unlike simply rereading your notes, forces you to synthesize information, which is what you'll be doing in the test itself. You complete your rehearsal by reconstructing your summary sheet entirely from memory. If you're able to do this, you'll be ready to recall the information when you need it.

Be sure to take another look at this chapter the next time you have an exam coming up. Follow all seven steps and you'll soon find yourself getting higher marks with less studying time.

How Smart Students Take Tests

THE PERFORMANCE

The last chapter told you what to get ready for an exam. By following the seven-step rehearsal system, you should be better prepared than ever before. This chapter will tell you what to do once you're actually sitting in that room. You've rehearsed well. Now it's time to perform.

IT'S NOT ENOUGH TO BE A GOOD STUDENT

You must also test well.

You often hear teachers or parents or even fellow classmates say of someone, "He's really bright and he works really hard; he just doesn't test well." Sorry, but testing is the name of the game. In many respects, school does mirror life; I can't think of a single job—from fry cook to chemical engineer—that doesn't at one time or another demand performance under pressure. Even papers are nothing more than untimed take-home exams. It doesn't matter how much you've learned or how well you've prepared if you can't perform where it counts—in the exam room.

But the notion that there are students who "just don't test well" is a false stereotype—with practice, anyone can become a good tester. This chapter provides all the skills. I'll show you how to put all your preparation together to maximize your performance on tests.

WHAT TESTS REALLY MEASURE

Most classroom examinations, especially at lower grade levels, consist of short-answer or multiple-choice questions. Such tests measure little more than your ability to recognize correct factual information. You can ace these with very little understanding of the course material if you can parrot what your teacher or textbook says.

But in higher grade levels, essay tests become the standard. These require more than simply memorizing and regurgitating. Essay tests require you to respond to ideas, interpret them critically, and apply them to new situations. In short, they require you to think.

All tests, however, measure not just what you know but how well you prepare for and take them. Smart students know how to prepare for a test, and perform their best while coping with the pressure everyone feels. Everybody gets nervous before and during exams, but smart students, like professional athletes and other performers, know how to perform despite their nerves. The pressures

It is not enough to be a good chess player, you must also play well.

SAVIELLY
GRIGORIEVITCH
TARTAKOWER

The defect in the intelligence test is that high marks are gained by those who subsequently prove to be practically illiterate. So much time has been spent in studying the art of being tested that the candidate has rarely had time for anything else.

C. NORTHCOTE
PARKINSON

are part of the package. The trick is learning to work in spite of them—even to be stimulated by them.

HANDLING YOUR NERVES

Text anxiety can reach terrifying proportions. I believe that Freud wrote about how common examination nightmares were even decades after an individual had left school! Again, the trick is to perform at your peak despite your fears.

Now, I'm sure you've heard the following well-intentioned but erroneous advice many times before an exam: "Relax. Calm down. Worrying about things won't help." This advice can fuel your nervousness like pouring gasoline on a fire. You now have something new to be worried about on top of the exam—you're worried about being worried!

Your posture during an exam affects your mood. It's easier to control your body posture than your emotions, so sit up with your back straight and lean over your test aggressively, even if you are terrified. Slouching only makes you feel worse.

Even the smartest of smart students sometimes let their nerves get the better of them. If you find yourself completely paralyzed by panic during an exam, adopt the following paradoxical attitude: resign yourself to failure! That takes the pressure off. Now look for the easiest question on the test, a question you *can* do. Say to yourself, "Well, I know I'm going to fail, but at least I can do *this* question." Once you've answered that question, look for another easy one you can do. Focusing on answering the questions takes your mind off failure, and answer by answer you will gradually get your confidence back.

Incidentally, overconfidence is as dangerous as panic. When you're too relaxed you're not as alert, and careless errors can creep in. In a study I did of high school students preparing for the SAT, I asked the following question:

> Compared with your performance on classroom tests, how do you do on standardized tests like the SAT?
>
> (A)   You do better on standardized tests because you try harder.
> (B)   You do about the same.
> (C)   You tend to freak out.

Now, which students do you think performed the best on the actual SAT? Surprisingly, it was those who answered (C)–the nervous students! Who did the worst? The overconfident ones who answered (A)!

THE MORNING OF THE EXAM

I touched on what to do the morning of an exam in the previous chapter. Wake up at your regular time and eat a normal breakfast. Don't overeat, and don't go wild on tea, coffee, or cola. Caffeine is a tricky stimulant, and you don't want to waste time later shuttling between the exam room and the bathroom.

Review your summary sheet casually, but do *not* quiz yourself on it. If you make any mistakes you'll just work yourself into knots. If you need to commit any last-minute facts or formulas to memory, do so as close to the exam as possible. Remember: short-term memory does not last very long.

Develop a regular routine for what you do on the morning of an exam. If you have a favorite pair of socks, wear them. Pack your lucky pen. Such routines and rituals help get you into test mode.

Before you leave your room for the exam, make sure you've got a watch (a digital is more readable), a couple of pens, a sweater if it's cold, and anything else you might need to be comfortable and prepared. Set these aside the night before so you don't have to think about such details the day of the exam.

WHAT TO DO WHEN YOU ARRIVE AT THE EXAMINATION ROOM

The best time to show up for an exam is a few minutes before it starts. If you get there earlier, avoid talking with other students, especially those who are doing some last-minute quizzing of each other or cramming. You don't need someone else's nervous energy upsetting your concentration. Bring your summary sheet with you if you have some time to kill before the actual exams are handed out. I'll say it again: any last-minute review should be casual; don't quiz yourself.

If seats are not assigned, choose one that allows you to concentrate. Where you sit is entirely a personal matter. I always tried to find a seat in the last row, preferably in the corner. If I sat anywhere other than the last row I would wonder what was going on behind me. Having a wall or window next to me instead of another student allowed me to turn away from the test periodically to regroup my thoughts without giving the proctor the impression I was cheating. But, obviously, sit where you are most comfortable.

Before the test begins, your teacher may give verbal instructions. Listen to these carefully. They may alter the written directions in the test or provide clues about what sort of answers the teacher expects.

THE FIVE STEPS OF TAKING EXAMINATIONS

There are many types of exams, but your general approach should be the same. Here are the five steps of taking exams.

> **Step 1:** Catch your breath.
>
> **Step 2:** Read the directions—carefully.
>
> **Step 3:** Skim through the test.
>
> **Step 4:** Budget your time.
>
> **Step 5:** Attack the questions.

We'll take a look at each of these steps before getting down to the specifics of taking the various types of test questions.

The brain is a wonderful organ. It starts working the moment you wake up and doesn't stop until you get to the office.
ROBERT FROST

STEP 1: CATCH YOUR BREATH

If necessary, begin by taking a couple of minutes to write down anything you are afraid of forgetting. Do this *before* you open your test booklet or the sight of the questions may rattle your short-term memory.

The moment you first open a test booklet is always a bit of a shock. The exam never looks or reads quite the way you expected. Ease yourself gently into the test, and resist the temptation to start answering the first question immediately. Don't worry about your panicked classmates who are already feverishly scribbling away. You'll be picking up speed shortly.

STEP 2: READ THE DIRECTIONS—CAREFULLY

You've heard this a hundred times, but make sure you read the instructions carefully. Look for the number of questions, whether you have any choice about which questions you can do, and the time limit. This will help you budget your time. The directions may also offer clues, sometimes quite explicit, about what the teacher expects your answers to be like.

STEP 3: SKIM THROUGH THE TEST

Leaf through the test to get an overall sense of the questions and their difficulty. Make sure that your booklet is complete. It's a good idea to check the last page: it's not uncommon for students to find themselves finishing the "last" question comfortably with a few minutes to spare, only to discover that they hadn't seen several questions on the last page!

Next, read each question that requires more than a short answer. Underline any key words and quickly jot down notes in the margin of your test booklet: points you want to make, formulas you'll need to use, facts you're afraid you'll forget, and so forth. These initial notes don't have to be complete or organized. You just want to get your mind working on the questions. You'll be adding to these notes and arranging them when you return to answer the question. In reading the questions through like this, you may find that one will trigger your thoughts about another question, or even provide subtle clues about possible answers.

Having skimmed through the test, you should return to the beginning for the next step.

STEP 4: BUDGET YOUR TIME

Unless you're doing a take-home exam, you'll have to determine quickly how much time you can devote to each question. This will depend on a number of factors:

- how much time you have for the entire exam
- the total number of questions
- the type and difficulty of each question
- the point value of each question
- how much you know

If the test gives you a choice of questions, decide which ones you intend to answer. Then decide on your question order. Attack first the questions you can answer the fastest or the most knowledgeably. This gives you more time to think about the difficult questions and boosts your confidence. Don't make the mistake of biting into the difficult questions first or you may find yourself without enough time to answer the ones you know best. Warm up with what you know.

A very common test-taking mistake is spending the most time trying to answer questions about which you know the least. Don't fall into this trap. Spend more time on the questions you know you can answer well. If, for example, a two-hour essay test consists of two questions, spend more than one hour on the question you know better and answer it first. The favorable impression this answer will make in your teacher's mind will earn you the benefit of the doubt on the other question.

As you're taking the test, you may find yourself falling behind the schedule you set for yourself, so stay flexible. **While taking a test, between questions ask yourself:** *What's the best use of my remaining time?*

STEP 5: ATTACK THE QUESTIONS

Read your first question carefully, again looking for any key words. Now think about the question and analyze it before you get into your answer. Get a sense of how long and detailed an answer your teacher expects. Teachers usually word their questions very carefully. A well-phrased essay question can tell you a lot about the answer's organization, content, and point of view.

Analyzing a question means facing it head-on with our tried-and-true method of asking questions. That's right, you ask questions about the question. Jot down your thoughts in the margin of your test booklet. We'll discuss analyzing questions in greater depth when we consider each of the different types shortly.

PUTTING UP A FIGHT: FIFTEEN STRATEGIES TO GET YOU OUT OF ANY JAM

As we noted in the previous chapter, no matter how well you've prepared for a test you will inevitably come up against questions that stump you. Sometimes you don't understand the question or can't remember the answer, or maybe you never knew the answer! Sometimes you just run out of time.

Intelligence is knowing what to do when you don't know what to do.

JOHN HOLT

189

Smart students don't always know the answer, but they are always resourceful! Being resourceful on tests means knowing what to do when you can't answer a question because you don't have enough time or information. Sometimes you just have to wing it and take your best shot.

Here are more than a dozen tips on how to get yourself out of a jam.

1. **Ask your teacher for help.** This requires some tact on your part. You can't ask for the answer, of course, but you can ask your teacher to clarify the question or to tell you about the kind of answer expected. Don't criticize the question; instead, ask your teacher to rephrase it. Sometimes a simple rephrasing of the question is enough to make you understand it or to make you remember information you had forgotten. Your teacher may also provide other clues if you pay close attention. If you have to wait for your teacher to come over after you raise your hand, move on to another question.

2. **Try rephrasing the question yourself.** Expressing the question in your own words sometimes jogs your memory.

3. **Postpone the question.** Your subconscious will continue to work on it while you move on to other questions.

4. **If you can't remember some fact, try visualizing where in the book or your summary sheet it was located.** Try to recall the time and place you last reviewed the fact. What were you wearing? What did your desk look like? Try to reconstruct the information using what you do know.

5. **Start writing something—*anything!*** If it's an essay question and you can't remember much, start writing down in your test booklet anything you know related to the question topic. Outlining your answer before you begin writing is ideal, but sometimes you just have to jump into the question. Once you start writing, other ideas will spring to mind.

6. **Think about a related question.** Perhaps you can answer a more general form of the question, or a part of it. That, in turn, may give you clues about the answer you need.

7. **Examine the precise wording of the question for potential clues.** Check out the instructions or even the wording of other questions, too.

8. **If you don't know the exact answer, write down your best *approximation*.** If you've forgotten, say, the formula for the volume of a sphere, estimate the answer. **Be sure you explain your reasoning.** Most teachers will be impressed by your resourcefulness and give you substantial partial credit.

I wrote my name at the top of the page. I wrote down the number of the question '1.' After much reflection, I put a bracket round it thus '(1).' But thereafter I could not think of anything with it that was either relevant or true.

WINSTON
CHURCHILL

9. **If you don't know some important information needed to answer the question, describe how you'd answer the question if you *did.***

10. **Think!** Use your common sense and general knowledge to answer the question as you would had you not taken the course at all. You'd be surprised how far this can get you.

11. **Replace the question with a related one that you *can* answer.** Your answer *must* let your teacher know that you are aware you aren't answering the question asked, otherwise it will just look like you didn't understand the question.

12. **If you don't know what something is, perhaps you can put down what it *isn't.*** If on a history test you can't remember which President was in office during the Great Depression but you know it wasn't Teddy Roosevelt, say so. Again, you're trying to show your teacher that you've at least learned something in the course

13. **If you know absolutely nothing about an essay question—I mean absolutely nothing—admit so, and use the time to answer your own question!** This takes nerves but it often works, and it's a lot better than leaving a complete blank. Show your teacher that you have learned something in the course, even if you can't answer this particular question. The question you replace it with should be an important one. (Don't try this more than once with a teacher.)

14. **If you're short of time on an essay question, scrawl a dramatic *Short of time!* and finish your answer in outline form.** Don't get in the habit of doing this on tests, but most teachers will award nearly full credit if your outline is complete.

15. **If it's not an essay test and you're running out of time, consider leaving some questions blank.** If you have ten minutes left for twenty questions, it is better to try fifteen of them and get most of them right, than to try all twenty and get most of them wrong. This is especially true on standardized multiple-choice tests like the SAT, GRE, GMAT, and LSAT.

As you can see, there's almost always something you can do when you're stuck on a question. **If you have the time, never leave a question blank without putting up a fight!** Teachers are interested not only in what facts you have learned in their class but also whether you have learned to think intelligently about their subject.

TRY NOT TO FINISH EARLY

Handing in your exam early may impress your classmates, but that kind of grandstanding doesn't win you extra points with your teacher. **So make sure you use every second of the allotted time!**

Use the time to review your answers, especially to the earlier questions. By the end of an exam new ideas will often pop into your head about questions you've already completed. Don't casually review your answers or you'll overlook your mistakes.

Look at the questions from a different angle. If you're solving problems, use a different approach; if you check your answer by repeating your steps, you'll probably repeat any mistakes you made, too.

You may sometimes wonder if you should change an answer that you're not sure about. The old saying "When in doubt, go with your first hunch" is positively *awful* advice on standardized tests, but on other tests it depends. While it's true that you can overthink a question and become confused, a well-designed test will have very few questions that can be dispatched with the first thought that pops into your head.

The best guide is your own experience. Keep a running total of the questions on which you seriously considered changing your answer. Over time you'll get a sense of when you should trust your first hunches and when you shouldn't.

THE DIFFERENT TYPES OF TESTS

The most common tests in high school and college are made up of essay, multiple-choice, short-answer, or true-false questions. Each type has special requirements. A test, of course, can have more than one type of question. We'll now survey the different types of exams and discuss the unique requirements of each.

ESSAY TESTS

Teachers give essay exams because they want to see if you can do more than simply recall information. Besides measuring what you know, essay exams measure your ability to analyze a question, organize an answer, and communicate well—and do it all quickly.

The next chapter covers in detail how to write essays. (You might want to read that chapter before continuing.) Writing an essay under time pressure is essentially the same process, though you obviously have to cut a few corners. You rarely get to choose your topic, and your first draft is your final draft. On the other hand, your teachers realize that you are working under pressure and do not have nearly as high standards.

In addition to the points made earlier about exams in general, keep in mind the following points about essay exams:

- **Don't worry about how you'll be able to write on a topic for one, two, or even three hours.** It's your teacher's job to give you a question you can sink your teeth into.

- **Examine the question closely and attack it with our trusty method of dialoguing.** Pay close attention to any key words in the question, especially those that tell you what to do such as *describe, discuss, explain, analyze, outline,* and *summarize.* Be careful because these words may be used ambiguously. *Discuss,* for instance, can mean any number of things. If you aren't sure what a question means, ask your teacher to be more specific about what he or she is looking for.

- **Spend *at least* a fourth of your time generating ideas and organizing your answers.** Begin by writing down all the points you'd like to make. Group them under headings if possible, and then arrange them in a logical order. Remember to consider different points of view to show your grasp of the subject.

- **The opening paragraph is the most important in your entire essay.** Use a sentence or two to introduce the topic, but get to the point quickly and state your thesis. **Whereas in papers you can afford a leisurely introduction to your thesis, in an essay exam you should get right down to business.** Don't begin your essay with a sentence like, "To answer this question, we must first examine what we mean by blah blah blah." Your teacher will assume you don't know the answer and are stalling. Answer the question first and then, if necessary, use the second paragraph to define any terms or examine any secondary issues.

- **Your final paragraph is the second most important.** An excellent way to conclude your essay is to mention briefly some topics you chose not to discuss because they were outside the scope of your essay. Apart from showing you know more than what was asked for, your teacher will conclude from your thoroughness that any points you neglected to mention were left out deliberately, and not because you simply forgot to include them.

- **The more distinct paragraphs you write, the better.** Each new point should get its own paragraph. Clear organization will help you make your points in a time-efficient manner. It will also make your test easier to read—a good way to impress your teacher!

- **If you don't have the time to organize your essay, start somewhere.** Once you get your ideas down, use the conclusion to organize the main points you've made.

- **The more you write, the better.** But don't overwrite; stop when you have answered the question.

- **If a thought occurs to you about another question while writing, jot it down on scratch paper before you forget it.**

- **Write on the right pages of your test booklet only.** Leave the left pages blank for any later thoughts you might want to make. It's also space your teacher can use for comments.

- **If you need to change your answer or correct misspellings, do so as neatly as possible.**

MULTIPLE-CHOICE AND TRUE-FALSE TESTS

Multiple-choice and true-false tests are easier than short-response or fill-in-the-blank tests because all they test is your ability to *recognize* the correct answer—you know *one* of the choices has to be correct. These tests do not require as much preliminary scrutiny as essay tests, but you should quickly leaf through the exam so you can get a sense of your overall time budget.

Here are some suggestion for handling these tests:

- **Read every word of the question and choices carefully.** Misreading a single word can cause you to pick the wrong choice, especially words like *not, always, never, all, every, only, some,* and *most*. Take such words literally, do not "interpret" them. The correct (or true) option often includes qualifiers like *most, some,* and *usually*. An incorrect (or false) option often includes absolutes like *all, every, any,* and *each*.

- **Take questions at face value.** Most teachers ask straightforward questions. Searching for hidden meanings by "reading between the lines" will generally get you in trouble.

- **After reading the question, anticipate the answer and look for it among the choices.** If you don't find your answer, it might be disguised as a paraphrase, so consider alternative ways your answer could be worded.

- **If you still can't find the answer, "back into" it by using the process of elimination.** Instead of trying to pick the answer, concentrate on eliminating the incorrect choices. The answer is the choice you can't eliminate. **The principle behind the process of elimination is that it is usually easier to say why an incorrect choice is wrong than why the answer is right.**

- **Read each choice.** Don't be too eager to pick the first one that looks good.

- **If you can't decide among the remaining choices after using the process of elimination, circle the question number and move on** *immediately*. You can't afford to waste time. Other questions may give you clues about the answer. Return to the question later, when you've had some time to think about it.

- *Always* **guess if you can eliminate at least one choice.** This is true even if a fraction of your incorrect responses is deducted from the total correct.

- **If a question seems suspiciously simple, ask yourself why anyone would ask it.** Be careful about selecting a choice that seems so obvious you can't understand why the teacher asked the question—you may be falling for a trap.

- **Choose the answer that the test writer (usually your teacher) thinks is right.** Don't overthink questions and don't be too clever.

STANDARDIZED TESTS

Standardized tests like the SAT and GRE are invariably used for placement or admissions purposes. How well you do on one can have a major impact on your educational choices. Here are some things you should know:

- *Never* **take a standardized test "just to see how you will do."** These test scores become a permanent part of your record. Yet each year tens of thousands of students sign up for tests without any sort of preparation. You should always prepare for any important standardized test, allowing at least a month or two.

- **The best way to prepare on your own is to practice on materials prepared by the same people who publish the actual test.** You can purchase books containing the *actual exams* given in previous years for the PSAT, SAT, ACT, GRE, GMAT, LSAT, and the MCAT. Beware: the questions in most how-to books and many prep courses have little in common with those on the actual test you'll be taking. **I'm prejudiced here, of course, but by far and away the best test preparation books are the ones I've written.** Look among the Princeton Review's Cracking the System series.

- **Don't rush to finish.** Most standardized tests are designed to prevent all but the very best test-takers from finishing. Be willing to leave some questions blank if you don't have enough time to finish. And unless you're aiming for a near-perfect score, you shouldn't have enough time to finish.

- **If you have the time, guessing rarely hurts.** Contrary to popular opinion, no standardized tests penalize *guessing*, including those that deduct a fraction of your errors. If errors are *not* penalized, always guess; if they are, guess if you can eliminate at least one choice.

- **Most standardized tests present questions in order of difficulty.** If a section has more than one type of question, the questions of each type will be arranged by difficulty. Don't rush on the easy questions in the beginning or you'll make many avoidable "careless" errors. And don't spend too much time on the most difficult questions at the end—questions that you are probably going to get wrong no matter how much time you have. Spend most of your time on the questions where it will make a difference—medium ones in the middle.

- **Trust your hunches on easy questions but not on hard ones.** The answer to a hard question on a standardized test is never—I repeat never—obvious. And remember: questions go from easy to hard.

A FEW WORDS ABOUT OPEN-BOOK TESTS

An open-book exam is one in which you are allowed to refer to your textbook and/or your notes. Some open-book exams allow you to refer to anything you can squeeze onto one sheet of paper. Teachers give open-book tests because they don't want you to overemphasize rote memorization.

A FEW WORDS ABOUT TAKE-HOME EXAMS

Treat take-home exams like papers. You will be held to much higher standards than on in-class exams. Prepare your answers carefully on scratch paper and then copy them over neatly in the test booklet. If appropriate, type your answers.

A FEW WORDS ABOUT MAKE-UP EXAMS

Teachers don't like giving make-up exams. It's a hassle and they resent the extra work. Do everything you can to avoid having to take a make-up. Make-ups are routinely more difficult than regular exams, and the grading is usually more strict.

TAKING TESTS: NUTS AND BOLTS

The following points covering general test mechanics are worth noting:

- **Print.** It's faster than script and easier to read. I've said this before but it's worth repeating. If you don't believe me check it out by clocking yourself. Compare how long it takes you to write a sample paragraph—legibly—using script versus printing. With practice your printing will become much more efficient than your script.

- **Don't squeeze your answers onto the page.** Make your exam easy to read.

- **Use a blue or black pen.** Avoid pencils or fountain pens.

- **Show all your work in your test booklet.** If you make a mistake your teacher can see where you went off track and still award some partial credit. Doing things "in your head" is risky; it's hard to check your work, and your teacher can't follow your thinking.

- **Write your name in all your test booklets.**

- **When possible, keep the questions after the test for future review.**

A TRUE STORY

A group of New York City high school students took a field trip to the Museum of Natural History to view the dinosaurs on display. Their teacher had prepared a room-by-room walking guide of the exhibits, with a fact sheet on each of the dinosaurs and questions for the students to investigate.

Susan, one of the students, had wandered away from the group to view the pterodactyl. She looked at her teacher's fact sheet. It listed the wingspan of this prehistoric flying reptile as fourteen feet. The official information plaque next to the exhibit, however, listed the wingspan as twenty feet. Susan looked at the life-sized replica, and to her the wingspan did indeed seem like twenty feet.

Puzzled, Susan brought the discrepancy to her teacher's attention. The teacher and the class walked over to the exhibit. The teacher read the plaque and then looked up at the pterodactyl. He held out his arms to estimate the creature's wingspan: "Let me see, if I'm six-foot one..." He hesitated for a moment. "Class, for the purposes of next week's exam the pterodactyl's wingspan is *fourteen* feet."

POP QUIZ

Question #1: Who do you think was correct about the wingspan, the museum curators or the high school teacher? (Fact: As far as scientists know, the wingspan of pterodactyls varied from one to twenty feet.)

Question #2: Which is more important, the teacher's opinion or the truth?

Question #3: Is it likely that next week's test will include a question regarding the pterodactyl's wingspan?

Question #4: Which response will receive credit on the teacher's test, fourteen or twenty feet?

Question #5: If Susan responds twenty feet on her test and then explains why she did so, will her teacher be impressed by her intellectual independence or deduct points from her score?

REVIEWING YOUR PERFORMANCE AFTER THE TEST

You've probably heard people say that taking a test is a learning experience. That's true if you treat it as one. Review your test thoroughly when it is handed back. Review the questions, your answers, your mistakes, and your teacher's comments. You'll not only gain a deeper understanding of the course material, you'll also discover how you can improve your performance on the next test.

Here's what you should be looking for:

- **What was your biggest problem overall?** Was it your understanding of the material, your preparation, your test strategy, or even your emotions?

- **Did you receive proper credit for your work?** Teachers can make mistakes correcting stacks of exams. Be very careful before you challenge your teacher, though—you'd better be *absolutely* sure unless you don't mind looking like a complete fool!

- **What types of comments did your teacher make?** Where did you lose points? Did the teacher expect more facts? More analysis? Review all your teacher's comments, even those on questions you got right.

- **What caused your mistakes?** Analyzing your mistakes is an important part of the learning process. Don't be too quick to dismiss your mistakes as "just careless." Assess them carefully. What kind did you make, and what should you do to avoid them on future tests? Were you rushing? Did you misread the question? Did you panic? If you examine your mistakes, you will almost certainly discover a pattern that sheds light on what kinds of questions you get wrong and what mistakes you make. Occasionally you'll simply mark the wrong answer, but this and other kinds of truly unavoidable random errors are quite rare.

- **Where did your teacher draw the test questions from: the textbook, the lectures, or somewhere else?** Were there any questions you did not anticipate? What does this test tell you about what to expect on the next one?

- **Did you find yourself less prepared than you thought you were?** If so, what steps will you take to prepare better for the next test?

DISCUSSING YOUR TEST WITH YOUR TEACHER

Sometimes you bomb. It happens. Most teachers are more than willing to discuss tests with their students. **Don't offer excuses (teachers have heard them all before) or plead for sympathy (it's unseemly).** On the other hand, if you knew the material, ask for another chance to prove it.

Keep in mind that you are not entitled to another shot (which will, after all, mean extra work for your teacher). So if this request is declined, accept the decision gracefully. Even so, most teachers cannot help but be impressed by your positive attitude and will be more on your side for the next test.

Maybe you didn't bomb. Perhaps you feel that your correct responses did not receive proper credit or your incorrect ones were unfairly penalized. You'd like a review. Be aware that asking teachers to review their grading is not without its risks. Grades, like some doors, can swing both ways. For all you know your teacher was giving you a break when marking your test; asking for a review could wind up lowering your score! So before you approach your teacher, describe your case to a friend or someone else who can be fair and objective. If this person agrees that you deserved more credit, schedule a meeting with your teacher; your grade is not something either of you will want to discuss in front of other students.

Teachers greatly resent pressure for higher grades. You will find them more receptive if your attitude is one of wanting to learn more about the material and improving your performance rather than merely trying to boost your grade. State your case calmly and be prepared to back up it up with hard evidence. Even though you disagree with your teacher's assessment, use tact and maintain a respectful tone. Don't blurt out confrontational statements like "I don't agree with this grade!" or "I don't see why I lost points here!" unless you want to alienate your teacher entirely. Even if you're right, it's not going to help you on this test or others to antagonize the person who determines your final grade. Instead, ask "How could I have improved my answers?"

If your teacher declines to change your grade but otherwise seems reasonable, you may want to suggest getting a second opinion. If there is an honest disagreement, your teacher should not object to having another teacher review your test. If, however, your teacher has been unreasonable and refuses to admit it, you are in a bind.

Ask another student or even a faculty member how you should go about challenging an unfair grade. There may be formal appeal procedures. Don't reveal your teacher's name before you see what your options are. (By the way, if a teaching assistant or some person other than your teacher graded your exam, your teacher is the first person you should appeal to.) If your teacher is really being unreasonable, you can go over his or her head by appealing to the head of the department. If your teacher *is* the head of the department, the court of last resort in high school is the principal; in college it's the ombudsman. (Most colleges have someone who acts as a student's advocate. Next to the president of a university, the ombudsman typically has more clout and authority than anyone else—and this person is your ally!)

Whatever you decide to do, consider the long-term consequences carefully. Appeals can backfire. In addition, you'll probably be stuck with the same teacher for the rest of the term. Don't lose the war trying to win one battle.

WHAT'S COMING UP

How Smart Students Write Papers is a long chapter and you've earned a little time out, so let's take another attitude check.

SUMMARY

Remember: test-taking is a skill. Of course you need to know your stuff. You also need to be good at taking tests.

This chapter presents a five-step method for successful test-taking. You'll notice that you don't actually begin answering questions until the fifth step. First you catch your breath, read the instructions, skim the test, and budget your time. These first four steps insure that when you do attack the questions (the fifth step), you'll be working efficiently, intelligently, and with your emotions in check (or at least under as much control as you can muster).

Different types of tests require different techniques and approaches, so this chapter details special methods for essay and multiple-choice tests. Finally, this chapter gives you fifteen fallback tactics for those inevitable occasions when you're drawing a total blank. Don't worry about memorizing this stuff now, but definitely review this chapter before your next important exam.

Intermission:
Attitude Check #3

TAKE THIS QUIZ!

Time for another attitude check.

ATTITUDE CHECK

Instructions: For each statement below, in the space provided indicate whether you agree (1) or disagree (0) with it. Again, choose the response that best reflects what you truly believe, not what you think is the "right" answer.

[ ] 1. In the right circumstances, most learning would be easy.

[ ] 2. Learning is often tedious and boring.

[ ] 3. How much you learn in school depends almost entirely on the kind of teachers you have.

[ ] 4. You find it very difficult to study subjects that don't seem relevant to your interests.

[ ] 5. Since you find some subjects less engaging than others, it's the teacher's responsibility to make them more interesting.

[ ] 6. School may not be perfect, but most of what goes on there promotes learning.

[ ] 7. How much (or how little) you learn in school is determined more by your natural talents than by any other single factor.

[ ] 8. Learning is inherently rewarding.

The "answers" to this quiz follow a brief discussion.

HOW SMART STUDENTS THINK ABOUT LEARNING

Not surprisingly, much of your attitude about learning has been shaped by your experiences in school. And yet, much of what goes on in school has *nothing* to do with learning, and everything to do with administrative convenience and the problems of teachers managing overcrowded classrooms.

In a typical class you and your classmates are thrust into a passive role—the teacher talks, and you have no choice but to listen. If you want to learn, you've got to accept responsibility for teaching yourself. And since no one learns quite in the same way as you, that means constantly experimenting with different methods to see what works best for you. Every smart student answers the twelve CyberLearning questions, but *how* they are answered differs from person to person.

It isn't easy to be an active learner. We've let our mind muscles get flabby. Nintendo, TV, Hollywood, and even many of our classroom experiences have conditioned us to expect entertainment. We're so bored we hope that if our teachers and textbooks don't entertain us, our classmates will.

Let's get something straight. Learning is not always easy. It often involves long, frustrating struggles. The subjects you're expected to learn won't always seem relevant to your life and interests. But look at it this way. You have two alternatives while you're in school: don't learn and be bored, or learn and be interested and challenged.

"Learning is its own reward." You're probably sick of hearing this cliché, and more than a little doubtful. That's because the way school is run has convinced you of precisely the opposite—that learning is anything but rewarding; that it's boring and sometimes excruciatingly mind—numbing. And that's a real tragedy. School turns off students from what should naturally be one of the most rewarding experiences in life.

Learning often takes a lot of hard work but it is always satisfying. Hard work isn't a drag. What's a drag is hard work without seeing tangible results. Nothing is so profoundly satisfying as being completely absorbed in productive hard work. Learning is not boring; not learning is!

If you're bored in class, it's a sure sign that you're not learning. **It's impossible to be bored while you're learning because you're too busy doing things and expanding your mind!** Don't wait for your teacher or your classmates to get you interested. That's your job. Start dialoguing!

"ANSWERS" TO ATTITUDE CHECK #3

Smart student responses are in brackets.

1. In the right circumstances, most learning would be easy.
    [0] Learning often requires hard work on your part. But that's okay. Hard work can be incredibly satisfying. **Remember Smart Student Principle #9: Few things are as potentially difficult, frustrating, or frightening as genuine learning, yet *nothing* is so rewarding and empowering.**

2. Learning is often tedious and boring.
    [0] Many students get this impression from school. But learning is rarely if ever boring and tedious—not learning is!

3. How much you learn depends almost entirely on the kind of teachers you have.

[0] Of course there are good teachers and bad teachers, but as a smart student you accept responsibility for teaching yourself. **Remember Smart Student Principle #1: Nobody can teach you as well as you can teach yourself.**

4. You find it very difficult to study subjects that don't seem relevant to your interests.

[0] Of course it's easier to study material that seems relevant, but how do you know what your interests will be in the future? Besides, as a smart student you know how to find a way to make any subject relevant to your interests. **Remember Smart Student Principle #8: Subjects do not always seem interesting and relevant, but being actively engaged in learning them is better than being passively bored and not learning them.**

5. Since you find some subjects less engaging than others, it's the teacher's responsibility to make them more interesting.

[0] There is no question that a dynamic teacher can make the dullest subject exciting, but consider yourself lucky if you have a teacher like that. It's your responsibility to take an interest in a subject, not anyone else's. The CyberLearning questions are designed to get you actively engaged in any subject.

6. School may not be perfect, but most of what goes on there promotes learning.

[0] A lot of what goes on in school has more to do with the administrative and bureaucratic problems of managing overcrowded classrooms than it does with learning. **Remember Smart Student Principle #12: School is a game, but it's a very important game.**

7. How much (or how little) you learn in school is determined more by your natural talents than by any other single factor.

[0] Of course your talents play a role in how much you learn, but it is far smaller than most students realize. **Remember Smart Student Principle #10: How well you do in school reflects your attitude and your method, not your ability.**

8. Learning is inherently rewarding.

[1] If you've gotten this far in the book, I hope you agreed with this statement!

Next up: How to write papers that knock your teachers' socks off!

How Smart Students
Write Papers

YOU'D BETTER BE ABLE TO WRITE

Writing well is one of the most important skills you need in school—not to mention an essential life skill—and that becomes more critical as your education advances. When you're in grammar school your grades are determined primarily by fill-in-the-blank-type tests. But in high school and college your grades are determined not just by what you know, but by how well you express that knowledge in your papers and on your essay exams. If you don't know how to write well, a B is the best you can expect in most courses, even if you have a good grasp of the material. If you do know how to write well, a B is the least you can expect, even if your understanding is a little shaky. **Writing well is so important to *all* your classes that you should take an expository writing course (not "creative" writing) as soon as possible if your papers are not consistently receiving A's.**

This chapter covers how to write papers. (**We've got a lot to cover; don't attempt to read through it in one sitting.**) You and I are going to write an essay together using the same seven-step approach used by smart students. As you'll see, writing academic papers makes heavy use of two skills you have already acquired: asking questions and organizing information.

THE QUIRKS OF ACADEMIC WRITING

Academic writing is different from the kind of writing you do naturally and informally, like writing letters to friends or entries in your journal. The most outstanding feature of academic writing is its unique vocabulary and style. Academic prose often violates ordinary standards of "good" writing, such as plain language and a conversational tone. At best this style can be described as formal; at worst it is jargon-filled, abstract, stilted, and pompous.

Academic prose style was mocked in a parody by George Orwell, the author of *Animal Farm* and *Nineteen Eighty-Four*. On the left is a famous passage, arguably one of the most moving and eloquent speeches ever written. On the right is the same speech as it would have been written using the diction (word choice) of your typical academician. Which version would get the A and which the C?

I returned, and saw under the sun, that the race is not to the swift, nor the battle to the strong, neither yet bread to the wise, nor yet riches to men of understanding, nor yet favor to men of skill; but time and chance happeneth to them all.	Objective consideration of contemporary phenomena compels the conclusion that success or failure in competitive activities exhibits no tendency to be commensurate with innate capacity, but that a considerable element of the unpredictable must invariably be taken into account.
Ecclesiastes 9:11	*George Orwell's academic version*

What's spooky about the parody is that it doesn't seem like one. It's the kind of writing—with enough inflated syllables to make you gag—that most students (and way too many academics) mistake for profound thought. The challenge of academic writing too often seems to be how to pack the smallest number of ideas into the greatest number of words, and then to disguise the fact by heaving in as much jargon and as many big words and vague abstractions as possible.

In addition to its unique style, academic writing is also more tightly structured than other types of prose. While teachers can give you many different types of writing assignments, they always expect your paper to be written in one way. The form virtually all academic writing takes, whether you are writing a 500-word response to a test question or a 5,000-word term paper, is the essay.

WHAT IS AN ESSAY?

Here's the dictionary definition:

> *An analytic, speculative, or interpretative literary composition on a specific subject or theme, generally from a particular point of view.*

Essays analyze or interpret a specific topic from a specific point of view. Your general aim in most academic papers will be to persuade your reader (your teacher) that something is true by presenting convincing reasons or other evidence. While you may occasionally be assigned to write a descriptive or informative piece, you'll usually be required to exercise your intelligence, formulate an opinion, and back up that opinion with a reasoned argument.

THE THREE PARTS

"Begin at the beginning," the King said, gravely, "and go on till you come to the end; then stop."
LEWIS CARROLL
Alice in Wonderland

All academic essays, from the simplest to the most complex, have the same basic three-part structure.

A beginning	You introduce your topic and then tell the reader what you think about it. You introduce your topic by providing *background;* what you think about it is your *opinion.* This part is also known as the *introduction.*
A middle	You explain why you hold that opinion. You do this by presenting your *reasons* or *evidence.* This part is also known as the *body* or *argument.*
An end	You summarize your opinion and reasons. Then you briefly discuss some of the larger issues your essay has raised. This part is also known as the *summary* or *conclusion.*

OTHER TERMS YOU SHOULD KNOW

In addition to the terms we have already discussed, here are some others we'll be using. Take a few minutes to acquaint yourself with them:

topic	The topic is the precise subject or theme your essay covers.
background	Background is the larger overall subject that includes your topic. Generally, you should begin your essay by providing background before narrowing in on your topic.
opinion	Your opinion (*stand, position, point of view*) is what you think about the topic.
qualify	To qualify an opinion is to restrict it or narrow it down. When you make an exception to a general rule, for example, you are qualifying that rule.
pros	The pros are the reasons or evidence supporting your opinion; they are the advantages of your position.
cons	The cons are the reasons or evidence against your opinion; they are disadvantages of your position.
thesis	The thesis includes both the opinion and an outline of the reasons for that opinion.
evidence	Evidence includes the particular facts, studies, details, and examples that an essay provides either to support or dispute a given position.
assertion	An assertion is a claim or opinion made without supporting evidence.
assumption	An assumption is a fact or reason that supports an author's claim but is usually left unstated.
conventional wisdom	The conventional wisdom on a topic is the commonly held or popular opinion; it is what most people think about a particular topic.
opposition	The opposition is the other side; it is all the opinions that differ from or oppose yours.
concession	To concede something (*to make a concession*) is to admit that yours is not the only opinion on the topic. You can make a concession by acknowledging the opposition or by pointing out the weaknesses of your position.
argument	An argument can be an individual reason for or against your position; more generally it can refer to all the reasons for and against your position.

Don't worry if you're not familiar with all these terms. They'll become clear as we use them throughout this chapter.

THE SEVEN-STEP FORMULA FOR WRITING ESSAYS

All right. Now that we know what essays are, we can discuss how to write them. Although the creative process of writing an essay is a fluid, dynamic one, there are a number of specific steps you must complete:

> **Step 1:** Choose your topic.
>
> **Step 2:** Explore the topic to generate ideas.
>
> **Step 3:** Organize and evaluate your ideas.
>
> **Step 4:** Take a position.
>
> **Step 5:** Back it up with specifics.
>
> **Step 6:** Write your first draft.
>
> **Step 7:** Revise, edit, and polish your final draft.

We will discuss why each step is important. Although these steps often overlap and their order may vary, I recommend that you try to stick as close to this order as possible.

As always, there is no need to memorize these steps; with a little practice they'll come naturally. **As you'll see, several of the steps involve the same process of asking questions, making connections, and organizing information that we use in CyberLearning.**

Okay! Let's work through the complete process of writing an actual essay step by step.

STEP 1: CHOOSE YOUR TOPIC

Since no one is giving us an assignment, let's say we have a week to write an essay at least 500 words long. Now all we have to do is decide on a topic.

How many times have you asked yourself, What should I write about? Sometimes your assignment is quite specific about both length and topic.

> ASSIGNMENT: Write a five-page paper comparing the theme of revenge in Shakespeare's *Hamlet* to that in *Romeo and Juliet*.

If so, your teacher has done the choosing for you, and you go immediately to Step 2. Such assignments, however, are rare. Usually teachers leave you some choice, as in the following general assignment.

> ASSIGNMENT: Write a paper discussing some aspect of Shakespeare's *King Lear*.

And sometimes the assignment is left completely up to you:

> ASSIGNMENT: Write a paper discussing any topic from our course on Shakespeare.

WHERE DO YOU LOOK FOR TOPIC IDEAS?

Start by reading through your summary sheet and revised notes. You've spent weeks or months asking questions of the subject matter; surely you've found numerous questions and topics worth investigating.

If the course has just started, however, you may not be familiar enough with the subject to pick a suitable topic. If so, here are some suggestions.

- **Your textbook is an obvious place.** Skim the index for a subject or category that catches your eye. Review the bibliography. The author will often include a list of suggested readings or related topics at the end of every chapter.

- **Read through your lecture notes.** Did the teacher ask questions or raise issues that seem promising?

- **Look over the list of outside or suggested readings.** Teachers often provide such lists, which usually include related topics or ones just outside the scope of the course. This is a fertile area for paper topics.

- **Check out the library, starting with the encyclopedia and various indexes.** Look up the major subject area. At the end of the entry you'll find a list of related articles that might give you some ideas. Check out the *Readers' Guide to Periodical Literature* for magazine articles that seem interesting. Most local and college libraries now have amazing computer data bases that will save you a lot of time searching for information. Ask the reference librarians for help. It's their job, and you'll get loads of good tips from them.

- **Examine a different subject you already know a lot about and look for areas of overlap.** Let's say you're in an English class and have to write a paper on any twentieth-century American author. If you happen to know a lot about political science, choose someone who wrote about political issues; if you know a lot about art, choose a writer influenced by painters.

- **If you really can't decide on a topic, ask your teacher.** Careful. Unless you want to lower your grade by a notch, the way *not* to ask for help is to blurt out, "I just don't know what to write about." You don't want to make it seem as if you're tossing the assignment into the teacher's lap. Instead, describe the topics you are considering and discuss why you are having difficulty choosing from among them. Your teacher will probably help you by asking questions that will help clarify your thinking.

WHAT MAKES A GOOD TOPIC?

When choosing a topic, here are some points to keep in mind.

- **If the topic bores you, it will bore your teacher.** If you've got some choice in the matter, why not select a topic you'd like to know more about? Using dialoguing, you should always be able to find questions that interest you about *any* topic.

- **Don't be too adventurous.** Pursuing a topic you know absolutely nothing about is risky and requires more work. Select a topic you can get a handle on.

- **Be original but not *too* original.** If you're doing a paper on ocean pollution and you decide to do it from the viewpoint of a fish, be sure you can pull it off or your teacher will think you're being a smart aleck (and grade you accordingly).

- **Keep it manageable!** Don't choose a topic that is either so broad that whole books are devoted to it or so complex that it overwhelms you. The more specific your topic, the better. You will not impress your teacher by selecting an overly ambitious topic if the result is an essay that falls short. It's best to keep it manageable and do a terrific job.

- **Choose a topic that will apply to more than one class.** If you're having trouble completing papers for more than one class, try to get more mileage out of your research. One smart student, for example, read a book on feminism that went towards a paper in art history *(The Depiction of Women in Modern Art)* and one in political philosophy *(A Feminist Utopia).*

- **A little controversy is good.** Few interesting topics are black and white. What makes a topic interesting is that people disagree over its issues. Your topic should not be strictly factual, but rather something about which people disagree. If the topic is simply a recitation of facts that can be found in an encyclopedia, your teacher will not find it interesting. What's more important, neither will you!

- **A lot of controversy is bad.** Avoid highly controversial topics or ones that your teacher feels very strongly about. Raising sensitive issues with the person who determines your grade is a big gamble, so why run the risk? There are plenty of other topics and you have more than enough work to occupy your energies without seeking conflict as an outlet.

In sum, you're looking for an interesting, familiar, manageable, and slightly controversial topic. These aren't really separate requirements. Beyond the form and facts, writing about something of interest guarantees your enhancing the essay with your personality and passion.

CHOOSING A TOPIC FOR OUR SAMPLE ESSAY

Since you and I are going to be working through the process of writing an actual essay together, I'm going to have to do the choosing. Since the topic must be something that a broad range of readers can relate to, after casting about I finally decided on the increasing trend of allowing students the use of calculators in mathematics classrooms, especially during examinations.

TURN YOUR TOPIC INTO A QUESTION

The trend of allowing the use of calculators during mathematics examinations is not the final form of our topic. **To give you direction, a topic should be in the form of a question.** You'll see why shortly.

Let's examine several question variations of our topic:

- *Is the use of calculators during mathematics examinations increasing?* This is too simple a question to form the basis of an interesting essay. It's not an issue reasonable people are going to disagree over. Note, however, that this may be an important background issue.

- *In what situations are students being allowed to use calculators during mathematics examinations?* Again, this is a background question.

- *Should students be allowed to use calculators during mathematics examinations?* Now we're getting somewhere. To answer this question adequately will take more than a simple yes or no.

So let's say for now the question for our paper is *Should students be allowed to use calculators during mathematics examinations?* Our goal is to write an essay that will convincingly answer this question one way or another.

YOU CAN ALWAYS CHANGE YOUR MIND

Our topic question may not be the one we wind up exploring in our final essay. The purpose of the question now is simply to give us a starting point for our investigations. We can modify or even drop it entirely if we decide later that we'd rather investigate another question. Starting is the important thing.

BEFORE YOU START WRITING, CHECK WITH YOUR TEACHER

Once you have selected a topic, run it by your teacher. Don't spend weeks researching a topic only to discover that your teacher finds it unacceptable for some reason.

DON'T JUMP TO CONCLUSIONS!

People tend to form their opinions quickly and will offer their views on any subject without a moment's thought. But a sound opinion is well reasoned; nobody is interested in your immediate emotional response to a subject. You may be entitled to your opinion, but your teacher wants to know what you *think,* not simply what you feel.

Don't confuse first impressions with an informed opinion. The trouble with first impressions is that they can prevent you from seeing other points of view. While you may have no problem putting your feelings aside and examining opinions that differ from your own, it isn't easy to examine all sides of an issue. Suspend your initial judgment so you can explore the topic objectively in the beginning. This approach will also serve you well in other areas of life.

EXTRA CREDIT

If you'd like to try your hand at writing an essay on your own before seeing how smart students tackle the project, take a stab at answering our topic question before continuing. It doesn't have to be perfect; an outline essay is acceptable.

STEP 2: EXPLORE THE TOPIC TO GENERATE IDEAS

Okay, we have our topic question. Now we have to figure out what we're going to say. We do this by our tried-and-true method of dialoguing (asking questions) and by conducting research. It's a good idea to dialogue before you do any research so that you'll have a clearer, more thorough idea of the various issues surrounding your topic. Like reading a passage, researching and writing one of your own should begin with this step to focus your thoughts.

DIALOGUING FOR IDEAS

Dialoguing in this prewriting stage is just like dialoguing when you're reading. While any questions you come up with are fine, the following questions are particularly thought-provoking for writing essays:

- *What does this remind me of? In what ways is it similar? In what ways is it different?*
- *Was this always the case? If not, why not?*
- *What will happen in the short term? In the long term?*
- *Is there an alternative or substitute? What are its advantages and disadvantages?*
- *Is this good or bad? For whom? Why?*
- *What are the exceptions?*
- *What broader issues does this raise?*

Don't try to be logical: your first question or answer will remind you of another question, and so on. Don't worry about whether these are good questions, or whether you can answer them correctly. The important thing is to keep asking and answering—to keep probing.

It's time to start getting this down on paper.

┌───┐
│   **EXERCISE #13**   │
└───┘

Instructions: Take out a sheet of paper. Print our essay question—*Should students be allowed to use calculators during mathematics examinations?*—in the center and draw a box around it. Write small and abbreviate, since you're going to be asking many other questions and you'll want to squeeze all your work on one sheet of paper. We'll call this our "dialoguing sheet."

Now, start asking and answering every question you can think of. (The previous questions are a good starting point and you might want to jot them down off to the side as a reminder.) Write these questions down around your main one. Spread them out, because you'll need room to list possible answers beneath each one. If you run out of space on this sheet, tape another piece of paper to it and continue the process.

An excellent way to start is to answer your initial question both ways—yes and no—and see where each road takes you. Here are a few starter questions and answers to give you an idea how they would appear on your sheet:

Should students be allowed to use calculators during mathmatics examinations?

<u>Yes</u>	<u>No</u>
Who thinks so?	Who thinks so?
Students everywhere, many teachers and some major test publishers	Those who believe that easier is not always better
Why?	Why?
Calculators are cheap; they free students from laborious computations	Students' basic math abilities have been declining for many years
In what situations should calculators not be allowed?	In what situations should calculators be allowed?
On basic arithmetic tests, when students are learning to calculate	On advanced math tests, after students have acquired a facility for calculations

---

And so on.

Another excellent point of attack is to consider individually each term or phrase in your initial question. If you break down our topic question, you get the following terms (some of which are phrases):

"should"

"students"

"be allowed to use"

"calculators"

"during math exams"

Now take each term, one by one, and start asking questions. Here are a few examples I came up with:

"should:"	*How widespread is the current use of calculators?*
"students:"	*At what grade level?*
"be allowed to use:"	*Should calculators be required?*
"calculators:"	*Any type? Hand-held computers?*
"during math exams:"	*All math tests? Any exceptions?*

Of course, you could brainstorm questions in a less structured way if you preferred, but attacking individual terms is systematic.

Here's what our dialoguing sheet looks like once we've transferred these questions and some answers. Again, I've had to reduce it to fit on this page.

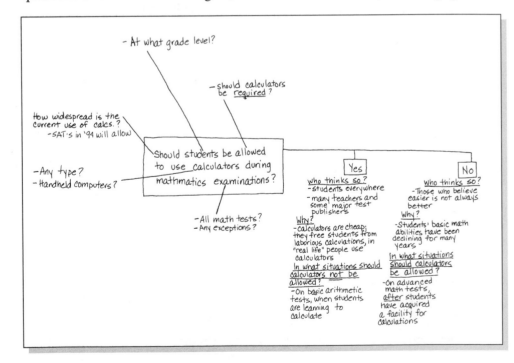

BROADEN YOUR PERSPECTIVE

Don't limit your initial search to your specific topic. Related topics and larger issues are also important. They stimulate your thinking and give you a broader perspective. Examining these topics will give you clues about the important issues in your specific topic question. **You'll also need to at least mention them in the background section of your introduction or in your conclusion.**

An effective way to discover such topics is to modify or remove certain terms from your initial question. For example, removing the term *mathematics* from our question gives us the larger topic, *Should students be allowed to use calculators during tests?* Someone who might oppose the use of calculators in math exams might have no objections to their use in, say, chemistry exams.

After including related topics, here's what our dialoguing sheet looks like.

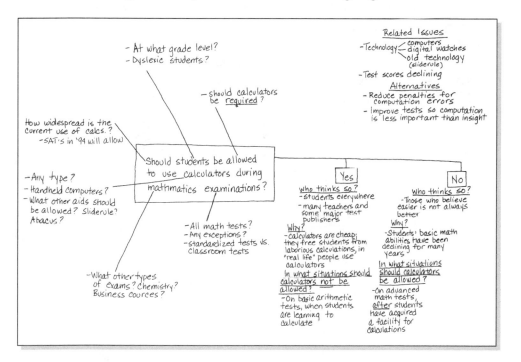

RESEARCHING FOR IDEAS

Now we're ready to begin some preliminary research. We haven't yet formulated our position, or decided which of the ideas we've generated will appear in our final essay. Once we've done that, we'll conduct more detailed research for specific details, examples, and evidence.

Start with the most general books and articles on the subject. Check out the indexes, introductions, conclusions, and bibliographies. You're looking for relevant questions and issues you haven't thought of. You're also looking for more answers to the questions you've included on your dialoguing sheet. As you begin to find answers to the questions you've raised, add them to your dialoguing sheet underneath.

I don't expect you to rush out to the library to research this topic, and we're trying to keep our essay simple. Let's just say our preliminary research revealed that beginning in the 1993–94 academic year, the SAT, taken by more than one million high school students each year, will allow the use of calculators.

DIG DEEPER

Don't stop with the first few ideas that occur to you. Continue applying this dialoguing and research process. More research will suggest more questions that will stimulate your dialoguing, which in turn will suggest other issues you might want to research. For our assignment this entire process should last a couple of hours or so; for a major research paper it might take a couple of months!

Your goal is to generate as many ideas as possible, not stopping until you have filled the page with questions. Don't worry if you can't answer all these questions, if you seem to have too many, or if some seem irrelevant. The next step will take care of that. Patience and sticking with the creative process are important. When you have a deadline looming you may be tempted to take shortcuts—avoid the temptation.

Here's what our dialoguing sheet looks like up to this point:

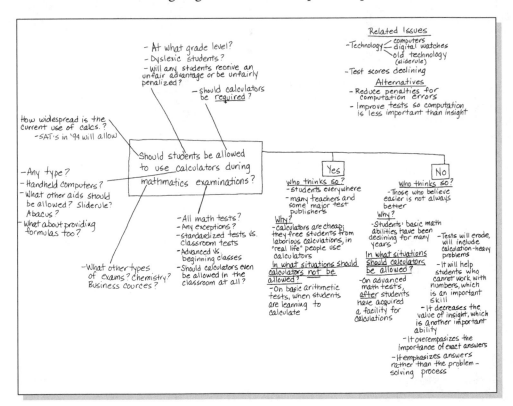

We may think of other things later but we have more than enough to work with. Let's move on and begin giving some shape and organization to our ideas.

STEP 3: ORGANIZE AND EVALUATE YOUR IDEAS

Okay. Once you've filled up your dialoguing sheet, it's time to organize that maze of ideas so you can write an essay your teacher can follow and understand.

This step is similar to the ninth CyberLearning question: *How is this information organized?* Here organizing your ideas means grouping similar ideas under the same heading. You then arrange the groups and the ideas within each group, in some kind of order.

After you've organized your ideas in this way, you can evaluate which ones seem appropriate for your essay. Let's take a closer look at how you should be organizing your ideas.

GROUP SIMILAR IDEAS UNDER MAJOR HEADINGS

You may have noticed that in filling out your dialoguing sheet, you began grouping similar ideas or questions. You'll now continue that process. The first thing is to divide all of the points on your dialoguing sheet into one of the following major categories:

- background/related topic/larger issue
- pro
- con
- example/detail/evidence/miscellaneous

This is just a preliminary grouping; you'll be getting more specific shortly. If you don't know where to classify an idea, toss it in the last category for now. You can think about it later.

Some of the points on your dialoguing sheet may seem irrelevant. If you aren't sure whether you'll need them for your essay, include them for now. Once you've organized all your ideas, it will be easier to decide which points do and don't belong.

By the way, keep in mind that not all academic papers are opinion essays. Sometimes you'll be required to write a strictly factual or informative paper. If so, your categories will be different from pros and cons, but the method of organizing your paper is exactly the same.

For example, let's say we were doing a paper on the causes of the American Civil War. The many causes could be grouped under the headings economic, social, and political. So instead of the body consisting of pros and cons, it would consist of these three types of causes.

EXERCISE #14

Instructions: Take another sheet of paper and divide it into five sections, one for each of the headings listed above (background, pros, cons, examples, miscellaneous). One by one, transfer each point from your dialoguing sheet to one of these categories. Since you may not have decided on your position yet, treat the pros as an affirmative answer to your topic question and the cons as a negative. Check off each point on your dialoguing sheet as you transfer it to make sure you haven't left out anything. Write small and abbreviate so you have enough room.

Here's what your worksheet with its preliminary headings should look like:

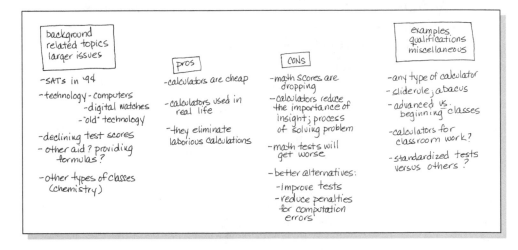

Don't throw out your dialoguing sheet; you might want to refer to it later.

SEARCH FOR MORE SPECIFIC CATEGORIES

Now that you've organized your points into the five initial categories, you're ready to organize the points still further. Choose any one of the major categories and see whether any ideas within that group can be combined and connected.

Question 9:
How can I organize this information?

As you may remember from our discussion of Question 9, you do this by asking whether any ideas have anything in common. Ideas that share something in common can form a subgroup. What these similar ideas have in common becomes the heading of their group.

Once you have completed grouping a major category, move on to the next and repeat the procedure. Continue doing this until you have completed grouping all the ideas within each category. You may feel as though you're doing a lot of preliminary work, but it's all a necessary part of writing. Concentrate your attention on the pros and cons. It is especially important to see whether you can create any subgroups for these categories. **As you'll see when we get to Step 6, the headings of each group of pros and cons will appear in your complete thesis statement.**

ARRANGE THE GROUPS AND THE IDEAS WITHIN EACH GROUP

Once you've collected your ideas into groups, it's time to arrange the groups and the ideas within each group in some type of logical order. It's not always possible to do this; but the more order your essay has, the more understandable it is—both for you to write and your teacher to read.

As you know from CyberLearning, ideas can be arranged in countless ways. You can arrange your points

- from the earliest to the latest;
- from the least expensive to the most expensive;
- beginning with causes and ending with effects;
- beginning with a problem and ending with solutions;
- in order of importance, ending with the most important;

and so on. How you arrange your ideas is up to you. The important thing is that the reader (whoever will be grading your paper) is able to follow what you're saying.

You may have heard that you should arrange the points in your papers from the weakest to the strongest, beginning with the weakest. This is good advice. **Readers are most likely to remember the last thing they read, so you want to finish with your strongest, most convincing point.**

This arrangement will not necessarily be the final one in your essay. You can always change your mind. It's simply a road map to get you started. As you begin the actual writing, you may discover that another order is better. Indeed, when you start writing your first draft, entirely new ideas may occur to you.

EVALUATE YOUR IDEAS

Until now your main concern has been to generate as many ideas as possible without being critical. Now it's time to get tough. Evaluating your ideas means deciding which ones you'll keep for your essay and which ones you'll toss. Not every idea you have come up with will be included in your final essay. Some of them may be unreasonable, inappropriate, or irrelevant. Others may be inadequately supported by evidence. Still others may be so broad or complicated that they require more analysis than you have space or time for

One point I decided to discard from my final essay was the belief that calculators, especially programmable ones, might encourage some students to cheat. Since I had no evidence for this belief, I dropped it from my essay.

Evaluating your ideas is not usually a separate step but a continuing process as your essay takes shape. When you start writing you may still be changing your mind about certain ideas and still getting new ones.

Okay then. Now that we've considered the various pros and cons and organized them into groups, we're finally able to formulate a reasoned opinion.

STEP 4: TAKE A POSITION

I know it hasn't been easy for you to explore your topic without forming an opinion. But it's important to look at a topic from as many points of view as possible before committing yourself to a particular position.

There's nothing wrong with taking a position from the outset if you are flexible and willing to change your mind. An initial position gives you a platform for questioning your topic in the same way that a hypothesis gives a scientist something to investigate. Good scientists, however, will abandon a hypothesis if new evidence should prove it wrong. They haven't got their ego wrapped up in any particular theory. They're concerned with finding "the truth," not "being right."

The problem is that most students don't like to change their minds because they feel it means they were "wrong" in the first place, or that they've wasted time. Smart students are always willing to change their mind.

FORMING YOUR OPINION

Think before you speak. Read before you think. This will give you something to think about that you didn't make up yourself—a wise move at any age, but most especially at seventeen, when you are in the greatest danger of coming to annoying conclusions.

FRAN LEBOWITZ

Well, you've explored your topic. Looking over your list of pros and cons, what do you think: *should* students be allowed to use calculators during mathematics examinations? If you can't make up your mind at this stage, you haven't generated enough ideas. Go back to your worksheet and list some more meaningful pros and cons.

As I noted earlier, not all opinions make equally good positions for academic papers. The three most important requirements are that your opinion be interesting, precise, and supportable.

YOUR OPINION SHOULD BE INTERESTING

Your opinion, like your topic, should be original. One sure way to grab your teacher's attention is to challenge the conventional wisdom. If, for instance, you know that most students wholeheartedly agree that they should be allowed to use calculators during math exams, your essay will stand out if your essay argues the opposing viewpoint.

The issue of originality brings us to the big question: if you know your teacher's opinion on a topic—and as a smart student you do—should you always agree with it? Let's say that your teacher thinks that Picasso is the greatest painter of the twentieth century while you think he has been wildly overrated. Is it wise to express your opinion in an essay? Challenging the conventional wisdom is one thing; challenging your teacher's opinion is another.

This is a toughie. Should you play it safe by siding with your teacher and getting a B, or should you go for the gold by being original? Being original means offering a unique opinion. The problem with that, of course, is that the reason your opinion is unique is that it can be proved wrong by the facts.

You know the answer: smart students play to win! Don't be afraid of taking a controversial stand. Your teachers aren't going to give you higher marks just because you agree with them anyway, so don't be a wimp. Of course, if you *are* going to disagree with your teacher, do so respectfully. Be sure you acknowledge your teacher's viewpoint and rigorously back up your own.

A well-reasoned paper will get you a B, maybe even a B⁺. But a well-reasoned paper backed by facts and good writing will get you the A. To get the A⁺, you must be original.

YOUR OPINION SHOULD BE PRECISE

Few issues are black and white. Even something as extreme as killing has exceptions. Murdering someone is against the law, but murdering in self-defense is not. There are *always* exceptions.

Let's say your position is that students should be allowed to use calculators during mathematics examinations. Do you mean *all* students on *all* math exams? Surely third-graders being tested on whether they can add a column of numbers should not be allowed to use calculators.

You make your opinion precise by asking questions that restrict or qualify it; *What are the exceptions?* is a good start. Ask questions that include words like *all, always, each, everyone,* and *everything.* Since you will inevitably find exceptions to questions with these words, use these exceptions to limit your opinion to precisely what you mean to say.

Compare the subtle difference in the following two statements:

> Students should not be allowed to use calculators during mathematics examinations.

> In general, students should not be allowed to use calculators during mathematics examinations.

Notice that the first statement is absolute; the second acknowledges that there might be situations in which students should be allowed to use calculators.

YOUR OPINION SHOULD BE DEFENSIBLE

One reason your opinion should be precise is that vague or absolute opinions are difficult to support. Do you have evidence and valid reasons supporting your point of view? If not, choose a different topic or arrive at a different opinion. Moreover, to support your opinion your essay must examine differing opinions and show why these are less supportable than yours.

YOUR OPINION IS YOUR THESIS

Once you have precisely formulated your opinion, you have established your thesis. The thesis is what you will try to prove in the body. As you write your essay, you may discover new ideas that force you to change your thesis. That's perfectly okay. Nobody is holding you to your first opinion!

STEP 5: BACK IT UP WITH SPECIFICS

Now that you know precisely what your thesis is, back up your points with specific details, examples, and other evidence. Your ideas form the basic skeleton of your essay; your specifics provide the meat. They enrich and clarify your essay and buttress your credibility—they tell your teacher you know what you are talking about. Instead of "test" say "SAT." Instead of "display" say "liquid crystal display."

When hearing an essay assignment, every student's initial reaction is *How am I ever going to write x pages on such and such?* The details, examples, and evidence you include in your essay are what largely determines its length. If you need to pad your papers with generalizations and rambling digressions, you aren't armed with enough supporting facts. Find them—they're out there.

BACK TO THE LIBRARY

Earlier, in your initial research, you were looking for general topic ideas. In a sense, you didn't know what you were looking for. Now you do. **Each point you raise needs to be backed up with details, examples, and supporting evidence. And don't forget to provide evidence for the *opposing* viewpoints your essay will include.**

ACKNOWLEDGE YOUR ASSERTIONS AND ASSUMPTIONS

If a point you are making is generally accepted or is common knowledge, you can assert it without providing evidence. Be sure you know the difference. When in doubt, back up your points.

If a point has no evidence or you want your reader to accept it for the sake of argument, there is nothing wrong with admitting so. Assertions and assumptions are perfectly acceptable provided you acknowledge them as such.

Again, compare the subtle difference in the following two statements.

> This knowledge cannot be gained by pushing buttons and watching answers magically appear on liquid crystal displays.

> It is hard to see how this knowledge can be gained by pushing buttons and watching answers magically appear on liquid crystal displays.

The first statement is an assertion that requires support. As such it is open to attack. By including a simple phrase in the second statement, the writer anticipates a possible objection. **If you're not sure that something you want to** say is a fact, do not use absolute words like *all* or *always* or *is*. Instead, use modifying words like *usually, typically, many, presumably,* and *appears.*

CITE YOUR SOURCES

Don't forget to copy down the title of any books or articles you consult, as well as the author's name and any other relevant information. Your essay should give proper credit for any important ideas that are not your own, any direct or indirect quotes, and any facts that are not readily available. If a fact or an idea is in every textbook or article on the subject, you probably don't need to cite any one source.

The citation should show the reader exactly where you got your information. Citing your sources is fair and thorough, and it helps support the credibility of your thesis.

STEP 6: WRITE YOUR FIRST DRAFT

We have our outline from Step 3, our thesis from Step 4, and our details and supporting evidence from Step 5. Now we're ready to write our first draft. Don't worry about style or the fine points of grammar now; all we're trying to do is get the basics down on paper. Once we've said everything we want to say, we can concern ourselves with how we want to say it.

Remember that your essay will consist of an introduction, a body, and a conclusion. The introduction will contain background information and your thesis. The body will contain the pros and cons of your argument. And the conclusion will contain a restatement of your thesis, and a brief expansion of it to related or larger issues.

WRITING THE BACKGROUND

Don't begin an essay by stating your opinion in the first sentence. Your reader needs to be warmed up and be told why your topic is important (even if the reader—your teacher—assigned the topic and "knows all this stuff"). Background information introduces your general subject and places your specific topic in a larger context, preparing the reader for your opinion. Gradually you narrow that subject to the specific area your essay will investigate. If necessary the background should define the issues under discussion and any terms that need clarification.

What background you provide is your call. We could open our sample essay in any number of ways; it's really a matter of personal preference. Keep in mind, though, that your teachers get their first impressions of your papers from the background. When you open with interesting background information, you are well on your way to a good grade. If your essay's background is weak, your teacher's initial reaction will be negative. **Since it is not always easy to decide what background to include, you may find it easier to write the background to your essay last—*after* you have written the rest of it.**

WRITING THE COMPLETE THESIS STATEMENT

The introduction to your essay will end with your thesis statement. The thesis statement "Students should not be allowed to use calculators during mathematics examinations," however, is incomplete. It expresses an opinion, but it does not provide reasons for that opinion or acknowledge opposing points of view. Your complete thesis statement should do more than tell the reader your opinion. It should also provide a basic outline of your reasons and acknowledge differing opinions. **Your complete thesis statement is a highly condensed version of your entire essay.**

You may need more than one sentence to complete your thesis statement. A complete thesis statement for our essay topic might read as follows:

> In general, students should not be allowed to use calculators during mathematics examinations. While calculators do indeed save time on lengthy or complex calculations, allowing widespread use will corrupt these very tests, lead to a faulty appreciation of exact answers, and contribute to the continuing atrophy of important mathematical skills.

This is a complete thesis statement. It expresses an opinion ("In general, students should not be allowed to use calculators during mathematics examinations"); it acknowledges another viewpoint ("While calculators do indeed save time on lengthy or complex calculations"); and it provides a basic outline of the writer's reasons ("allowing widespread use will corrupt these very tests, lead to a faulty appreciation of exact answers, and contribute to the continuing atrophy of important mathematical skills").

Notice that the thesis statement still requires clarification and that certain terms must be defined. For example, when should students be allowed to use calculators"? What does the writer mean by "a faulty appreciation of exact answers"? What important mathematical skills have atrophied? These are questions the rest of your essay will go on to answer. One of the functions of a successful thesis statement is to raise questions in the reader's mind—to make him or her curious.

WRITING THE BODY

The body examines the arguments both for and against your opinion. To convince your teacher that your opinion is reasonable, make sure you examine the flaws or disadvantages in *your* position, and acknowledge that other points of view exist. If your essay supports the use of calculators, you should concede that this has some drawbacks. Doing this will not weaken your position, but *not* doing it will greatly weaken your essay and credibility. If your essay advocates limiting the use of calculators, it should recognize that calculators do offer some advantages.

Generally, the best way to develop the body is to begin by presenting the cons rather than the pros. You immediately disarm any potential opposition if you open with all the reasons against your viewpoint. As strongly as you can, list all the shortcomings of your thesis, beginning with the most serious. The more forcefully you present the other side's case, the more fair and convincing your position will ultimately be.

After you have presented the case for the opposition, point out all of its limitations. Then, having disposed of the cons, present the pros. As we mentioned in Step 3, start with your weakest argument and end with your strongest. Devote at least twice as much space to the pros as the cons.

It is not absolutely necessary to list all the cons before stating the pros. A common variation is to alternate between the pros and cons. If you choose this method, follow each con with a pro.

WRITING THE CONCLUSION

The conclusion begins by summing up your basic claim or thesis, but it also serves two other purposes. First, it wraps up any loose ends. If there are any further qualifications to your thesis or any final concessions you want to make, now is the time to do so. Acknowledge your assumptions if you didn't earlier. And if there are still unanswered questions relevant to your topic but beyond the scope of your paper, mention them in passing. For example, should calculators be allowed in examinations other than those in mathematics? What about allowing other aids in the exam room like laptop computers for essay exams?

You don't need to answer these questions; just state they are beyond the scope of your essay. Bringing up unanswered questions has the added benefit of suggesting to your teacher that if you failed to address a key issue, you planned it rather than forgot it.

Second, your conclusion should answer the question that's probably on your reader's mind: "So what?" That is, your conclusion should show the importance or significance of your thesis. One way to do this is to expand your thesis and show how it affects related or larger issues. In the introduction you narrow a general subject area to a specific theme or topic; in the conclusion you reverse the process, expanding the scope of your paper and placing your thesis in the context of the big picture.

Though your conclusion might be only a paragraph long, it is as important as your introduction. Remember: first and last impressions have the biggest impact on your teacher.

STICK TO THE BLUEPRINT

All your essays should follow the same format—introduction (background, thesis statement), body (pros and cons), conclusion (thesis summary, significance to other issues). You may find this format too rigid and "uncreative." The basic structure can be modified, of course. You may decide in a particular paper to open immediately with your thesis and follow it with background information. In another you might decide to postpone your thesis until the conclusion. Be sure there is justification, however; departing from the formula should strengthen, not detract from, your points.

Vary the structure at your own risk. Keep in mind that writing an essay is a complex task. You must explore a topic, generate ideas, develop your argument, consider other points of view, arrange the sequence of ideas, and write well while keeping your reader's interest. Following the essay blueprint enables you to express your opinion creatively while accomplishing all of these things.

Here's the blueprint you should follow:

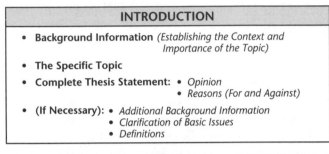

INTRODUCTION

- **Background Information** *(Establishing the Context and Importance of the Topic)*
- **The Specific Topic**
- **Complete Thesis Statement:** • *Opinion*
  - *Reasons (For and Against)*
- **(If Necessary):** • *Additional Background Information*
  - *Clarification of Basic Issues*
  - *Definitions*

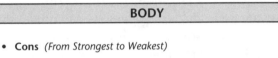

BODY

- **Cons** *(From Strongest to Weakest)*

- **Pros** *(From Weakest to Strongest)*

CONCLUSION

- **Restatement of Your Thesis**
- **(Possibly):** • *Your Assumptions*
  - *Any Unanswered Questions*
  - *Further Qualification of Your Thesis or Concessions*
- **Relevance of Your Thesis to Related or Larger Issues**

This diagram indicates roughly the relative size of the three sections. The introduction and the conclusion should be approximately equal in length, while the body should take up about three-fourths of your essay.

CONGRATULATIONS!

You have completed your first draft. If you've used a word processor—as I strongly recommend—double space the lines and print out a copy. Set it aside for a couple of days so you'll be able to edit it with a fresh perspective. (Of course, if you're writing your term paper the night before it's due, you won't have much time to get a fresh perspective!)

STEP 7: REVISE, EDIT, AND POLISH YOUR FINAL DRAFT

Your primary concern in writing the first draft was to make sure you said everything you wanted to say. Now your concern is making sure you said it well. **Don't skip this step!** Editing and proofreading are clearly more important for major assignments like term papers, but all your papers deserve some editorial review.

GET FEEDBACK

Your teachers give you their comments when they return your papers, but by then it's too late—they've already graded them. The time to get feedback is before you hand in your work.

Show your essay to someone whose opinion you value. If you're asking a friend, make it clear that you are more interested in constructive criticism than praise. People who know nothing about the subject can make excellent readers because they often ask questions you wouldn't think of asking. Those who are more knowledgeable, of course, can be quite helpful, too.

Here are some useful questions to ask a reader:

- *What is the main point of my essay?* (If your reader can't summarize your argument, check your introduction and conclusion.)

- *Where is my essay unclear?* (Clearing it up may require editing as well as elaboration.)

- *Does my essay flow logically?* (If not, try rearranging your points.)

- *Where do you lose interest?* (Perhaps your topic is too "safe.")

- *What do you disagree with?* (You may need additional evidence.)

- *Does my essay omit any important points?* (If so, continue dialoguing.)

- *Do I present opposing views convincingly?* (Be fair to the other side.)

Criticism is not always easy to take, but really try to listen to what your readers tell you. Not every comment they make will be valid; sometimes they will simply disagree with your thesis. If, however, more than one reader tells you the same thing—and you're sure it's not a personal reaction—listen up!

Let your readers mark up the paper. They should be looking for more than spelling and grammatical errors. Remember that your teacher is concerned with your ideas, your facts, your persuasiveness, and your style. Ask your readers to put a question mark next to any point they don't understand or disagree with.

EDIT FROM THE BIG PICTURE DOWN TO THE DETAILS

When you start revising your essay, don't agonize over making sure each sentence is perfect. Begin with an overview of the entire paper. Read it through quickly, trying to get the overall structure, organization, and "feel." What are your general impressions? Are there any major problems? Does the entire thing hang together?

Once you've gotten the big picture, work your way down from the overall structure to each paragraph to each sentence to each word.

Let's take a closer look at this review process.

CHECK YOUR ESSAY'S OVERALL STRUCTURE AND ORGANIZATION

On your first critical reading look for general impressions. Is your essay understandable? Have you supplied evidence and details for all the points you make? Is the general tone appropriate? Is the organization logical? Are the transitions between sections clear? Do any further thoughts occur to you that you should incorporate?

After you're satisfied with the general structure and organization of the whole, tackle each section—the introduction, the body, and the conclusion. Are the sections distinct? Do they flow logically? Is each section complete?

CHECK YOUR PARAGRAPHS

A paragraph is a group of sentences organized around a central point. Each paragraph should contain one major idea. The topic sentence of a paragraph expresses that main idea, while the other sentences elaborate on it. Tackle each paragraph one by one. Does each one express a complete thought? Is each paragraph coherent?

Indent your paragraphs clearly. **Studies have shown that the number of paragraphs in your paper significantly affects your grade.** The more paragraphs your paper contains, the more organized it seems, and the easier it is to read, the higher your grade.

CHECK YOUR LINKS BETWEEN PARAGRAPHS

Each paragraph should follow the previous one in a smooth and logical way. If necessary, introduce a paragraph with a sentence or two that link it to what was just said. Linking usually requires identifying or repeating a concept, if not the actual words, used in the previous paragraph. Sometimes you will find you need to go off the track for a paragraph or two, in which case the current paragraph will be connected to something said two or three paragraphs earlier.

CHECK YOUR TRANSITIONS

To help your reader follow your essay, use transition words to make clear the introduction of a new thought or idea and the connection to the preceding one. The following are some ways you use transitions:

- Listing points: Use words or phrases like *first, second, next,* and *finally.*

- Introducing a different point of view, making a concession, or qualifying an idea: Use words or phrases like *of course, to be sure, granted, it must be admitted that, it could be argued that,* and *obviously.*

- Rejecting a different point of view or returning to yours: Use words or phrases like *however, although, still, nevertheless, nonetheless, on the contrary, on the other hand, despite, yet,* and *notwithstanding.*

- Emphasizing a point: Use words or phrases like *moreover, in addition, similarly, furthermore, indeed, also,* and *as well.*

- Summing up: Use words or phrases like *as a result, in sum, thus, therefore, in conclusion, in the final analysis,* and *finally.*

CHECK YOUR LINKS BETWEEN SENTENCES

Sentences, like paragraphs, should follow one another logically. Your thoughts may have tumbled awkwardly onto paper when you wrote the first draft, even if you followed an outline. Now you may have to rearrange sentences within paragraphs or add a sentence or phrase so everything flows gracefully.

CHECK YOUR SENTENCE STRUCTURE

Now look at individual sentences. Does each follow logically from the preceding sentence? Like most people, you probably have a few pet sentence patterns that you use over and over. Your sentences should vary in both structure and length, so become aware of the sentence patterns you favor.

CHECK YOUR DICTION AND STYLE

I wish I could recommend that your essays be written in a simple and natural style. I know I'm going to get heat for saying this, but here goes: most teachers are not nearly so impressed with statements like this:

> Americans tend to believe that all technological progress is good.

as they are with ones like this:

> In America, the prevailing ideology is that all technological progress is good.

But don't be afraid to sound like yourself. Show some self-assurance. Even a sparing use of slang is good, showing your teacher that you are so confident in what you are saying that you don't have to hide behind long words or academic jargon. Find the right balance between normal, everyday speech and formal, academic prose.

No matter what your topic, make sure your essay includes at least a few buzz words and key concepts emphasized in the course. Teachers like to see that you have learned something from them in their class and that you are applying it in your papers.

And while the best word is the word that says precisely what you mean, there is no denying that big words impress teachers. I'm not suggesting that you *always* try to use the longer, more difficult word when a shorter substitute is available, or make the mistake of replacing as many of your words as possible with sophisticated-sounding synonyms. I do, however, suggest that your essays include enough impressive-sounding words that your opinion appears to have some authoritative weight behind it.

168 WORDS AND PHRASES THAT REALLY IMPRESS TEACHERS

I am a Bear of Very Little Brain and long words Bother Me.
A. A. MILNE
Winnie-the-Pooh

I've selected the following words because you can work any one of them into any essay on any subject you find yourself writing about. They're also great words to know in any event.

Don't be obvious when you use these words in your papers. You have to be casual about it, as if these were the sort of words you use every day to communicate your many profound thoughts. So don't overuse them—lobbing in one every page or so should do the trick. Since your opening and closing paragraphs create the biggest impression, make sure you use one or two in each.

You'll be amazed at what a different reception your ideas and papers will receive from your teachers. They figure that anyone who uses words like these must know what he or she is talking about. Of course, as a smart student, you do!

Whatever words you use, make sure you use them correctly. Not all dictionary definitions give you a clear idea of how a word can and cannot be used. Beware also of thesauruses. It is rare to find synonyms that mean precisely the same thing. Finally, be sure you can pronounce these words correctly—they can be dropped in class discussions, too! (In the next intermission I'll tell you how to choose a good dictionary and thesaurus.)

aberration	dispassionate	intrinsic	ramification
adherent	dogmatic	invoke	rationale
advocate	dubious	ipso facto	rebut
ambivalent	eclectic	irrevocable	recapitulate
ancillary	elicit	juxtapose	reciprocal
anomaly	empirical	lucid	redundant
antipodal	endemic	manifest	refute
antithesis	ephemeral	marginal	repercussion
apocryphal	epistemological	non sequitur	requisite
apposite	equivocal	nuance	rhetorical
archetype	esoteric	obfuscate	schism
ascertain	euphemism	objectivity	scrutinize
ascribe	evoke	obscure	sine qua non
astute	exemplify	orthodox	singular
axiom	exhaustive	ostensible	specious
broach	exigency	paradigm	status quo
categorical	expedient	paradox	stratify
circumscribe	explicate	parallel	subjective
cogent	explicit	parochial	subsidiary
cognizant	exposition	partisan	substantiate
comprehensive	extraneous	patent	subtle
conjecture	extrinsic	pedantic	sui generis
consensus	facet	peripheral	superfluous
construe	fallacy	pertinent	supposition
contention	flagrant	peruse	surmise
corollary	fortuitous	pervasive	surrogate
correlate	generic	pivotal	synthesis
corroborate	germane	platitude	tacit
crux	gestalt	plausible	tangential
definitive	hyperbole	postulate	tangible
delineate	ideology	pragmatic	tantamount
depict	impartial	precedent	tenable
dialectical	implication	preclude	tenuous
dichotomy	implicit	premise	transitory
dictum	incontrovertible	presuppose	truism
didactic	indigenous	profound	ubiquitous
digress	ineluctable	proponent	underlying
discern	inevitable	propound	verisimilitude
discrepancy	inexorable	purported	vestige
discriminate	infer	putative	viable
disinterested	inherent	qualify	weltanschauung
disparate	integral	quintessential	zeitgeist

CHECK FOR GRAMMATICAL ERRORS

Grammatical errors are not easy to spot, especially in lengthy or complicated sentences. Some mistakes cause you to say something completely different from what you think you're saying! In a tight, logically structured argument, this could be disastrous. Like your sentences, your grammatical errors fall into predictable patterns. If you look over your previous papers, you will discover what types of mistakes you tend to make. Avoid them in your future papers!

CHECK FOR SPELLING ERRORS

A spelling error is like a red flag to your teacher. If your essay contains more than one or two, your teacher will assume that you didn't take the assignment seriously and will penalize you accordingly. (True story: I know of a college student who handed in an art history paper with both *Renaissance* and the professor's name misspelled on the cover page. He gave it an F without opening it!)

Spelling errors or typos are tough to catch. Professional proofreaders sometimes read each sentence backward to spot them! **Read through your paper** *at least once,* **looking** *only* **for spelling and typing errors.**

If you do your writing on a computer, most word processors today include spell checkers. Spell checkers match every word in your paper against an internal dictionary in a matter of seconds. If the computer can't find a match for a word, it flags the word for you to verify. It doesn't mean the word is spelled incorrectly, because the spell checker's dictionary doesn't contain every word in the English language.

You should be aware that this software will not catch *all* the errors in your paper. For example, a spell checker catches misspelled words but it can't catch *misused* words. If you type *their* instead of *there* or *they're,* or *them* instead of *then,* the spell checker will not flag these errors, because the words you've mistakenly used are themselves valid words. A spell checker will also overlook any times you've *omitted* a word. In short, spell checkers do not catch your grammatical mistakes. (By the way, grammar checkers are also available, but most today are relatively unsophisticated.)

FOLLOW AN ACCEPTED STYLE FORMAT

While there is no one correct way to format academic papers, most teachers insist that you follow their guidelines. They may mark off if you deviate from them. Before you hand in your paper, find out

- how your sources should be listed in the bibliography;
- whether footnotes should be at the bottom of every page or at the end;
- what information the cover page should include;
- what the correct margin settings should be.

And so on. Courier twelve-point is the standard type font. If your teacher does not require a particular format, choose one that is commonly accepted at your school and use it consistently.

GIVE IT ONE FINAL REVIEW

After you've looked over your essay from the overall structure down to the spelling of individual words, give it one final reading from beginning to end. You might have introduced new errors in the editing process. If you've made more than a few minor changes, have a friend read it one last time as well.

WHAT YOUR TEACHER EXPECTS TO SEE

"How long does it have to be?" is usually the first question a teacher hears when assigning a paper. Length, however, is the least of your concerns. Sometimes your teacher is quite specific about length (*In not more than 500 words, discuss the causes...*), but generally the length of your paper will not affect your grade as much as other factors.

Your teachers assign essays to see if you can organize information, formulate a reasoned opinion, and present that information and opinion coherently and persuasively. **How you say it is just as important as what you say.** Your teacher will be grading not only your essay's facts and ideas but also its organization and writing style. Here's what all teachers look for.

- **Your ideas are the most important part of your paper, even more important than your facts.** Are they coherent, logical, and convincing? Did you consider opposing ideas or viewpoints?

- **Your ideas must be supported with facts.** Are your facts accurate, relevant, and relatively complete? If this is a research paper, are your facts documented with sources?

- **Your essay's organization and style should conform to the generally accepted academic model.** As we have discussed, teachers expect your essays to have a very specific organization and tone. The better your essay matches up to the blueprint, the better your grade. As for tone, you don't have to sound as ridiculous as Orwell's parody but neither should you be too "familiar" with your reader. Ideally, your papers should strike a balance between conversational informality and academic formality.

Besides these considerations, each teacher also has personal expectations. The precise wording of the assignment will give you clues about these, as will your teacher's comments on your previous papers. Study them carefully.

THE MOST IMPORTANT PARAGRAPHS OF YOUR ESSAY

Consider that some teachers, especially in overcrowded classrooms or lecture halls, might not have the time to read every paper as carefully as they would like. No matter how much time they have, however, they will always give your introduction and your conclusion the closest scrutiny. By the time they finish your essay's introduction, they have already formed a good idea of the grade they think you deserve. They may skim the rest and then slow down at the conclusion, but basically they are looking to confirm their initial impression.

From your teacher's often harried point of view, the beginning and end are the most important parts of your essay.

THAT'S IT! YOU'VE FINISHED THE FINAL DRAFT!

Here's how our final essay shaped up:

Calculators in the Exam Room

Affordable technology is continually reducing the amount of thinking we need to do in daily life. With the widespread popularity of digital watches, for example, we do not have to know how to tell time anymore. Computers, another thought-saving device, are becoming ever more sophisticated with the advent of artificial intelligence software. Recently, technology has been creeping into the classroom. Increasingly, teachers are allowing the use of calculators in mathematics classes even during examinations. Even the Educational Testing Service, publisher of the influential SAT, is bowing to the times: beginning in the 1993-94 academic year, students will be allowed to use calculators on the SAT.

This trend has dangerous, long-term consequences. In general, students should not be allowed to use calculators during mathematics examinations. While calculators do indeed save time on lengthy or complex calculations, allowing widespread use will corrupt these very tests, lead to a faulty appreciation of exact answers, and contribute to the continuing atrophy of important mathematical skills.

Admittedly, calculators are cheap; a decent one can be purchased for less than the price of a movie ticket. Permitting their use would greatly reduce simple computational errors and allow test-takers to devote more time to important mathematical concepts rather than the "grunt work." Basic computation is relatively mindless and needlessly time consuming. Besides, in everyday life people use calculators, why shouldn't students?

1

Students should refrain from overusing calculators for a number of reasons. First, the excessive amount of computation required on many tests is not an argument for calculators, it's an argument for better tests. Allowing the use of calculators in the examination room will just make it easier for math teachers to fall back on problems that emphasize number crunching instead of insight and higher-level thinking. Furthermore, the point of many questions is to reward insight rather than brute force computations. A calculator would allow a student without insight into such problems to solve them just as fast as a student with insight does.

Second, calculators reinforce the notion that the answer is the crucial thing; rather, it should be the problem-solving process itself that is emphasized. Instead of allowing calculators, why not simply eliminate penalties for computational errors?

Third, calculators promote the false impression that precision and exactness are the paramount concerns of mathematics. As Bertrand Russell, the famous philosopher and mathematician, once said, "Although this may seem a paradox, all exact science is dominated by the idea of approximation." Real life is also dominated by approximations since our information is rarely completely accurate. What is the point of calculating an answer to ten decimal places when the inputs themselves may only have been ballpark estimates. The ability to approximate answers is yet another vital, neglected skill that calculators will further push into the background.

Last, and most important, students' computational skills have been steadily eroding for decades. SAT scores, which measure basic mathematical skills, have recently sunk to all-time lows.

2

235

Being able to compute is an important skill. Knowing how numbers behave is useful even in some branches of advanced mathematics. Previous generations of students have gained a "feel" for numbers by working with them manually. It is hard to see how this knowledge can be gained by pushing buttons and watching answers magically appear on liquid crystal displays. Moreover, how will students know the answers they obtain by calculators are correct if they cannot verify these answers by hand? If the wrong numbers are punched in or the right numbers are entered in the wrong order, the calculator will give an incorrect answer. "Garbage in, garbage out," as they say in the computer field.

The dangers of calculators in the exam room far outweigh any supposed benefits. I see nothing wrong, however, with their use in upper-level math courses such as trigonometry or calculus, where computational competence can (one hopes) be assumed. Nor do I see anything wrong with their use in nonmathematics courses that entail complex calculations; chemistry is a prime example.

I am not against machines' doing some of our thinking for us; I just want to be sure we don't forget how to think altogether. Of course, not all technology does away with thinking, and therein lies a potential compromise. Before cheap electronic calculators became commonplace, students used the slide rule. And before the slide rule, there was the abacus. To benefit from the technology of *these* calculators, however, students still had to think. To use an abacus, you had to keep in mind the number system; to use a slide rule, you had to estimate and think in terms of logarithms and decimal places. For students who want to avoid "mindless" computation, I wholeheartedly recommend allowing the use of either of these humble yet effective anachronisms.

3

NOTE CARDS, TYPING, AND WORD PROCESSORS: NUTS AND BOLTS

Everyone has special writing preferences. Some students love note cards; others prefer legal pads. Some students feel that using a pen and paper helps them think; others have no problem with typing. (Personally, I alternate between legal pads and my word processor as I write).

Find out what methods work best for you. Having said that, I offer the following observations based on long experience:

- **Use a pen rather than a pencil.** It will be easier on your eyes and won't smudge as much.

- **If you take notes on 3-by-5 cards, write the general subject on top.** Later you can sort and group these titles and get a basic structure for your essay.

- **Do all your writing in the first draft stage on one side only of each sheet of paper.** That way you'll be able to spread out your note cards or paper on a desk and see everything at once. I like taping outlines to the wall in front of my desk so I can refer to them as I write. Some people put sentence ideas on Post-it notes, which they then arrange and rearrange on a wall or bulletin board.

- **If you don't know how to type, learn.** Typed papers are easier to read and convey an air of professionalism. I don't know of any conclusive studies of this, but I'd be willing to bet that neatly typing a paper is worth half a grade or more.

- **Word processors and computers are a godsend.** As someone who swore by pen and legal pad, I dismissed word processors for years. But I finally gave in. Word processors allow you to get your thoughts down on paper quickly and then edit them later. And you'll never have to retype anything. Rearranging sentences, changing words, and correcting typos are a snap. In fact, one of the disadvantages of word processors is that it's too easy to change what you've written! You can spend ten minutes deciding where to place a single comma in a sentence. Such perfectionism can add hours of time to the rewriting process. Another danger is that in cutting and pasting chunks of words, you will inadvertently leave gaps or forget to include needed transitions in that draft.

NOTE CARDS, TYPING, AND WORD PROCESSORS: NUTS AND BOLTS (CONTINUED)

- **If you use a word processor, get a surge protector and save your document frequently.** It's not a bad idea to print out a hard copy every once in a while, too. Once a friend accidentally tripped over the power cord to my computer. Zap—ten hours of work lost forever! Now I save my documents every few paragraphs, or whenever I need to stop and think. At the end of each session, back up your document on another floppy disk. If your hard drive crashes, even saved documents can be destroyed. (If this happens, don't touch a thing! Immediately call one of your techie friends to look over the damage. Sometimes it's possible to retrieve information you've accidentally "erased.")

GETTING IT DONE ON TIME

Don't procrastinate. While writing under pressure can help focus your ideas and lend a certain forcefulness to your prose, I don't recommend waiting until the last minute for every assignment. All-nighters take their toll.

Teachers usually specify the approximate number of words or pages they expect your papers to be. My personal rule of thumb is to allow at least two days for every page (250 to 300 words), but your rate may be different. Don't be too optimistic, and leave some room for the inevitable screwups. However long you think it will take you, double that estimate to be on the safe side.

It's a good idea to start investigating the topic at the earliest possible moment, even if you think it won't take long. Getting a head start allows you to see what you're up against and gets your thinking process started.

WHEN YOU GET YOUR PAPER BACK

Review your teacher's comments so you can improve your performance on your next paper, even if you got an A! Did your teacher point out any issues or questions that your paper overlooked? What was your paper's chief weakness—the ideas, the facts, or the style?

If you disagree with the grade your paper received, request a meeting with the teacher. You can do this even if you think the grade is fair. For a more complete discussion of how to handle this situation, see page 198.

WHAT'S COMING UP

I think a break is in order. The next *Intermission* covers some of the tools you'll need in your smart student arsenal.

SUMMARY

This has been a long, possibly overwhelming chapter. You may be wondering if you really have to go through all that to write a paper. Remember, though, that academic writing demands a very specific style. The seven-step writing process smart students use will guide you there.

You begin by choosing an interesting topic. It should be something that can be asked as a question—controversial but not too controversial.

Steps 2 and 3 ask you to brainstorm as many ideas about your topic as you can, and then to organize these ideas into a coherent structure. You may have noticed that this process has much in common with several CyberLearning questions.

Step 4 asks you to find your opinion: should calculators be used in classrooms or shouldn't they?

Step 5 asks you to find specific arguments to back up your opinion; counter arguments as well as supporting arguments are vital to academic writing.

Not until Step 6 do you write the first draft, but by now you've done the hard work. You just need to put your thoughts in place according to our blueprint.

Finally, in Step 7, you put on the polish, editing and proofreading your final version.

You'll soon find, by the way, that the seven-step process isn't so much work after all. Like most techniques in this book, it will quickly become habitual and make your writing assignments much easier. As always, smart students don't waste time.

Don't forget to stick to our blueprint for academic essays. Your teachers expect a certain formula. If your paper matches up to the standard academic model your teachers are looking for, they will have no choice but to give you high marks. It works. Use it. Once you've mastered the basic formula and all your papers are receiving A's, you can attempt more sophisticated variations.

Intermission:

Other Skills and Resources
You'll Need as a Smart Student

TOOLS OF THE TRADE

As a smart student, you'll need a few reference books and other resources. Some of these are "must" items; others are strongly recommended:

- **A good, hardcover dictionary.** Look for a college edition that includes etymology as well as a discussion of synonyms for important words. Ideally it should also include illustrative sentences and discuss proper usage. *Webster's Tenth New Collegiate Dictionary* (by Merriam Webster), *The Random House Webster's College Dictionary,* and *The American Heritage Dictionary* are excellent choices. *The Oxford English Dictionary,* or *OED,* is the mother of all dictionaries. English and literature majors will need to refer to it, but for most students the *OED* is unwieldy and expensive. You might also want to get a cheap paperback version to carry around. I recommend *The American Heritage Dictionary* (based on the second college edition) and *Funk & Wagnalls Standard Dictionary* since they include etymology, but even paperbacks that can fit in your jeans' hip pocket are okay in a pinch. (Note: Merriam Webster publishes an outstanding dictionary and thesaurus; don't confuse them with other "Webster's" dictionaries—anybody can publish a Webster's dictionary since the name is not copyrightable.)

- **A good thesaurus.** A good thesaurus lists more than a few synonyms for each word and also includes antonyms, slang, and related words. Get one that lists words in alphabetical order rather than the original Roget classification scheme. *Webster's Dictionary of Synonyms* (by Merriam Webster) is my personal favorite since it distinguishes between synonyms and gives illustrative sentences.

- **A usage guide.** The problem with most dictionary definitions is that they do not have enough space to tell you precisely how a word can and cannot be used. The classic *Fowler's Modern English Usage, The Dictionary of Contemporary Usage* by William and Mary Morris, and *Webster's Dictionary of English Usage* are highly recommended.

- **A general one-volume encyclopedia.** This isn't absolutely necessary, but it comes in handy and saves trips to the library. Many are surprisingly complete considering their size. Check them out and choose one that suits your needs. They aren't adequate for serious research, but they're helpful for looking up things quickly when you don't want to lose your train of thought. You can also find paperback encyclopedias for individual subjects from philosophy to art history.

- **A style guide.** You'll need to refer to one when you type the final draft of serious papers. *The Chicago Manual of Style* is popular; look also for *Webster's Standard American Style Manual.* Since each teacher has different style preferences and since you won't need to refer to a style guide that often, you may want to save your money and use one in the library.

- **A grammar guide.** Your grammar (as well as your vocabulary) is an important skill. If you're going to be a smart student, you'd better speak and write like one! Unfortunately, most students are turned off by grammar sometime in the fourth or fifth grade by books that use words and phrases like *antecedent, copulative verb,* and *predicate nominative.* Finding a book that explains grammar without such jargon isn't easy, so use one that at least offers numerous paired examples of correct and incorrect usage. By seeing enough such examples you can figure out the rules without needing to wade through Greek terminology.

IF YOU CAN AFFORD ONE, GET A COMPUTER

Prices seem to drop almost weekly, and student discounts are frequently available. You can get a complete system—with printer—for under $1,000. I realize that's not chump change, but it's an investment that will last years. Laptops are somewhat more expensive, but the portability is sometimes worth it if you do a lot of work in the library or away from your desk.

With the pace of technological developments accelerating, it pays to get the latest model. Do your research and shop around for the best price. Apple computers are currently much easier to use than any DOS-based PC machine, although PC's are catching up with Windows-based software. Ask a computer jock for advice. Explain what you'll be using the computer for so you don't buy more than you need. High-end systems are rarely necessary unless you're doing graduate work in science or taking advantage of advanced graphics software.

As for software, you'll need a word processing program at the very least. If you're in college, acquaint yourself with what spreadsheet, data base, and graphics software can do; you'll be amazed.

As I recommended in the last chapter, **learn to type.** You'll have a hard time getting through high school, much less college, depending on others to type your papers. By the way, he computer uses the same keyboard as a typewriter.

WORK ON YOUR VOCABULARY *DAILY*

You simply can't know too many words. No matter what you're studying now or what profession you eventually enter, a large vocabulary is an invaluable asset. **Numerous studies have shown that a person's vocabulary is one of the most important factors in determining his or her success.**

Get started today! Don't try to set aside special time for this; vocabulary building is an excellent way to exploit the spare moments in your day. Make a point of looking up every word you don't know as soon as possible after you encounter it. You don't have to stop what you're reading; just jot down the word and look it up later.

I may as well plug my two best-selling vocabulary books: *Word Smart I* **and** *II.* The words in these books were carefully selected to include only those that are frequently found in educated usage. Each volume includes hundreds of the words you are most likely to encounter in high school and college. I you compare other vocabulary books to mine, I think you'll find mine are the most practical for students. Each book also includes a list of the words that appear most frequently on standardized tests like the SAT and GRE.

WHAT'S COMING UP

The hard work is behind you. By now you should have a firm grip on all the techniques smart students use to maximize their grades and optimize how much they learn. *Part V: How Smart Students Put It All Together* shows you how to minimize the time all this will take.

How Smart Students Put It All Together

How Smart Students Manage Their Time

GETTING YOUR WORK DONE (SO YOU'LL HAVE TIME LEFT OVER FOR A LIFE)

If your success in school is all up to you—and it is—you'd better plan to make it happen. You are assigned a lot of schoolwork, and the workload increases every year. Getting everything done without being overwhelmed requires a systematic approach that includes hard work, discipline, planning, and prioritizing.

It doesn't take an iron will. Acquiring effective, and often easy, little habits and routines can make the hard work a lot easier. It can also make big differences in your academic performance. Smart students are willing to work hard, but they don't want to work any harder than necessary. They are always looking for more efficient ways to learn. Everything they do in school is done with some purpose or goal in mind.

Planning means gathering information, looking ahead, and taking in the big picture—the long view. You must be flexible and willing to invest some time and energy in the short term in order to save a lot of time and energy in the long run. Planning is especially important in college. First, you have more work than in high school. Second, without the threat of daily pop quizzes, the temptation to procrastinate is all the greater. And since less of your time is structured than in high school, it's easier to goof off.

Smart students know how to set academic priorities, and they budget their time accordingly. **Of course, the real reason you should manage your time is so that you'll have more of it to pursue your own interests.** Your outside interests, in turn, will provide some structure to your daily and weekly activities that will help get your schoolwork done. It's true: as long as you're not overloaded with after-school activities, the busier you are, the more you get done! If you're an athlete or if you take part in some other seasonal activity, you've probably found to your surprise that it's harder to keep up with your assignments when the season is over. Somehow all that extra time you have on your hands just gets wasted.

In this chapter I'll show you how to harness all the elements of CyberLearning into a systematic approach that will save you time and energy. Remember: smart students don't work any harder than necessary to get the job done.

Work expands so as to fill the time available for its completion. General recognition of this fact is shown in the proverbial phrase "It is the busiest man who has time to spare."

C. NORTHCOTE
PARKINSON

HOW *NOT* TO PLAN YOUR TIME

Some students try to map out each minute of the day with schedules that look something like this:

	MON	TUE	WED	THUR	FRI	SAT	SUN
7:00 am	shower & breakfast	shower & breakfast	shower & breakfast	shower & breakfast	shower & breakfast	sleep	sleep
8:00am	study english	read newspaper	study english	read newspaper	study english	sleep	sleep
9:00 am	ENGLISH	study biology	ENGLISH	study biology	ENGLISH	sleep	sleep
10:00am	ALGEBRA	BIOLOGY	ALGEBRA	BIOLOGY	ALGEBRA	dance class	sleep
11:00am	review algebra	freetime	review algebra	BIOLOGY	review algebra	dance class	sleep
12:00 pm	lunch	lunch	lunch	lunch	lunch	lunch	brunch
1:00 pm	study history	prepare bio lab	study history	review biology	study history	photo-graphy	brunch
2:00pm	HISTORY	BIO LAB	HISTORY	freetime	HISTORY	photo-graphy	community service
3:00pm	study italian	BIO LAB 3:30 LIT. SEM.	study italian	debate team	study italian	darkroom	community service
4:00 pm	ITALIAN	literature seminar	ITALIAN	debate team	ITALIAN	darkroom	homework
5:00 pm	photo-graphy	dance class	dance class	dance class	photo-graphy	freetime	homework
6:00pm	dinner	dinner	dinner	dinner	dinner	dinner	homework
7:00 pm	freetime	freetime	freetime	freetime	freetime	freetime	dinner
8:00pm	school newspaper	homework	school newspaper	homework	take newspaper to printer	freetime	write letters
9:00 pm	school newspaper	homework	school newspaper	homework	freetime	freetime	freetime
10:00pm	watch news & call friends	watch news & call friends	watch news & call friends	watch news & call friends	freetime	freetime	plan next week
11:00pm	sleep	sleep	sleep	sleep	freetime	freetime	sleep

There's no way anyone is going to stick to such a schedule for more than a week without going absolutely insane. You *should* try to stick to some kind of routine, but it doesn't have to be nearly so detailed and inflexible. You don't have to map out each and every minute of every day. Give yourself a break.

HERE'S WHAT YOU'LL NEED

When you're studying a subject, you have to keep your eye on the details as well as the big picture. It's the same with managing your time and planning your activities. To keep a perspective on each day, each week, and the term as a whole, you'll need the following lists and schedules:

1. **A daily "to-do" list.** Divide this into sections: must get done today, must get done soon, if I have the time. In other words, *prioritize.* Remember Smart Student Principle #3.

2. **A "clean" weekly class schedule (nothing on it but your classes).** Use a week-at-a-glance calendar. You can color-code classes, especially those that typically require special preparation.

3. **A general wall calendar.** Use this for your assignments as well as your outside interests and personal affairs.

4. **A "clean" calendar reserved exclusively for all the major tests and papers that term.** This should show the entire term at a glance, and have *nothing* on it but your scheduled papers and exams. Some students color-code different courses, papers, and exams depending on how far in advance they'll have to start preparing. Post this calendar on the wall where you'll see it every day; over your desk is a good spot. If you don't plan ahead, you'll find yourself in the last few weeks of the term trying to write two term papers while studying for three final exams (a common and unpleasant end-of-semester predicament)!

You'll find these calendar items at any store that sells stationery or school supplies, or you can make up your own.

MEETING DEADLINES

Everyone—and I mean *everyone*—underestimates how long assignments take to complete. It is especially hard to gauge completion time at the beginning of a course when you are not familiar with either the material or your teacher's workload. You'll get a better idea as the term progresses and you learn what you're up against. In the meantime, estimate how long it will take to complete a paper or lengthy assignment and then *triple* that figure. (Really.)

One of the reasons it's hard getting started on major assignments is that they seem so formidable. Here's some good advice. If you break down large tasks into manageable units and chip away at them in spare moments, you'll be amazed at how much you can accomplish in a short time.

Another benefit is that you'll be distributing the work over a longer period of time. For some reason your brain takes a certain amount of days, weeks, months, or even longer to "get" certain types of information. It's called a "learning curve," and everyone's is different (another reason why *you* are your best teacher). If you're tackling a complex assignment that will take, say, twenty hours to complete, spreading those hours out over several weeks is more efficient than trying to cram them into a long weekend.

GETTING INTO A ROUTINE

Habits and routines help structure your time and get you in the right frame of mind. Figure out how and when you study best. Some people work better during the day, others at night. Some prefer lengthy study sessions for each subject, but others learn best in short bursts. So experiment with different schedules and study conditions to find what works best for you.

Obviously one of the major things you'll have to work around is your class schedule. Some students are highly disciplined and can make use of the blocks of time between classes. If you find you need more time to "get in the groove" and the time between classes is a loss, try to schedule your classes with as little time between them as possible. I'll have more to say about class schedules in the next chapter when we discuss how to choose your courses.

Adopt a regular place of study. Personally I always found the quiet in a library maddening, where the loudest sound was the overhead buzzing of fluorescent lights. But to each his own. Just find a place where you can get your work done. You'll need a flat surface and a hard chair. You should be comfortable but not too comfortable; a little muscular tension helps keep you alert. Avoid couches, beds, and soft chairs—studying is hard enough without the temptation of falling asleep.

How long you study in a given session will depend on any number of factors—the subject, your energy level, whether you're preparing for an exam, and so on. You'll have to find out what works best for you. It takes me a while to get in the groove; I am much more efficient in the second hour than the first. Generally, however, an hour or two is the maximum you should spend studying any subject before switching to another.

Two important exceptions to this rule are when you are studying for a major exam or when you are writing a paper. In both cases you have to juggle vast amounts of information and complete a number of steps at almost the same time. In such situations the more time you can spend in one sitting the better.

When you sit down to study, don't wait to be inspired. Clear away any potential distractions from your desk and get down to business. You won't always be in the mood, but it's your responsibility to learn. Once you've been at it for half an hour or so, you'll find yourself absorbed in your work. Getting started is the hardest part, but there's no getting through without it. As the folks at Nike say, "Just do it!"

If you really can't concentrate, switch to a different subject or take a break. **Don't take breaks for more than five or ten minutes, or you'll lose your concentration level.** And don't think that every break means calling a friend or putting on your headset and listening to some music. This is the kind of break (in concentration) you don't need. You can lower the intensity level and continue to review the material while munching on a sandwich or whatever.

HOW YOU CAN PICK UP AN EXTRA DAY EACH WEEK!

Routines are important, but so is flexibility. Don't wait for the ideal conditions to work (because you'll be waiting forever). If you're like most people, you probably waste five or ten minutes an hour. That's one or two hours every day. Assuming that the workday is eight to twelve hours long, the average person wastes one day a week!

You may not be aware of this time because it doesn't fizzle away in one big chunk. Rather, it's the total of lots of short moments throughout the day: waiting for the bus, waiting for the teacher to arrive, traveling to school, standing in a movie line.

Win back these wasted moments by using them to

- chip away at lengthy reading assignments;
- memorize information;
- jot down thoughts for a writing assignment;
- update or review your summary sheets;
- work on your vocabulary.

Make sure you're always carrying a pen and something you can work on during such moments. Some smart students even prepare their own flash cards. You'll be surprised how valuable this reclaimed time will prove to be.

I'm not saying that you should be obsessed with getting something done by utilizing each and every spare moment in your day. Some moments should be wasted. Relax. Daydream. Whatever. But do become aware of how much time you now fritter away unintentionally.

THE 80-20 RULE AGAIN

The 80-20 rule advises you to figure out the few important things that must get done and make sure you get them done first. If you give everything the same time and energy, you'll be wasting time on unimportant matters and shortchanging the important ones. **Learn to set course priorities or you'll never get everything important done on time.**

HERE'S YOUR GAME PLAN FOR EACH WEEK

You may not be able to stick to this schedule, but here's the ideal:

- *Before* each class you should review your notes from the previous class as well as the assigned reading.
- *After* each class, or as soon as possible, you should combine your class and reading notes (page 93).
- At *least* once a week you should consolidate your notes and update your summary sheet (pages 122-125).

Tackling what you know you have to do incrementally is manageable; confronting a large block of neglected work is overwhelming.

My father must have had some elementary education for he could read and write and keep accounts inaccurately.
GEORGE BERNARD SHAW

HERE'S YOUR GAME PLAN FOR THE TERM

The beginning and end of each term are critical; make sure you work during these times. Most students float through the first few weeks of school, figuring that the hard stuff will come later. True enough, but it's during the first few weeks that the groundwork is established and your teachers make up their minds about what kind of student you are. You can have this bias working for you or against you for the rest of the term. Don't blow off the first month of school!

Before the term begins, you should have

- started checking out what courses you intend to take so you don't enter a course four lectures in (pages 255-260).

In the first few weeks of the term, you should have

- worked out the expert questions (pages 67-68);
- found at least one supplementary source of information (pages 60-61);
- created your initial summary sheet (page 122);
- discovered whether copies of your teacher's previous exams are on file somewhere (page 179);
- gotten an overview of the entire course (pages 122-123);
- signed up for an extra course or two (page 259);
- made up your mind about the courses you want to take or which ones you might want to change during the drop-add period (page 259).

By the last few weeks of term, you should have

- reduced your summary sheet to one page (page 124);
- begun preparations for your final exam (pages 177-184);
- decided what courses you want to take next term and, if necessary, contacted the appropriate teachers or department heads (page 259).

SUMMARY

Smart students strike a balance between routine and flexibility. Daily to-do lists and a calendar of the semester are absolutely necessary. You need to prioritize your responsibilities so you get the important stuff completed on time. You should also know when your major assignments and tests are coming, and allow plenty of space to prepare.

On the other hand, you can go way too far with schedules. Flexibility allows you to use unexpected bits of time—and allows you to keep your sanity. Once you get into the habit of exploiting all the spare moments that now go to waste, your workload will seemingly take care of itself. Remember: smart students are able to get their work done with plenty of time left over to have a life.

The last point we listed above—deciding what courses you want to take—is our next topic.

How Smart Students
Choose Their Courses and Teachers

CHOOSING YOUR COURSES IS AN ART

I don't care how smart you are—if you take a course you're not ready for or one taught by the wrong instructor, you're asking for trouble. And yet some students give less thought to their choice of courses than they do to making a selection from the menu at a fast-food restaurant. One of the reasons smart students do so well is the considerable thought they give to planning their curriculum.

A student should not be taught more than he can think about.
ALFRED NORTH WHITEHEAD

Don't expect your adviser or anyone else to do this for you. Nobody has quite your perspective or interest in you. What's more, to plan your curriculum for this term means looking ahead at least for the next year or two!

THERE'S A LOT TO CONSIDER

At the beginning or end of every semester, depending when the sign-up period is, you are faced with the traditional question, "What courses should I take next term?" When you ask for advice, the typical suggestions generally run something like this:

- "Take courses you're interested in; don't worry about whether they're practical." versus "Hey, you've got to be practical—take courses that fit in with your future career goals."

- "Go for courses that challenge you." versus "Stay away from courses that might lower your grade point average."

- "The whole point of a liberal education is to take a wide variety of courses; you never know what you'll become interested in." versus "The important thing is to concentrate your courses in a specific area; be sure you're an expert at something."

As general guidelines, there's some truth in all this conflicting advice. You should take courses that interest you; but you should also be practical. You should take courses that challenge you, but you should also keep an eye on your grade point average. You *should* take a variety of courses, but you should also specialize in something so that you have a strong point.

But there's a lot more to the decision process than these considerations. In addition to the course's subject matter, you've got to consider the following:

- **the instructor's teaching style**
- **your graduation or other course requirements**
- **the various grading options**

- when and how often the class meets
- whether the course fits into your schedule
- whether you should take the course this term or later
- whether you can handle the course workload on top of all your other courses.

Knowing how to choose your courses and teachers is a vital skill. You have many more options once you get to college, but even in high school you have some serious choices to make. In this chapter I'll show you what questions you need to answer and how to go about making an informed decision. (The previous chapter—*How Smart Students Manage Their Time*—contains some information relevant to choosing courses, so you may want to review it briefly.)

DOES THIS COURSE HELP YOU MEET YOUR GRADUATION REQUIREMENTS?

Whether you're in high school or college, you must satisfy certain course requirements to graduate. You may be required to take a certain number of core courses, as well as meet distribution requirements. In college, your major will require still other courses. Courses that satisfy requirements get priority over electives.

HAVE YOU TAKEN THE REQUIRED COURSES FOR THIS CLASS?

To take calculus, for example, the instructor will expect you to have completed advanced algebra and trigonometry. These official requirements are generally published in the course guides, or you'll find out in the introductory lecture. Some instructors will exempt you from requirements if you convince them you can handle the work (can you?), but check with the head of the department first.

ARE YOU *READY* TO TAKE THIS COURSE?

Just because you've taken the required courses for a class and done well in them does not mean you're ready to take the class. Those mandatory requirements should be treated as *minimum* requirements because it often helps to have taken still other courses to increase your understanding of the material. Most calculus courses, for example, do not require students to have taken physics. If you haven't, however, you're at a distinct disadvantage since many of the examples in class are taken from physics. You've also got to watch out for courses recent for majors of a certain field. If it's not your field, the pace and competition in such classes can be brutal.

These "quasi" requirements are rarely mentioned either by the instructor or in the course catalog. You'll get some idea if you look at the course textbook, but your best bet is to ask students who've already taken the course. Start with courses you know something about and build from there. If you've never taken an art course and you're considering taking Renaissance Art, it would help if you've taken a history course that covered the Renaissance.

WHAT ARE YOUR GRADING OPTIONS?

How are grades determined? Is there a curve? How strict is it? Should you audit this class? Should you take it pass/fail?

WHAT'S THE TEACHER LIKE?

What is the instructor's teaching style? Does he or she communicate well? Brilliant professors do not necessarily make engaging or even understandable lecturers (and keep in mind that in college many of your classes may be taught by teaching assistants). Is the instructor organized? Beware the teacher, for example, who has a history of falling behind the syllabus schedule and yet holds the class responsible on the final for topics that were never covered.

How demanding is he or she? Is the instructor fair when it comes to grades? How tough are the standards? (See pages 258-259 for tips on using course guides and other clues to a teacher's reputation.)

Finally, do you *like* the teacher? Sometimes there's a personality clash or something else that just rubs you the wrong way. I once had to drop a great course in college because the professor spoke in-an-ag-on-iz-ing-ly-slow-mon-o-tone-that-was-driv-ing-me-cra-zy.

WHAT ARE THE CLASS DYNAMICS LIKE?

Do you care how many students are in the class? Are they encouraged to ask questions and participate in discussions? Is the instructor accessible after class for students who need extra help?

HOW DEMANDING IS THE COURSE?

Each subject presents different kinds of demands on your time, energy, and intellectual resources. Chemistry classes require lab work; literature courses require heavy reading; art and architecture courses require studio time; language and music classes require a lot of practice. You'll recall from the exercise you did on page 142 that there are certain types of subjects you have an affinity for and those to which you have an aversion. Even if you find it easy to learn problem-solving techniques, for example, it's probably not a good idea to take algebra, physics, and a computer science course all in the same term.

In addition to a subject's demands, there is the workload of the particular course and instructor. How much reading or homework is assigned? How many papers and tests are required, and what type?

By the way, introductory classes are typically the most demanding of all! The subject is unfamiliar, there's new terminology to master, classes are usually larger and more impersonal, and grading is usually based on a strict curve. Sometimes teachers and department heads are trying to see which students are serious enough to stick it out and possibly become majors. Don't give up on a subject on the basis of the first course you take in it.

HOW WILL IT AFFECT YOUR OVERALL COURSE LOAD?

Consider how your total workload will stack up with this course. You should try to balance, for example, the number of courses that require final papers with those that require final exams. If you don't, you'll find yourself overwhelmed trying to prepare for five finals during the last few weeks of the term. Papers can be finished earlier in the term or if you have to you can possibly take an incomplete or work out an extension, leaving you more time to concentrate on preparing for your exams during the crunch period.

WHEN AND WHERE SHOULD YOU TAKE THE COURSE?

Should you take it during the regular school year or in summer school? Be aware that summer school courses can be particularly difficult. You're cramming months of work into a few week, so watch out—class has barely started before you're taking your final exam. Be prepared to give up a lot of your vacation time to studying. The flip side, of course, is that you'll be able to concentrate on one or two courses.

Also, your school may allow you to take courses at other schools. If your school doesn't offer a class you need at a time when you can take it, shop around.

CAN YOU FIT IT INTO YOUR SCHEDULE?

Once you decide on the courses you want to take, you've got to do some juggling to see whether you can fit it into your schedule. There's bound to be some scheduling conflict among all the classes you want to take. So it's a good idea to narrow your search to a few *more* courses than you intend to take. This way you can drop one or two that you can't squeeze in. Consider also the time of day the class meets. If you're a late riser, you may just have to pass on that early-morning course you were really looking forward to taking, The Comic Book as American Literature. Maybe next semester it will be given in the afternoon.

Finally, keep in mind how your overall schedule will look. Some smart students prefer spreading their courses out so they'll have time to study in between classes, while others prefer keeping their class schedule as compact as possible so they can get into either class or study mode.

DOING THE DETECTIVE WORK

Faculty members such as teachers, department heads, or even your college adviser can provide some general guidance, but you'll have to look elsewhere for the information you need. Descriptions in course catalogs are about as helpful as advertisements in the Yellow Pages.

See if your high school or college has a course handbook written by students. These "inside guides" can be ruthlessly accurate. If your school doesn't have one, ask students who have already taken the course you are considering. Students who have taken *other* courses by the same instructor can also provide useful insights.

Remember that courses and instructors can change from one year to the next, so your information can become dated. If a teacher is too easy one year, he or she may decide to get tough the next—possibly in reaction to a "gut" rating in the student course guide!

Finally, check things out for yourself. Sit in on the class the previous semester if the course is a "definite maybe." Get a copy of the syllabus, the reading list, and even previous exams.

START YOUR SEARCH EARLY

You'll have to plan ahead. By the first day of classes, and certainly by the end of the first week, you should have made up your mind.

The best courses and instructors can have long waiting lists. It sometimes helps to contact the instructor a term or even a year before you consider taking the class. If there's any problem getting in, you now have an ally.

SIGN UP FOR AN EXTRA CLASS OR TWO

Most schools have a drop-add period during the first few weeks of a semester during which you can switch classes. Since you can never be completely sure beforehand, some smart students make a habit of signing up for an extra class so that they can drop the one they like least. In this way they're sure they won't get shut out of a class that they might want to take.

(True Story: One smart student at a famous Ivy League school which begins with "H" found herself trying out an exciting course in astrophysics. The professor wore costumes, told jokes constantly, and showed film clips from Star Trek episodes. She decided to remain in the course. The *day* after the drop-add period, the professor lowered the boom on everyone. He put away the film projector, pulled down the blackboard, and began writing complex equations. The moral of the story is that some teachers don't always play fair—do your detective work!)

You teach your daughters the diameters of the planets, and wonder when you have done that they don't delight in your company.

SAMUEL JOHNSON

IF YOU DON'T GET WHAT YOU WANT

Sometimes you find yourself stuck in a class after the drop-add period has ended. You still have options. If you don't like your teacher, you can possibly sit in on another class or try transferring to a different section. If the class is too difficult, speak to the teacher. If necessary, take up your case with the department head, the principal, or the ombudsman. If you can't drop the class, consider the pass-fail option if you have a really bad feeling about a class or teacher.

WHAT'S COMING UP

One more *Attitude Check* and then a final (brief!) look back over what we've covered.

SUMMARY

If you remember one thing from this chapter, it should be this: don't blow off course selection. There's a lot to consider: What's the professor like? Can you handle the workload during term? How will this course affect your workload during the final few weeks of school? And so on.

Being careless and taking one wrong course can turn your entire semester into one long nightmare, so spend some time on this step. Talk to your friends and older siblings about teachers and classes. Of course, try to pick courses you're interested in. Some courses are required but most schools offer at least a few interesting and cool electives. One of these each semester could be enough to change your attitude dramatically towards the required courses.

Intermission:
Attitude Check #4

TAKE THIS QUIZ!

Time for our final attitude survey.

ATTITUDE CHECK

Instructions: For each statement below, in the space provided indicate whether you agree (1) or disagree (0) with it. One more time: choose the response that best reflects what you truly believe, not what you think is the "right" answer.

[ ] 1. From a learning point of view, much of what goes on in school seems like a complete waste of time.

[ ] 2. When a teacher asks a question in class, you are usually one of the first few students who raises his hand.

[ ] 3. When your teacher praises you, it increases your self-esteem.

[ ] 4. School is designed to maximize the potential of students.

[ ] 5. Working hard at learning is not especially satisfying, but you do it primarily because you know it's important to your career plans.

[ ] 6. You know you could do better in school but you refuse to play by its rules.

[ ] 7. You are reading this book because your parents expect you to.

[ ] 8. If grades did not go on your permanent record, you would still be interested in learning as much as you could.

The "answers" to this quiz follow a brief discussion.

SCHOOL IS A GAME

To embrace the notion that school is a game no doubt flies in the face of everything you've been told since kindergarten. You've been conditioned to believe that school is designed to promote learning, and that your grades are objective measures of how much you've learned. Somewhere along the line, however, you probably began to suspect that genuine learning is not one of the chief goals of school. In fact, you've probably discovered that it is quite possible

Intermission

to receive high grades without learning or understanding very much. You want to learn and you're frustrated that so much of school seems to prevent that.

Many students resent that school is not connected in any meaningful way to their lives and interests. They are angered by the lies and hypocrisy they perceive in the school system. They realize that school is one colossal game, and they refuse to play by its rules.

This is not how smart students respond. But how do you stay interested in something when you're not interested? While smart students realize that school is a game, they also realize that playing it well will have a significant impact on their life. Even though school is not a situation of your choosing, you now know ways to make it relevant to your interests and goals. It isn't always possible, however, to relate to every subject you are studying. Still, school is a game you can't avoid playing. You can't take it too seriously, but never forget its serious consequences. I know this isn't easy while you're in school but try to keep it in perspective.

WHY SMART STUDENTS PLAY THE GAME

The most important motive for work in the school and in life is the pleasure in the work, pleasure in the result, and the knowledge of the value of the result to the community. In the awakening and strengthening of these psychological forces in the young person, I see the most important task given by the school. Such a psychological foundation alone leads to a joyous desire for the highest possessions of men: knowledge and artist-like workmanship.

ALBERT EINSTEIN

"Motivation" is a reason people frequently cite when discussing how well students do in school. Students who do well are considered "highly motivated," whereas those who don't do as well are less motivated, and those who do poorly are dismissed as "unmotivated."

But the motivation factor explanation misses the point: all students are motivated; the question is, what are they motivated to do? If you observe infants or young children, you notice that curiosity and a desire to learn are natural human traits. Every individual is motivated to learn, to make sense of his or her world. The fact that many students are not so motivated to be told what and how to learn is another matter.

Why do you want to do well in school—to please your teacher, to impress your classmates, to satisfy your parents, to get into a good college, to get a good job? These reasons are well and good, but they should not be your primary goals. The bottom line is that doing well should make *you* feel good.

The best work is done for the love of it, not for external rewards like praise or grades. You should want to learn to please yourself, not others. Unfortunately, too many students are motivated by external factors. Ironically, those students who depend on external rewards such as grades or acceptance are less likely to achieve them than are students who see excellence as its own reward. Working for high marks or teachers' praise puts your self-image and self-esteem at the mercy of things outside your control.

Of course, it's a kick getting straight A's or becoming the class valedictorian. But if you're working hard for external factors like those, you haven't yet learned a principal messages of this book: the learning process itself should absorb you to the point where you are no longer aware of external considerations. There is simply no way you can be asking the twelve questions actively while you're also wondering what your teacher thinks or what kind of grades you'll be getting.

The irony is that students who worry about these things aren't doing what they need to do to achieve them! Lose yourself in the learning process *completely.* I promise that the grades and the approval of the people you care about will follow automatically.

"ANSWERS" TO ATTITUDE CHECK #4

Smart student responses are in brackets.

1. From a learning point of view, much of what goes on in school seems like a complete waste of time.

   [1] Not only seems, much of it *is* a complete waste of time. **Remember Smart Student Principle #12: School is a game, but it's a very important game.**

2. When a teacher asks a question in class, you are usually one of the first few students who raises his hand.

   [0] How much thought can students who raise their hands immediately have given to the question? More often than not these are the students who are most desperate for the teacher's approval. **Remember Smart Student Principle #11: If you're doing it for the grades or for the approval of others, you're missing the satisfactions of the process and putting your self-esteem at the mercy of things outside your control.**

3. When your teacher praises you, it increases your self-esteem.

   [0] Praise is a double-edged sword. Teachers mean well by it, of course, but the result is often making students dependent on it. Your sense of self-worth should come from inside, not outside. As a smart student, you work hard because you find the hard work of learning profoundly rewarding, not because you've gotten a gold star or a pat on the head.

4. School is designed to maximize the potential of students.

   [0] I'll bet you didn't have to give this one a lot of thought.

5. Working hard at learning is not especially satisfying, but you do it primarily because you know it's important to your career plans.

[0] Doing well in school *is* important to your future career plans, but as a smart student you know how to redesign your school experience so you are extracting satisfaction *today*. You're not going to last too long if school is something you're tolerating solely for the sake of some long-term goal. **Remember Smart Student Principle #8: Subjects do not always seem interesting and relevant, but being actively engaged in learning them is better than being passively bored and not learning them.**

6. You know you could do better in school but you refuse to play by its rules.

[0] As a smart student, you now know how to do well in school on its terms as well as your own. **Remember Smart Student Principle #12.**

7. You are reading this book because your parents expect you to.

[0] Perhaps you started that way, but I sincerely hope that you've finished it for yourself.

8. If grades did not go on your permanent record, you would still be interested in learning as much as you could.

[1] You might not be interested in learning the way school insists, but you would be interested in learning. **Remember Smart Student Principle #11.**

A Parting Look at What Smart Students Know

YOU'VE COME A LONG WAY

In the beginning, as a smart student-in-training, you may feel as if you're putting in more time and effort. You will be. You're still learning the finer points of a whole new approach to school and putting it into action. You're also experiencing a radical shift in your perception of your teachers and yourself.

Change is hard and we resist it. But if you stick with CyberLearning, in a short while you'll see a vast improvement in how much you learn and the grades you receive. If you've gotten this far, you've got the drive it takes to be a smart student. It may take some time for you to become comfortable with all the techniques, but the hard part is over. As learning becomes easier and your grades improve, you'll move from one success to the next.

ONCE MORE WITH FEELING: ATTITUDE + TECHNIQUE = SMART STUDENT

I've certainly presented you with a lot to digest. You may be wondering whether you'll remember all the tips, techniques, and strategies in the coming weeks and months.

Don't worry if you can't remember all the techniques—the important thing is that you see yourself as a smart student. **Attitude is much more important than technique.** Once you see yourself as a smart student, you'll act and learn like one.

Before we close, let's take one final look at the Twelve Principles.

Principle #1: Nobody Can Teach You as Well as You Can Teach Yourself

Because you know this, you control any learning situation. While teachers tell you *what* you have to learn, *how* you learn that material is your business. You adapt situations to your learning needs, not the other way around. No teacher, no matter how gifted or dedicated, knows how you think and process information better than you do.

Principle #2: Merely Listening to Your Teachers and Completing Their Assignments Is *Never* Enough

Because you know this, you do whatever it takes to learn the material in a course. Think of your teachers and assignments as the framework around which true personalized learning is built. You are constantly on the lookout for new and better sources of information and new and better ways to learn. After all, that's why you worked your way through this book.

Principle #3: Not Everything You Are Assigned to Read or Asked to Do Is Equally Important

Because you know this, you set priorities and plan ahead. You budget your time and focus on the most important tasks on your agenda. And you apply this principle to your studying as well. You know the value of concentrating your learning efforts on the most important aspects of a course rather than becoming overwhelmed by trying to absorb everything.

Principle #4: Grades Are Just Subjective Opinions

Because you know this, you don't get overly upset with bad grades (or overly excited by good ones). Besides, you're not in it for the grades (Principle #11). Since grades are important, you also make it a point to get to know the personal likes, dislikes, and biases of the person who decides them—your teacher. But doing the best you possibly can—mastering a subject to the best of your ability—is your true goal.

Principle #5: Making Mistakes (and Occasionally Appearing Foolish) Is the Price You Pay for Learning and Improving

And it's a price you're more than willing to pay. In the learning process, mistakes are as important as successes. Young children have a nearly unlimited aptitude for learning owing to their willingness to make mistakes. Observe them some time.

Principle #6: The Point of a Question Is to Get You to Think—*Not* Simply to Answer It

Because you know this, you are always looking for different perspectives, different answers, and different methods to solve problems. You see questions as challenges, not threats, and you approach obvious answers with skepticism.

Principle #7: You're in School to Learn to Think for Yourself, Not to Repeat What Your Textbooks and Teachers Tell You

I respect faith, but doubt is what gives you an education.
WILSON MIZNER

Because you know this, you take nothing at face value. You question everything, especially authority and most especially yourself. And I hope you've questioned the ideas I've presented in this book. Only through constant challenging and reaching beyond limitations does anyone learn anything of significance.

Principle #8: Subjects Do Not Always Seem Interesting or Relevant, but Being Actively Engaged in Learning Them Is Better Than Being Passively Bored and Not Learning Them

Because you know this, you are willing, even eager, to learn things that other students might find boring. Few things are boring to you. You may not be interested in the subject, but you are always interested in your questions about it. If you are bored or distracted in class, you realize it means you aren't learning—and you do something about it. You know that learning is an ongoing dialogue and investigation, and that you must uphold your end or discovery comes to a screeching halt.

Principle #9: Few Things Are as Potentially Difficult, Frustrating, or Frightening as Genuine Learning, Yet *Nothing* Is So Empowering

Again, it's a price you're more than willing to pay. Learning does not end when the bell rings or you grab your diploma. It literally is the stuff of life. The alternative to questioning, grasping, and moving forward every day of your life is much more restful but far less exciting and gratifying. It takes courage and hard work to tackle the unknown, but each time you do it will be easier and less frightening—and soon you'll be hooked.

Principle #10: How Well You Do in School Reflects Your Attitude and Your Method, Not Your Ability

Because you know this, you don't take academic mistakes or disappointments personally. There's nothing wrong with you; it's just your attitude or method that needs adjusting. The material is the material; there will always be something you don't understand. You are what is constantly changing. Once you begin to see all classes and topics as within your control, you can work on fine-tuning what you must do to master them.

Principle #11: If You're Doing It for the Grades or for the Approval of Others, You're Missing the Satisfaction of the Process and Putting Your Self-Esteem at the Mercy of Things Outside Your Control

Because you know this, you work hard for yourself first. Of course it's nice to get good grades and to impress those who care about you. But that can't be why you work so hard. You work hard and you excel because it makes you feel good, and because you realize that you alone will live with the consequences of your education. Praise is great but its flip side is disapproval, which can derail learning and undermine your sense of yourself and your abilities. As a smart student you know that true gratification—like true learning—is something that comes from within.

Principle #12: School Is a Game, but It's a Very Important Game

Because you know this, you keep everything in perspective. Even though you know that a lot of what goes on at school has nothing to do with learning, you play the game anyway. And you play to win.

WHY I REALLY WROTE THIS BOOK

Our entire school system is based on the notion of passive students that must be "taught" if they are to learn. Unfortunately, most students have become indoctrinated with this insidious message. So they sit patiently (or not so patiently) in class, waiting for their teacher to give them an education. They listen to what their teachers say and they do what their teachers tell them to do. And they wonder why they aren't learning much and why their grades aren't as high as they'd like. The result, on a national level, is a steady erosion of academic standards for the past few decades.

This is the first book that shows students what it means to learn. I wrote it to free students from their over-reliance on teachers by showing you how to teach yourself. This is also the first book that recognizes that learning tools are useless unless students have the courage to accept responsibility for learning, and are willing to put in the hard work that genuine learning entails. Once you've internalized the Twelve Principles, you'll be ready to take charge of your own education.

Look, the real reason I wrote this book is that I hate what school does to students. Our country spends tens of billions of dollars each year not just giving students a second-rate education, but at the same time actively preventing them from getting an education on their own. And I'm angry at how school produces submissive students with battered egos. Most students have no idea of the true joys of learning, and of how much they can actually achieve on their own.

I wrote this book to give you some idea of your true potential. I wrote this book to set you free.

THE CENTRAL MESSAGE

Education is an admirable thing, but nothing that is worth knowing can be taught.

OSCAR WILDE

If you learn only one attitude in this book, I hope you've learned the following message. **Your success in school—your grades, how much you learn, and how you experience the process—is** *entirely* **up to you.**

Your success is your responsibility, not your teachers' and not your parents'. In the past you might have blamed your lack of interest or success in a subject on a lousy textbook or a boring teacher, but that doesn't change the fact that *you* have to finish the course. From now on there are no more excuses. No more slipping through school passively. You're going to take an active role, and you're going to do whatever it takes to learn and succeed.

WHAT'S STOPPING YOU?

You now know *everything* you need to know to excel in school. Go for it!

The Myth Behind the Education Crisis (and What's Really Wrong)

An Open Letter to Parents, Educators, Business Leaders, Politicians, and Policymakers

By now we're used to reading gloomy headline statistics of the ongoing education crisis:

SAT Scores Slump to All-Time Lows!

One High School Student in Four Now Drops Out!

Study Finds Tens of Millions of Adults Are Functionally Illiterate!

*American High Schoolers Rank Near the Bottom in Math and
Science Ability Internationally!*

With headlines like that, you'd think that parents would be worried and students would be embarrassed. Curiously, the opposite seems to be the case.

In international academic rankings, American students routinely place somewhere at the bottom of the top ten nations (okay, okay, so I exaggerated—we're not even among the top ten). Yet despite their dismal showing, our students are quite satisfied with their academic accomplishments, thank you very much. Just ask them. The Educational Testing Service did.

ETS recently conducted a national survey in which eighth-graders were asked to fill out a questionnaire before taking a math test. Many of the students who had described themselves as math "whizzes" in fact achieved abysmally low scores on the accompanying test! This gulf between actual ability (very low) and perceived ability (very high) has been confirmed by other researchers. It's got to make you wonder.

Parents are remarkably unperturbed by this state of affairs; perhaps they are simply unaware of the truth. In one survey, American parents were far more likely to report that they were "very satisfied" with their child's education than were, say, Japanese parents (whose children's academic performance, by the way, ranks near the top internationally).

Corporate leaders, however, cannot afford to be so sanguine. They see the effect of the education crisis every day firsthand—in the workplace—and they are terrified of the mounting international economic competition we face. With an undereducated work force, we're simply not equipped to fight back. Some major corporations spend millions of dollars annually just trying to teach their workers to read and write.

Did our schools produce this crisis? And if they did, where did they go wrong? One problem is that many features of a student's academic experience are dictated not by conventional educational considerations, but by political, bureaucratic, custodial, and administrative ones. With millions of students in crowded classrooms, our overworked teachers are often reduced to just keeping the peace. Workbook exercises might not enhance learning, but they do keep students quiet and busy. Multiple-choice tests might not require much intelligence, but they are certainly easy to grade. Textbooks and workbooks might not be the ideal educational vehicles, but at least we know that everyone is "learning" the same thing.

All the blame cannot be placed on teachers—many of whom, of course, are superb. Teachers are doing their best to cope with pressures from assorted parties and interest groups: parents, administrators, school boards, textbook publishers, and the testing industry, not to mention local, state, and federal governments. And to be sure, schools are struggling in socially and economically troubled times.

It's not as if all this bleak news has discouraged the optimists. Indeed, they believe that schools should reach for even loftier goals. According to some, public education should strive not merely to enhance students' intellectual development, but their personal, social, civic, and vocational development as well. Wonderful—the same schools that currently have trouble teaching students to read, write, and reason competently should also be trying to teach ethics, interpersonal relations, and career strategy. Given our school system's dismal results on the academic front, these aspirations are either astonishingly farfetched or unabashedly hypocritical, depending on your point of view.

Let's face reality—most schools are doing a terrible job. Numerous solutions and education reforms have been proposed, including the following:

- decreasing federal control over local schools
- tying teacher pay to student performance
- providing more money
- mandating a tougher curriculum of required courses
- creating a series of national standardized exams
- relying more on computers and multimedia technology
- establishing longer school years
- providing more money
- allowing "school choice"
- allowing competition from for-profit schools
- requiring minimum competency testing of students
- insisting on tougher standards for everyone
- providing more money

Take your pick.

These proposals are all well-intentioned. Most, however, will do little to raise the quality of education. Indeed, some are sure to lower it. There is no question that many schools are in desperate need of greater funding, especially those in inner cities. But money alone is not the answer.

Keep in mind that any improvements to the school system will take years to implement. Remember too that the goal of our school system has less to do with education than its institutional survival. As a bureaucracy, the school system has an interest in blocking any reform that would threaten its its monopolistic control over education. By its own institutional standards, our education system is a major success: it graduates a majority of students, and keeps itself in business.

The assumption behind most proposals for educational reform is that schools are doing an okay job. According to conventional wisdom, all schools need is a few alterations, tougher standards, more money, and some prodding from marketplace competition and they'll soon be back on track toward fulfilling their noble mission. Yet I am convinced that even if we doubled the number of teachers in the classroom tomorrow, the impact on education and academic performance for most students would be negligible.

The truth is this: our education system rests on erroneous assumptions about how students think and learn. It doesn't matter how much money is poured into schools, the vast majority of students will continue to learn little until schools overhaul their fundamental beliefs about the learning process. This is unlikely to happen any time soon.

The real myth lurking behind the education crisis is that academic standards in this country will not improve until our school system improves.

Nonsense! Tens of thousands of students manage to learn a great deal and excel, no matter what's going on in school. These are the smart students. This book shares what they have always taken for granted—that knowledge and understanding are not bestowed by the teacher, but generated by the student. Smart students aren't any "smarter" than other students. They just realize that it's their responsibility to learn. Smart students do not rely on teachers because one day they discovered a fundamental truth: nobody can teach you as well as you can teach yourself. And it wouldn't matter if all their teachers were brilliant and charismatic—smart students would *still* be teaching themselves.

Because of the way school is structured, most students see themselves as passive passengers in the learning process. They think it's the teacher's job to teach and their job to listen and learn. So they sit back and wait for learning to happen. But learning doesn't just happen—the student must make it happen.

In the classic movie *The Wizard of Oz*, Dorothy, Lion, Scarecrow, and Tin Man journey together on an odyssey to a distant land. Despite their fears, they endure hardships, overcome obstacles, and fend off great dangers. Why? Because they have heard that there is a great wizard in Oz. Once there, however, they discover that the man behind the curtain cannot grant their wishes. Instead he gives them something far more valuable: the knowledge that they were always able to get what they wanted on their own.

The message of this book is that teachers are not wizards; and that if students want to learn, they must teach themselves. To do this they must become aware of the process of learning, and of the satisfactions and empowerment it brings. If at times I sound preachy, my gospel is only that forgotten American virtue: self-reliance.

We face a serious education crisis. All the solutions proposed to date assume that students are incapable of learning without "innovative" programs or inspired teachers. Sure our classrooms are overcrowded—especially if we view teachers as the exclusive givers of knowledge to row after row of passive students. Smart students learn what they need to know no matter what's going on in class.

I propose that we shift our focus by reframing the education problem. Instead of viewing students as passive receivers of knowledge, we see them as knowledge creators. Smart students have always seen themselves in this light; my goal is to inspire all students to see themselves in the same way. This attitude shift will not be easy to achieve since almost everything about the way school is run conspires against the student trying to learn on his or her own.

Hundreds of billions of dollars and millions of man-years are being wasted annually, all in the name of education. As Albert Einstein once said, however, "There is too much education altogether, especially in American schools." Improving our education standards will require an enormous coordinated effort from government and business as well as the education community.

And yet the most important initiatives will come from the students themselves. While we work toward improving the school system for tomorrow, this book shows students how to teach themselves and get an education today. And when that happens, we will produce an educational transformation that will astonish the world. (Ssshhh, if you're quiet you can hear the rumblings of the coming educational earthquake.)

Index

What follows is a brief, user-friendly index of the major topics in this book. It's short enough that I recommend your reading through it entirely to look for areas that pique your curiosity. If you don't find something, look for it under synonyms (tests, for example, are listed here as exams).